Vision and the
emergence of meaning

Vision and the emergence of meaning

Blind and sighted children's early language

ANNE DUNLEA

Division of Social Sciences, University of Southern California

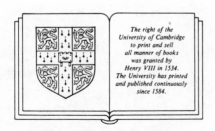

The right of the
University of Cambridge
to print and sell
all manner of books
was granted by
Henry VIII in 1534.
The University has printed
and published continuously
since 1584.

CAMBRIDGE UNIVERSITY PRESS

CAMBRIDGE

NEW YORK · PORT CHESTER · MELBOURNE · SYDNEY

Published by the Press Syndicate of the University of Cambridge
The Pitt Building, Trumpington Street, Cambridge CB2 1RP
40 West 20th Street, New York, NY 10011, USA
10 Stamford Road, Oakleigh, Melbourne 3166, Australia

First published 1989

Printed in Great Britain at the University Press, Cambridge

British Library cataloguing in publication data

Dunlea, Anne
Vision and emergence of meaning: blind
and sighted children's early language
1. Blind Children. Language skills.
Acquisition
I. Title
401.'9.

Library of Congress cataloguing in publication data

Dunlea. Anne.
Vision and the emergence of meaning: blind and sighted children's
early language / Anne Dunlea.
    p.   cm.
Bibliography.
Includes index.
ISBN 0-521—30496-2
1. Language acquisition.   2. Children, Blind – Language.   3. Speech
acts (Linguistics) I. Title.
P118.D86   1989
401'.9 – dc 19   88–34636 CIP

ISBN 0 521 30496 2

VN

Contents

Preface

One of the ultimate mysteries for anyone who wants to understand the remarkable human capacity for language is to discover how language is acquired by children and how it is integrated with other areas of cognition. This is certainly the central issue in child language research where there are two views that, in their strongest forms, appear irreconcilable. There are those who believe language is a special capacity, separate from other areas of cognition and learning, and there are those who believe language is one part of a larger, more general cognitive system. This study does not unravel the mystery, but in a very important way it is this central question that motivated the study in the first place.

Language is probably related in some interesting ways to conceptual development. It is not a trivial matter that language and other areas of cognition are mutually informative and that discoveries in one domain can lead the child to related discoveries in another domain of intellectual development. This relationship is not unidirectional, but rather it is symbiotic. Very simply, learning terms for, say, time may lead the child to grasp abstract concepts of temporality. Discovering that small items can be contained in larger ones may lead the child to discover words, such as *in*, that encode this idea.

With congenital blindness nature has created children whose representations of the world and paths to understanding the world are necessarily a little different from those of seeing children. This situation provides some intriguing possibilities for exploring the elusive relationship between language and other areas of development. Are there any interesting differences in the kinds of strategies blind children bring to the language learning task? Are there any significant correlations between language and other intellectual achievements? If blindness impacts upon development in one domain of thinking, then are there related effects in language?

Perhaps visual information itself is important in early language. Not all children learn language in precisely the same way and science has yet to delimit the range of individual variation that is possible among children. The ways into language seem to rely heavily on exploiting the non-linguistic context, on the immediate environment, and on utilizing visually based strategies for gaining and directing attention. They also seem to involve some basic understandings about people, objects and events and how these fit together. Visually based strategies and information certainly seem to facilitate the usual course of language acquisition. How can these be circumvented by children who have no vision? To some extent, the congenitally blind test the flexibility of the kinds of information and strategies required for learning language.

Some years ago, in 1978, my friend and colleague Elaine Andersen and I were pondering these lofty questions when we realized how important it was to examine language development in blind children. At the time blind children's language had been of little interest to linguists. Only in the past few years have researchers turned to this population. That discussion led to a comprehensive longitudinal investigation at the University of Southern California on language development in several blind, partially sighted and sighted children. It was jointly conducted by Elaine Andersen, Linda Kekelis (now at the University of California, Berkeley) and myself. While the study has been very much a collaborative effort, each of us initially focused on a particular aspect of development. Kekelis is especially interested in mother–child interaction, Andersen in sociolinguistic and socio-interactive skills as well as general issues in psycholinguistics, and I in early semantic and pragmatic development. While the data have been gathered, at the time of writing this book various analyses continue.

The present study represents one aspect of this investigation and is based on a doctoral dissertation submitted to the University of Southern California in 1982. The discussions and some of the other material have been revised and expanded since the earlier version to reflect my current thinking about language and vision and thought.

The most important issues are the processes and not the end products of learning language. After all, blind children *do* learn to talk. Yet we are at best only able to speculate about what these processes might be. Here, in this special population, we find a few clues about how language and cognition may converge in development: about some of the non-linguistic information that may aid the child in learning language, about some of the purely linguistic accomplishments that occur despite some seemingly large obstacles placed by blindness and somewhat lagging conceptual and social development, and indeed about some areas where language cannot progress without a supporting conceptual framework.

Acknowledgements

The children and their families made this study possible and it is to them that my first and deepest gratitude goes: to Teddy, Lisa, Julie, Lydia, Brett and Bonnie (the names are pseudonyms). The families were very generous in sharing their children's early years and the triumphs, accomplishments and occasional disappointments. In part as a way of thanking these families, the products of this research not only go to exploring academic issues, but also to finding new ways to aid blind children.

This investigation received financial support from several sources. The analysis and data collection specific to the study of meaning were supported by a grant from the National Science Foundation and by a Morkovan Research Fellowship from the University of Southern California. The larger project on the emergence of communicative competence in blind children, of which this study is one part, was supported by a grant from the Spencer Foundation to Elaine Andersen.

Elaine Andersen and Linda Kekelis are very much a part of this study. Together we visited the families and shared the tedious tasks of transcribing and preparing the data. We also shared the challenges and frustrations of this kind of research and best of all the excitement of discovery. I especially want to thank Elaine who has stimulated my thinking in many ways, first in supervising my doctoral dissertation, then as a colleague and always as a friend.

Over a dozen student research assistants gave many painstaking hours to help prepare transcripts for the larger project. I am especially grateful to Martin Lampert who helped me code the data on semantics and pragmatics and to Marie Taillard who helped with some of the home visits. I would also like to thank the faculty and staff of the Blind Children's Center in Los Angeles where I learned so much.

I am also grateful to several colleagues for their thoughtful comments, and sometimes lively discussions, after reading earlier versions of this material: Lois Bloom, Bernard Comrie, Sue Foster, Alison Gopnik, Patricia Green-field, Randa Mulford, Ann Peters and Cathy Urwin.

I would like to thank Penny Carter of the Cambridge University Press for her interest in this book, for her help during preparation and for her patience when completion of the manuscript took a little longer than originally planned.

Finally, infinite thanks to John Hawkins for surrounding me with his keen intellect, lively wit, peaceful nature and gentle spirit.

Symbols

Phonetic symbols (American pronunciation)

Consonants						Vowels			
p^h	pill	t^h	till	k^h	kill	i	beet	ɪ	bit
p	spill	t	still	k	skill	ey	bait	ɛ	bet
b	bill	d	dill	g	gill	u	boot	ω	foot
m	mill	n	nil	ŋ	ring	o	boat	ɔ	bought
f	feel	D	rider	h	high	æ	bat	a	pot
v	veal	s	seal	?	bottle	ʌ	but	ə	sofa
θ	thigh	z	zeal	l	leaf	ai	bite	aw	bout
ð	thy	č	chill	r	reef	ɔi	boy		
š	shill	j	Jill	j	you				
ž	azure	ʍ	which	w	witch				

Other symbols

[ ]   Material contained within these kinds of brackets is written in the phonetic alphabet

/   To mark the end of an utterance, e.g.: drop the horsie/

≠   Utterance boundary, but no pause, e.g.: We better go ≠ Right now!

╱   Similar to an accent mark but placed above several letters at the end of a word or phrase. Indicates a rising intonation contour, e.g.: drop the horsie/

*   Ungrammatical or unacceptable

⊃   Implies

≥   Used here to mean 'appears before or at the same time as'

>   Before or greater than

((SNG)) Sings, or singing (appears in some transcripted material)

((LF))   Laughs, or laughing

((SHT)) Shouts, or shouting

((SW))   Spoken sweetly

((EI))   Exaggerated intonation

((FS))   Fussing or fussily

Main codes used in various analyses

(See indicated chapter and section for definitions)

Semantic case roles and grammatical categories (chapter 5, section 5.3.1)

Agt	Agent
A/S	Action or State
Attr	Attributive
B	Benefactive
Com	Comitative
Conj	Conjunctive
Dat	Dative (Recipient)
Dem	Demonstrative
E	Experiencer
Ent	Entity
FR	Formulaic Request
I	Instrument
L	Locative
N	Negation
O	Object
Poss	Possessor
Possn	Possession
Q	Question
Rec	Recurrence
StSp	Stereotypic Speech

Type of utterance and its discourse status (chapter 6, section 6.3)

B	Babbling
B+	Babbling with Expressive Jargon
BW	Babbling or Jargon with some real words
F-I	Frame Insert
IM	Imitation
IV	Interactive Vocalization
R	Reiteration

RIM   Requested Imitation
SP   Sound Play
SpL   Spontaneous Language
TG   Turn using conventionalized gesture (but not language)

Type of fundamental illocutionary act (chapter 6, section 6.3, and see table 6.1)

Asst   Assertion
Attn G   Attention Getting
Dr Attn   Draw Attention (to something other than self)
I/D   Identification or Description
Id +   Elicited identification or description
N-Resp   Verbal Response of negation
No I F   No Illocutionary Force
Off/Sh   Offer or Show
P/R/R/D   Protest, Refusal, Rejection or Denial
Q   Question
Resp   Response
Rout   Routine
Rq Act   Request for Action or Activity
Rq Obj   Requestion for Object
Rq Rout   Request for Routine
Soc   Social Routine
U I F   Unspecifiable Illocutionary Force (reflects interpretation problems)

1 Introduction

> If we tried to picture the most precocious child orator, we should think of a blind girl, the only daughter of wealthy parents.
>
> George Miller (1963, p. 157)

This provocative statement culminates a discussion of individual differences in language learning in Miller's pioneering text, which first appeared in 1951, for a fledgeling discipline that was to become known as developmental psycholinguistics. The book was the first to bring together various approaches for studying and analysing children's language and it was to influence several generations of child language researchers. While research techniques and the theories motivating them have changed, the text remains a fascinating historical document, articulating some important underlying assumptions about language learning.

Miller's description of the precocious child orator stems from an examination of factors in a child's environment and background that seem to be related to rapid language development. High family income, being a girl and being an only child have all been correlated, at least in surveys, with slightly facilitating language learning. But what possible advantage might blindness give a child?

In fact, the suggestion is derived from two interacting ideas about language acquisition. The first is what Miller calls "ear–voice reflexes" or the "ear-to-voice link" in infancy. Babbling stimulates a baby acoustically and kinesthetically, thereby encouraging the infant to continue making sounds. Eventually the child imitates sounds spoken by others and begins to learn words. Miller proposes that the blind may develop more rapidly in this area because of their verbal dependence on others. The second factor is an implicit assumption that once a child makes sounds and learns a few words, the course of language development will progress in a predictable and unremarkable way.

This line of reasoning motivated several decades of research into language development in deaf children, but until the late 1970s there was a total lack of interest in how blind children learn language. The neglect reflects the assumption that blindness should have little impact on language. Even more

1

importantly, it reflects a bias toward isolating language from its social context and conceptual underpinnings. Congenital blindness affects both cognitive and social development (see chapter 2 and Warren, 1985). Examining language acquisition in this population can thus provide a unique opportunity for evaluating whether and how language intersects with other capacities.

Moreover, since the mid 1970s, there has been growing evidence suggesting that vision itself plays an important role in the emergence of communication. An obvious corollary is that the absence of vision may have an impact on the course of language development.

Visual information has been implicated as an explanation for many facets of the process of language acquisition as it normally progresses. It is thought to be important in fostering early parent–infant interaction, in providing the child with a stimulus for hypothesizing about what language encodes, and in supplying the parents with clues about what a young child's early verbalizations mean. Furthermore, vision seems to be crucial in the infant's conceptualization of the environment, on which early language development is thought to depend.

The basis of early interaction between parents and their infants depends on visually based strategies. Stern (1974, 1977) points out that the infant's first exposure to the human world is composed of his mother's activities, especially her repertoire of "infant elicited behaviors." These center on exaggerated facial expressions, accompanied by vocalizations and gazing at the infant. The human neonate has a strong propensity to observe and even imitate these expressions (Meltzoff and Moore, 1977), with the result that they form the core of interactive play. The play episodes themselves are typically initiated by caregivers using a combination of eye gaze and vocalization in which the objective is to obtain mutual orientation in a face-to-face position with the infant (Stern, 1977; Tronick *et al.*, 1979; Kaye, 1979). Once the infant is attending, a play-dialogue ensues until the infant disengages by glancing away. The best predictor of when a mother will respond again to the infant is the moment that the infant's gaze again focuses on her (Brazelton *et al.*, 1974; Stern, 1974; Fogel, 1977). Thus, visual attention on the part of both the caregiver and the infant is crucial in initiating and maintaining early exchanges. These rudimentary exchanges are structured along the same lines as the adult discourse system and they develop very quickly into a communicative framework which increasingly permits linguistic interchanges. Without access to visual information, the structure of these interactions is necessarily disrupted and there seems to be no substitute for their effectiveness in establishing a bond between parents and infants, and in initiating the human infant into the social world from which language emerges (Fraiberg, 1977).

As the child begins to use language, visual information seems to provide an important stimulus for building hypotheses about meaning. For example, in ascribing meaning to words, the child appears to abstract certain salient attributes from early referents and uses these as a basis for extending the domain of application for words (Bowerman, 1976, 1978; Clark, 1973; Nelson, 1973a; Rescorla, 1980). This process is essential in helping the child move from using a word as a "name" for a specific referent, to using words as symbolic vehicles to denote a heterogeneous class of referents. The overwhelming evidence is that such visually based properties as shape, size, and movement are the most important criteria used in constructing these classifications. Not only is visual information important in the child's organization of referent properties, but it appears to underlie adult categorization and the structure of many lexical fields as well (Andersen, 1978; Clark, 1977b; Rosch, 1975, 1977). Some of the evidence for this comes from the analysis of classifier systems in a variety of natural languages. Classifiers are expressions which group together entities that share some particular attribute. English does not exploit these, though the principle can be seen in the utterance "She bought four *lengths* of material." Some languages classify all varieties of countable objects yielding such sentences as "She has seven *round-things* eggs." Clark's (1977b) analysis of classifier systems reveals that perceptual information, again largely visual, is the primary basis of groupings. The features round, long and flat are especially important. For example, the Indonesian language groups such objects as fruit, peas, eyes, balls, and stones together on the basis of roundness; Nung groups together trees, bamboo, thread, nails, and candles on the basis of length; Kachari groups together leaves, fans, and cloth on the basis of flatness. Even in cultures which do not have classifier systems, these features are important. As the result of a number of experiments conducted in a variety of cultures, Rosch (1973, 1975, 1977) has found that people tend to group objects on the basis of perceptual features, especially the visual perception of shape. Thus, there appears to be a human propensity to exploit perceptual features in constructing sets of objects and in defining lexical classes which operates from infancy on, and visual information seems to be central in this.

Vision is an important basis for concept development in general. During its first year, the infant comes to learn a great deal about the physical environment in which it lives. The Piagetian notion of interaction with the environment as the basis of sensorimotor intelligence specifically involves perception, especially visual attention to objects and events, as well as purely motoric behavior. Moreover, visual information coordinates other schemata (Piaget, 1927, 1951, 1952a, 1952b, 1955; Piaget and Inhelder, 1969). In particular, the infant attends to the movements that entities can perform, identifies the relationships between people and objects, and recognizes and comes to know how things are used. The quantity and quality of the information available without the aid of vision is drastically reduced and it appears that the course of development is hampered for infants who are born blind (Piaget and Inhelder, 1969). This is significant for the present discussion, since language acquisition seems to depend on the emerging conceptual system and the young child's developmental task involves matching linguistic and cognitive structures (Clark, 1977a; Nelson, 1974; Pylyshyn, 1977). One area where this is particularly evident is in the child's early expression of semantic roles in which such fundamental relations as Agent + Object or Agent + Action are thought to reflect the child's understanding of and experience with his immediate environment.

Perhaps the most frequent explanation for how very young children come to understand and produce language is that they depend on the "here and now," which has been defined as "whatever is directly under the child's eyes" (Clark and Clark, 1977, p. 322). The child learns about the matching of language and world largely through context. A now classic example is Shatz's (1974) analysis of how toddlers successfully respond to such directives as "Can you shut the door?" Basically, the child maps maternal speech onto the objects and actions he sees in the world with the aid of the mother's non-verbal clues. In this instance, the child follows his parent's eye gaze and gesture which are directed toward the door, a strategy which crucially depends on vision. The child's previous observations and explorations equip him with the knowledge that doors can be opened and closed, and the child may pick up the parent's intonation and recognize the utterance as a directive. (Stern and Wasserman, 1979, among others, have presented considerable evidence that infants as young as six months old are sensitive to basic intonational contour, though they do not associate it with grammar until much later.) If the door is open, the child closes it. We do not infer that the toddler understands the grammatical components of his parent's utterance, or the meaning of each word, or how the meanings are combined, but through context, the child comes to solve the puzzle of language. Much of this context, and certainly most of the parent's non-verbal clues, depend on vision for their interpretation. Similarly, the "here and now" provides parents with clues that enable them to interpret their infant's first efforts to communicate. In particular, they rely on eye gaze and the children's conventionalized gestural complex (e.g., pointing, reaching) in order to understand early vocalizations and to distinguish the focus of their child's attention (see Bates *et al.*, 1979; Carter, 1978, 1979; Pechman and Deutsch, 1980; and many others). Without the aid of vision, these clues are lost.

Taken together, the evidence strongly suggests that visual information is crucial in the development of fundamental social, cognitive, and linguistic structures, and it is not surprising that vision has been inferred as an underlying mechanism in the process of language acquisition. But there has been little effort to test this by examining how development progresses when visual information is not available. The motivation for the present investigation is precisely this. It is an effort to begin to evaluate the extent to which visual information can account for the process of language acquisition.

Three key areas were selected for investigation: *the acquisition of early words, developments in the use of illocutionary force,* and *the emergence of propositional structures.* These form the core of the study of meaning in semantic and pragmatic approaches to linguistic theory and they represent those areas in ontogenesis in which concept development and linguistic development seem to be most interrelated. Lexical acquisition is intimately related to category formation; the use of illocutionary force involves the ability to exploit various aspects of the context to convey messages and to use language to gain access to the environment; propositional structures represent the ability to encode relations which obtain between elements of the environment. A synopsis of the principal issues considered in each of the chapters follows.

Chapter 2 presents a summary of general development in the young blind child. It begins by discussing the common causes of childhood blindness and the effects of that blindness on sensorimotor and early cognitive development. In particular, the central role of haptic-kinesthetic information in the construction of concepts is examined. The chapter concludes with a review of what is presently understood about the emergence of language in young blind children.

Chapter 3 is a description of the methodology used in the present study. The work is based on media recorded samples made during regularly scheduled home visits, and is supplemented by parental diaries and individualized experiments. The structure of these visits is outlined and the way in which the data were gathered, transcribed, and prepared for analysis is discussed. Each of the children who participated in the study is introduced: two are totally blind, two have minimal residual vision, and two are fully sighted.

Chapter 4 examines the earliest form of conventionalized meaning: the emergence of words. Drawing largely on data from diary records kept by mothers, the acquisition of each child's first 100 lexemes is documented. The first use of a word and the way in which its meaning evolved and was extended is considered. Since visual information seems to provide the sighted child with criterial information for extending the domain of application for early words, and since it seems to be a stimulus for the sighted child's developing hypothesis about the nature and meaning of words, this chapter explores the extent to which the absence of vision alters the process of lexical acquisition in the blind child. In doing this, we can begin to assess the extent to which visual information can explain lexical development as it generally progresses.

Chapter 5 investigates a further aspect of semantic meaning: the expression of semantic roles and the development of propositional structures.

It also examines a strategy that seems to be unique to the blind children – the incorporation of stereotypic maternal speech patterns into their communicative repertoire – and discusses how this may influence other aspects of language and conceptual development. Drawing on transcripts of the home visits, the content of the first proposition-like structures occurring in sequences of related single word utterances is evaluated and the semantic roles that are expressed in early multi-term utterances are analyzed. Children in a variety of cultures have been observed to encode the same fundamental relations early on – relations which directly reflect information about objects, entities, and activities that they have observed in their environment. The child without vision has much less information available. By exploring the differences in the kinds of semantic relations that are encoded by blind and sighted children, we can begin to determine the extent to which visual information is a catalyst for the emergence of apparently universal semantic categories.

Chapter 6 explores a more pragmatic aspect of early meaning: the communicative function of the child's utterances. The semantic content of an utterance is only part of its meaning; also important is the kind of message that is intended by the utterance (i.e., whether it is an assertion, a request, a greeting, and so on). This chapter uses transcripts of the home visits to consider how access to visual information affects the way in which children use language. It identifies some of the strategies that are available to young blind children to help them express the communicative force of their utterances in lieu of the gestural and eye-gaze clues that are exploited by sighted children. It also considers how blind children use language to increase their access to the environment. Since there is no fully comparable work evaluating the development of illocutionary force in young (sighted) children, a system for conducting a fine-grained analysis of early communicative intent is developed and presented. Its application reveals an ontogenetic progression in the use of illocutionary acts that has not been previously appreciated.

Chapter 7 summarizes the principal findings of the study. It draws them together and identifies a number of recurrent themes which point to an interaction between concept development and language acquisition and it articulates how visual information plays an even more important role in explaining the emergence of meaning than has previously been proposed.

2 Blindness and childhood

This chapter briefly considers the meaning and consequences of congenital blindness in order to provide a framework from which the present research can be better understood. It defines "blindness," discusses the effects of blindness on selected aspects of cognitive organization, and discusses the development of very young blind children, culminating with a summary of research on language acquisition in this special population.

2.1 The nature of blindness and its prevalence in childhood

Most people think of blindness as the total absence of visual sensation and they imagine that a blind person is someone who experiences the world through a kind of black void. In fact, blindness cannot be viewed in terms of an absolute dichotomy between the presence and absence of visual information. The popular conception of the blind person characterizes only a very small proportion of the blind population, since the vast majority of "blind" individuals experience and utilize some visual information, though this may be limited to sensing direct light.

The generally accepted legal definition of blindness in the United States requires that central visual acuity in the better eye with best correction be no more than 20/200 Snellen. The Snellen measurement is derived from the familiar Snellen eye chart, developed in 1862. The person with 20/200 visual acuity is able to recognize from a distance of 20 feet objects which those with average vision see at a distance of 200 feet, and would only be able to identify the letter corresponding to a 200 foot distance on the eye chart.

While the Snellen measurement describes the sharpness of visual perception, the integrity of the visual pathway is evaluated in terms of the visual field which refers to that portion of space which the fixed eye can see. Normally the eye can see a nearly complete circle or approximately 330° in the vertical plane. The thirty degree "blind spot" is the optic disk where the head of the optic nerve enters the retina, thereby preventing stimulation of this section of the retina. (We are completely unaware of this blind spot.) Anomalies of the visual field can occur in the central field, in the periphery or

7

in both, and severe field defects are also used to classify individuals as legally blind.

It is worth noting that in 1966 the World Health Organization listed 65 different definitions of blindness and visual impairment throughout the world. Because there is no universally accepted definition of blindness, cross-cultural comparisons of development in blind children, as well as more general epidemiological studies, are not reliable.

The extreme case of blindness is one in which a child is diagnosed as being totally congenitally blind, or who has minimal light perception (LP) which enables him to recognize the difference between light and dark. Light projection (also generally designated "LP") makes it possible for the individual to orient toward a strong source of light such as a window through which direct sunlight enters a room or a lamp lit in an otherwise dark room. Light perception is thought to be similar to the kind of vision we experience with our eyelids closed. It is useful in mobility, since large objects placed between the individual and the source of light will disrupt the stream of light and thereby alert him to a possible obstruction. Progressively higher levels of visual function include: (1) sensing shadow motion of near objects such as a hand moving in front of the eye (2) sensing the basic form of light, and possibly the number, distance and pattern of the form (3) sensing the color of the form, and (4) sensing increasingly accurate patterns of shape and distance, ultimately permitting a legally blind person to function with printed material using visual aids. A summary of the hierarchy of visual function appears in table 2.1.

In 1967, the annual incidence of congenital blindness in the United States was calculated to be 14.9 per 100,000 live births. With advances in prenatal and neonatal medical care, the incidence of congenital blindness has generally declined during the past century. But during the late 1940s and early 1950s the rate rose as high as 8 per 10,000 because of the profound effect of retrolental fibroplasia (RLF). RLF is caused by the administration of excessive oxygen to incubated premature babies which results in the formation of an opaque fibrous membrane over the retina. The damage is severe and irreversible. (The risk of blindness from RLF is not completely absent and today it accounts for approximately 4% of congenital impairments.[1]) The incidence of congenital blindness since the mid-1950s has remained constant, whereas the prevalence of childhood blindness is increasing, largely due to advances in pediatric care enabling more children to survive who formerly would have died (see Robinson, 1977). Consonant with this trend, the majority of visually impaired children today are multi-handicapped. For discussions of the causes of congenital blindness see Hatfield (1972, 1975) and Robinson (1977).

Unless there are obvious anatomical anomalies, the diagnosis of con-

[1] Strictly speaking, RLF is not congenital since it develops during the neonatal period, but it is typically grouped with congenital disorders in the literature.

Table 2.1. *Hierarchy of visual function*

Absolute blindness		No light perception	
Relative blindness	1	Light perception (LP)	} Light sense
	2	Light projection	
	3	Hand motion	} Motion sense
	4	Shadow perception	
Low vision	1	Finger counting	Form vision
	2	Snellen Visual Acuity at the following levels:	
		20/800 Travel vision	
		20/400	
		20/200	
		20/70 Visual disability	
		20/50 Reading vision	
Functional vision		20/40 Driving vision	
		20/30	
		20/25	
Normal vision		20/20 Standard vision	
		20/15	
		20/10	

Based on information provided by the Southern California College of Optometry, Fullerton, California.

genital blindness is usually made when the infant is four to five months old, and the news is devastating. Generally the parents suspect something is wrong earlier, but because the symptoms of visual impairment are minimal, many physicians reassure families that everything is fine (Jan *et al.*, 1977). In the months following the initial diagnosis the parents often seek various miracle cures. Family reactions to handicapped children in general typically involve parental depression, especially in the mother; anxiety and guilt at the time of discovery of the handicap; and later, compensatory attitudes of rejection or overprotection (Lairy and Harrison-Covello, 1973). These reactions are frequently amplified when blindness is the diagnosis, in part because our cultural mythology associates blindness with punishment, incest (Oedipus), madness, castration, and at the same time with a strange kind of wisdom and omnipotence – "the blind prophet" (see Lairy and Harrison-Covello, 1973; Lowenfeld, 1974; Urwin, 1978a). Until the modern era, blindness was viewed as the greatest misfortune that could befall an individual; for many it was worse than death. Today some families are never able to cope with the impairment and healthy parent–child relationships fail to develop, with devastating results for everyone. Perhaps the most poignant and frank expression of what it means to come to accept the blindness of one's own child is from one of the mothers in our study who confided that: "You have to mourn the death of your perfect child and then come to love the child you have."

2.2   The basis of concept formation in the blind and the hypothesis of sensory compensation

We all know what vision is. Because of its importance to us, we surmise that the absence of vision must have devastating consequences and that congenital blindness must inevitably lead to the construction of a rather different perspective of the world. Consider for a moment the nature of vision. It is the form of information input that allows the easy summation of simultaneous spatial reality independent of time. Vision, then, enables us to establish and maintain a coherent concept of the environment and our existence in it without struggling with memory and information retrieval. Quite simply, the blind must remember what the sighted can effortlessly reconstruct with a single look. Above all, vision has the outstanding and unique quality of simultaneity. In the absence of vision, all the other modalities put a tremendous burden on the mind's ability to synthesize a coherent sense of the objective environment and one's position in it.

To better understand the development of the blind child, it is useful to characterize the basis of the blind adult's conceptualization of the world, since the blind child's developmental target is not wholly equivalent to the sighted child's. The blind build up a conception of the world based on tactual, auditory, and kinesthetic experiences. Hearing, which gives clues in regard to distance and direction, does not often convey concrete information about unfamiliar objects. It is primarily useful as a means of verbal communication and in locomotion. While obviously useful, hearing is not quite as central to the blind as many sighted individuals suppose. Perception of the spatial qualities of objects, if sight is lacking, can only be achieved by touch in which kinesthetic sensations participate.

Tactual perception requires direct contact with the object to be "observed." Certain objects are therefore inevitably inaccessible – distant objects (sun, moon, stars); large objects which cannot be perceived in full (mountains, rivers, large buildings); fragile objects (soap bubbles, smoke, fog); and minute objects (fleas, dust). Moreover, certain objects under certain circumstances are inaccessible to tactile exploration (burning fuel, boiling water). Thus, a great many experiences taken for granted by sighted children are difficult or impossible for blind children. Another difference between sight and touch is that visual perception goes on throughout the waking state, whether or not one fully attends to it, whereas hands as touch organs need to be actively applied and the scope of their application is limited to one arm's length without moving. The act of touching and feeling is a *search* for information; it implies a conscious effort to obtain sensory stimulation. Just in terms of *time* the sighted person is able to obtain enough information to grasp the reality of experiences much more quickly than a blind person, especially a blind child.

For the congenitally blind person, an object, for example a table, is haptically representable by its texture, density, and tactual form. By calling together all the tactual–kinesthetic impressions associated with tables, a blind person can develop a haptic concept of a table in a way that is analogous with the sighted person's visualization of a table. In the sighted, videation or "optification" is the ability to transfer all non-visual sensory data (haptic, auditory, gustatory, olfactory) into a visual perceptual field. For example, for a sighted person the fragrance of a banana typically conjures up the visual image of a banana. It is believed that blind people have a similar process which pulls all available sensory information into a haptic representation (see Kidwell and Greer, 1973).

It has been suggested that there are significant "phenomenological" differences between visual and haptic representation, though these have not been explicated (Kidwell and Greer, 1973; Lowenfeld, 1956). Some evidence for this comes from congenitally blind individuals who have undergone corrective surgery and are suddenly able to see (see Valvo, 1971 for discussion). After surgery, haptically familiar objects are indistinguishable on the basis of visual information without considerable training and experience in learning to interpret visual information. (The philosophical questions about the transfer of information from haptic to visual space following sight restoration is known as the Molyneux problem after the 18th century scholar who originally posed the question.)

An interesting question is whether or not there is much difference in the haptic abilities of the blind and sighted child. Gottesman (1971, 1976) has found that blind and sighted children between the ages of two and eight, representing different stages of development, demonstrate similar abilities on a Piagetian task of haptic preception. Several other studies have also failed to show significant differences in form perception between blind and sighted subjects (Eaves and Klonoff, 1970; Ewart and Carp, 1962; see Warren, 1977, 1985 for review).

For centuries, people have believed that the blind are endowed with superior non-visual senses which compensate for the absence of sight. In fact, the notion of sensory compensation is a myth. Repeated scientific investigations indicate that the acuity of the intact senses cannot be increased in either the congenitally or adventitiously blind, but they have shown that these senses can be used more efficiently. Perhaps the most famous form of sensory enhancement is the so-called "blind man's sense" which enables the blind to avoid obstacles in their path. Until recently this was thought to be "facial vision" since both blind and blindfolded individuals reported pressure sensations on the temples, forehead, and cheeks. In fact, the sensations are acoustic in nature and the ability is now recognized as echolocation, similar to the sonar navigation system used by bats, dolphins, whales, and other animals (Kohler, 1964).

Echolocation is a process by which the location or distance of near objects is determined by the reflection of sound waves off the object. Random noises such as breathing, footsteps or the rustling of clothing provide some information but specific sounds such as hissing, snapping fingers or tapping are more accurate. Useful sounds are in the range of 8,000 to 10,000 cycles per second (Welsh, 1964). Jan *et al.* (1977) report that bright and mobile blind children at one-and-a-half to two years of age spontaneously begin producing sounds, such as clapping, to aid in echolocation. Blindfolded sighted individuals can be trained to efficiently use echolocation (see Jan *et al.*, 1977).

In terms of other intact senses, few differences have been demonstrated between the blind and the sighted. Research on cutaneous sensitivity and on various forms of tactile discrimination tasks reveals only slightly superior skills in blind adults compared to sighted adults, and in fact indicates that blind children under 11 years old may actually tend to be inferior in tactile perception when compared with their sighted peers (see Warren, 1977, for an extensive review). A study of auditory abstraction (the ability to recognize a three to five note pattern within a longer tune) found that blind adolescents did perform better than sighted adolescents (Witkin, Olfman, Chase, and Freedman, 1971). In contrast, the blind performed poorly on auditory localization tasks. There is certainly no evidence that the visually impaired are musically gifted.

2.3   Development of blind infants

Although it is of considerable theoretical and practical importance, there is surprisingly little research on the effects of blindness on development in the age range between infancy and five or six years. There are at least two reasons for this. First, pre-school children are relatively inaccessible, whereas there are many residential and special schools for older children (Warren, 1977; Urwin, 1978a). Secondly, adapting research methods to blind infants is unusually difficult (Warren, 1977). For example, almost all of the eliciting situations in the Užgiris and Hunt Scales, and similar tests of infant development, crucially involved visual information such that the infant is required to observe various kinds of object manipulations (Užgiris and Hunt, 1975). Similarly, recording visual attention and the imitation of various gestures is an important means of evaluating an infant's social behaviour (Bullowa, 1979; Schaffer, 1977). In neither example can auditory or tactile information be a complete substitute for the visual information.

The information that is available on early development tends to evaluate children in terms of their performance on certain standardized scales, including two scales that have been normed for use with blind children: the Maxfield–Buchholz Social Maturity Scales for Blind Children, which is an adaption of the Vineland Social Maturity Scale (Maxfield and Buchholz, 1957) and the Reynell–Zinkin Scales for Young Visually Handicapped

Children (Reynell, 1979). For an extensive review of development in blind children see Warren (1977, 1985).

Motor development in the first few months appears to progress similarly for blind and sighted infants, possibly because many of the activities are reflexive in nature or result from predictable neuro-muscular maturation. Motor delays, but not postural delays, may be present in some older infants and children up to about three years (Fraiberg, 1977; Reynell, 1979). Delays in directed reaching have received a fair amount of attention, in part because of their hypothesized relationship with the development of object concepts (Fraiberg, 1977; Bower, 1974; Bigelow, 1983).

The emergence of the object concept in blind children is generally viewed in terms of the onset of ear–hand coordination and it is regarded as parallel to eye–hand coordination in the sighted child. But, while sighted infants reach and grasp for objects by four or five months, in blind children this development may appear considerably later. In Fraiberg's study the median age for coordinated reaching was 0; 8; 27 (range 0; 6; 18 to 0; 11; 1).

It appears that auditory cues are not an effective substitute in blind infants for the role that visual cues serve in stimulating reaching for objects in sighted infants. This has led several researchers to discuss inherent differences in visible and audible information (Warren, 1970; Bower, 1974).

In fact, young infants, both sighted and blind, often reach toward objects in response to sounds but the behavior disappears fairly quickly. Relatively few objects actually emit sounds and frequently those that do are not graspable (televisions, stereos, doorbells and so on). The result is that many early attempts at reaching toward sounds lead to unrewarding results.

Fraiberg suggests that the late re-establishment of sound–prehension coordination is due to a conceptual problem. Since sound does not necessarily signify presence of a graspable object, she argues that the infant must have some kind of object concept *before* auditory–manual coordination develops.

Both Bower and Fraiberg imply that the blind infant must have tactile experience with objects in general and with sound making objects in particular before ear–hand coordination can be expected. But, it appears that tactile exploration is itself delayed in blind infants. Fraiberg suggests that this is a direct effect of blindness since the biological program "intends" tactile exploration to develop in synchrony with vision when the tonic neck reflex brings the infant's head to midline, thereby expanding the range of vision. Ultimately this leads to eye–hand coordination. But, this inducement to begin tactile exploration is lost on the blind infant.

Although the process of development is somewhat different, blind babies do develop a coordinated reach, typically before their first birthdays (Fraiberg, 1977; Reynell, 1979; Bigelow, 1983). Directed reaching may in turn be a prerequisite to locomotion in blind children since mobility directly follows the achievement of prehension, especially in Fraiberg's study.

The emphasis in the literature on the later developments of coordinated reach and the onset of mobility tends to portray a rather grim picture of the blind baby which is not entirely warranted. While we do see lags in areas which are normally visually based but must now be served by audition, auditory discrimination abilities in and of themselves are not impaired by lack of vision. Freedman (1964) reports that early on the infant smiles in response to his parents' voices. At eight months stranger anxiety is observed in response to a new voice (Fraiberg, Siegal and Gibson, 1966). At seven months there is attention to sounds created by actions of the infant's hands (Burlingham, 1964). Babbling and imitating sounds typically occur within the same age range as for sighted children and "expressive jabbering" may actually emerge earlier in blind children than in sighted ones.

On the other hand, blind infants lack precisely the mechanism which appears most crucial for the development of early parent–infant interactions. The importance of an infant's attending to its parents' faces, of its imitating their facial expressions and smiles, of visual regard and visual co-orientation are amply documented in the literature on early interaction (see chapter 1).

With the absence of sight, infant-elicited social behaviors (see Stern, 1977) fail to properly emerge. And the situation is frequently exacerbated when parental grief prevents the usual bonding. It is not until the second half of the first year, when the infant begins to vocalize, that a suitable channel for interactive exchanges becomes available. As a result, language development takes on an added importance for the blind infant and its family (see Urwin, 1978a, b).

2.4   Blind children's language

The importance of language for the blind has long been recognized by clinicians and educators, but it is only in the last decade that the question of how blind children learn language has attracted the attention of linguists. Clinicians have documented the attainment of such language milestones as appear on the Bayley Scales (Bayley, 1969) and have discussed "irregularities" in the blind person's use of language.

The two most frequent "irregularities" are echolalia and verbalisms. Echolalia, the parroting or repeating of words and phrases, is in fact observed in many very young children (see Piaget, 1926 for one early account of this), but it is more common and more pervasive in blind children. It becomes problematic when it is maintained until an older age and is characterized by longer echoic utterances, pronominal confusion, delayed echolalia and the like (Fay, 1973). In fact, excessive echolalia is associated with autistic symptomology and appears to be limited to a disturbed subgroup of blind children (Fraiberg, 1971; Freedman, 1971; Fay, 1973).

Verbalisms refer to the tendency of the blind to use words for which they have no first-hand sensory information, for example talking of "red" roses, "twinkling" stars or using the word "see." Some clinicians are concerned that verbalisms indicate incoherent and loose thinking and a tendency toward unreality (Cutsforth, 1951). In fact, the use of visually based terms by the blind is not necessarily meaningless, though the meanings are obviously not the same for blind and sighted people (Nolan, 1960; Landau and Gleitman, 1985). It should also be remembered that all children use words facilely which they don't completely understand.

Speech production has also been of interest and some reports point to a higher incidence of disorders involving stuttering, voicing and articulation in the blind compared with the general population. However, it is difficult to interpret these data because of the presence of confounding neurological or physiological handicaps, in addition to blindness, in the sample populations (e.g., Stinchfield-Hawk, 1944; Miner, 1963). Clinical studies have not shown a positive correlation between the degree of visual impairment and the presence of speech disorders, suggesting that blindness alone is not the decisive factor (Brieland, 1950; Rowe, 1958).

Speech development is also of interest. Blind children must depend on acoustic imitation since they cannot observe the muscular movements that accompany articulation. The most detailed examination of phonetic development is presented by Mills (1983b, 1987) who compares three sighted and three visually impaired children learning German. The sighted subjects learned sounds with visible articulatory movements, such as *b* and *w* more quickly and with less error than the blind subjects. Mills also observed different patterns of phonological substitution (substituting one sound for another in saying words, a common characteristic of children's language).

The blind children were more influenced by acoustic similarity of sounds (*m, n*) whereas the sighted children's sound substitutions may also involve visual similarities in the way sounds are made (*b, m*).

Fraiberg (1977) used the Bayley Scales to document language acquisition in ten blind subjects who were participating in her developmental/psychoanalytic study of blindness in children. The Bayley items record only the very broadest achievements (e.g., "says two words") and are limited to the very earliest aspects of language. The results suggest language development in blind children progresses at a normal pace, though different skills may have ontogenetically differing significance for the two groups. For example, Fraiberg's subjects are precocious in their attainment of the items "jabbers expressively" and "imitates words" while they are delayed in "says two words" and "sentences of two words". The first differences may indicate the importance of acoustic signals to blind children, whereas later acquisition of words and word combinations is in line with the reported delay in object concept for blind children.

Language acquisition in blind children

During the past few years several investigations of language development have appeared in the linguistic literature, notably Urwin (1978a), Rowland (1980), Mulford (1980, 1986), Kekelis (1981), Mills (1983b), Landau and Gleitman (1985), Wilson (1985) and Bigelow (1987).

The way into language may be somewhat different for blind and sighted children. Urwin's pioneering study reveals that nursery rhymes incorporating body actions, such as clapping or rocking, provide an unusually effective means for parents to gain and maintain their blind infant's attention. These routines may then become the basis of social play and provide a means for the blind children to initiate and control interaction during their second year. Interestingly, nursery routines became less important for one subject Urwin studied who had some residual vision, a pattern more typical of sighted children. Language itself seemed to evolve out of these rituals for her subjects; a number of early words and phrases derived from familiar routines. Nursery routines may thus provide an alternative to the visually based pointing, gesturing and offering games that evolve in interactions with sighted children and that seem to facilitate language (see Ninio and Bruner, 1978; Masur, 1982).

The impact of verbal routines may in fact be quite pervasive. Urwin suggests that the beginnings of representational play in her blind subjects were not in games with objects, but in reconstructing conversations. Beginning at $1\frac{1}{2}$ years, one subject actually used different voice qualities to mark different people's speech: for example, a gruff voice for his father and a low voice for his mother. The important point here is that blind children may use language to begin to engage in role-play and possibly to represent themselves. This contrasts with Fraiberg's (1977) view that self representation (and correct use of pronouns) evolves much later in blind children and may be associated with object play. Urwin also found that a rapid expansion in vocabulary at about 18 months occurred concurrently for her children with the emergence of representational play. This play involved objects for the child with residual vision but mainly verbal role play for the totally blind children. However, other research indicates that a close examination of role-play speech reveals some difficulties blind children have in understanding reversibility of perspective and the shifting meanings of some words, especially deictic terms (Andersen, Dunlea and Kekelis, 1984).

Just as verbal role-play may be characteristic of blind children, there is also a tendency for them to engage in a considerable amount of sound and word play not directed to others and there is a striking tendency to reproduce segments of speech that sound like their caregiver's language (Urwin, 1978a; Wilson, 1985; Fraiberg, 1977). This characteristic is what some clinicians call "delayed echolalia" but it is important to distinguish between children whose language is almost exclusively echoic and children who use language in many situations including echoically. Only the former is regarded as pathological. Moreover, sighted children also pick up and use unanalyzed chunks of language which they eventually dissect (Peters, 1977, 1983).

The nature of interactions between blind children and their sighted caregivers poses some potentially interesting challenges since neither partner can fully appreciate the other's perspective and experiences. Mothers appear to compensate for their infant's visual impairment by using greater physical contact and vocalizing to respond not only to their infant's vocalizations, but also to their smiles and other behaviors (Urwin, 1978a; Rowland, 1980, 1984). Language inevitably serves an important function in maintaining contact. Speech directed to blind children may be more centered on the children themselves than on their activities with objects (Urwin, 1978a; Kekelis, 1981; Andersen and Kekelis, 1982). In comparison with sighted children, blind children seem to receive fewer statements describing activities and events and more labels for objects or requests for the child to identify objects. Kekelis suggests that this is because it is more difficult to direct blind children's attention outside themselves and to monitor their attention to events. In general, she suggests these strategies appear to encourage visually impaired children to take an active role in conversations, but they may also limit the kinds of information provided to these children.

After a possible mild delay in beginning to say words, blind children seem to acquire 50 or so words in the usual amount of time reported for sighted children – a few months – then, as their vocabularies expand, they begin to say two- and three-word phrases. Several researchers looking at the early stages of language development have found blind and sighted children's language fairly similar (Bigelow, 1986; Landau and Gleitman, 1985). The strongest claim comes from Landau and Gleitman who argue that "the blind learner can surmount whatever obstacles diminution of experience places in her path, acquiring her native tongue in a largely unexceptional fashion" (p. viii). They later suggest that blind and sighted children are linguistically indistinguishable by 36 months. Such claims are based on surveying the content of early vocabularies and the semantic roles expressed in early multi-word phrases and by calculating mean length of utterances.[2]

A number of researchers have found the content of blind children's early vocabularies fairly similar to sighted children's when classified along the lines proposed by Nelson (1973a) (Bigelow, 1986; Landau and Gleitman, 1985; Urwin, 1978a). In combining data from a number of sources,

---

[2] "MLU" as described by Brown (1973) measures the average number of morphemes in 100 consecutive utterances produced by a child. The chief advantage is that it counts morphemes, the smallest units of meaning including prefixes, suffixes, inflections and basic words rather than simply counting words. It therefore better reflects a child's linguistic sophistication in the early stages of language learning. For example, "I play car" and "Freda's parrot sings" both have three words, but the former has three morphemes whereas the latter has five.

including some unpublished data from the present study, Mulford (1986) found the most notable differences were a relatively high proportion of specific nominals and action words in the blind children's vocabularies, a lower proportion of general nominals and surprisingly few function words (e.g. "more," "what," "all gone").

There are fewer studies of blind children's early multi-word language. Landau and Gleitman report that the three children they studied expressed similar types of semantic roles to the sighted children studied by Bloom, Lightbown and Hood (1975). Unfortunately, the scale of the graphic representations in which the comparative data are presented is so small that it is difficult to interpret the findings (see Landau and Gleitman, p. 37). There are, however, differences across subjects. In particular, the vague category "other" is relatively large for the blind children, leading the reader to wonder if some interesting differences remain undiscovered. Indeed, some differences are suggested by Urwin, who classified the two-word combinations produced by her oldest subject according to Brown's (1973) semantic categories. While all of the categories were attested, locative relationships were rarely expressed and the utterances often referred to the child's own activities. As we shall see later, this hints at an important thematic difference in the way blind and sighted children use language.

The greatest delay reported at the multi-word level is Landau and Gleitman's finding that their blind subjects were late in acquiring auxiliary verbs. They attribute this to a proportionally greater number of declaratives in mothers' language to their blind children and a correspondingly fewer number of yes–no questions. In English, auxiliaries are stressed in yes–no questions and are therefore relatively salient in these structures, which would presumably aid children in learning them.

This is not to say that there are no other areas in which blind children's language development is seen as different from sighted children's. In particular, Mills' discussion of phonology (1983a) and Mulford's work on reference (1980, 1983) suggest some difficulties. Mulford's investigation of referential terms in three to five year old blind children indicates that pronoun use appears to be the same for her blind subjects as for the sighted five year olds described by Wales (1979). However, she did find the blind children making semantically based errors. Moreover, exophoric pronominal references, those which relate to experience and the situational context, were less frequent than endophoric references for the blind children. Endophoric references relate to language and the linguistic context, and may therefore be more accessible to the blind. Perhaps most interesting, Mulford found that the blind children used deictic terms such as "this" and "there" as names for locations and entities but were not sensitive to the relative value of deictics with respect to the speaker. Mulford's analysis demonstrates the importance of delving beneath the surface to examine qualitative differences in use that may be obscured by simple counts of frequency or merely looking for the presence or absence of certain structures.

Reports of early lexical and semantic development in blind children provide an interesting initial survey, but they are generally too superficial to shed light on the possible roles of visual perception (and conceptual development) on language acquisition. For the most part the studies focus on the end product. This raises important questions about subtle differences in the relative use of various types of words and semantic categories and, more importantly, about some of the processes involved in getting to these end points.

In fact, understanding more about the language-learning process is a principal concern of Landau and Gleitman. The bulk of their study documents how one of their three blind subjects came to understand and use such visually based expressions as "look," "see," and color terms. They assume that the task is one of mapping, that is, that the subject had a concept for, say, "explore with the hands" and that she was motivated to discover which word in English expressed the meaning. Landau and Gleitman demonstrate that their subject interpreted "look" as meaning roughly "explore haptically." We should note at this point that not all researchers regard lexical development as a mapping of words on to pre-existing concepts. Other views regard language and cognition as mutually informative and do not necessarily give priority to conceptual development. (See Gopnik and Meltzoff, 1985a for one discussion of this.) In any case, the interesting question becomes: How did the blind child come to attach meaning to the word "look"?

Landau and Gleitman consider sentential context more important than situational context and propose that knowledge of the syntactic properties of verbs, principally subcategorizational restrictions, permits the blind child to deduce the meaning of visual terms. They begin by wondering if the mother's use of "look" occurred mainly when objects are touchable and whether that alone would distinguish "look" from other verbs, such as *give*, *put* and *get*, that might mean "explore with the hands." They find this criterion inadequate for distinguishing the various verbs. They then consider syntactic co-occurrence restrictions for the verbs. It so happens that the syntactic frames are of a certain sort in these particular data. Of 25 maternal utterances containing the verb "look," 18 are interjections and it is also the case that the referents of these 18 interjections are near and touchable. Landau and Gleitman give primacy to syntax, but in fact there is nothing privileged about the syntax in this situation. For example, in some linguistic environments (e.g., "look at x") the object ("x") is syntactically required, but *look* as an interjective is much looser (e.g., "look, I have a headache"). It just so happens that the set of x is usually *semantically* constrained in this particular universe of discourse by things which can be haptically explored.

Obviously, the blind subject is attending to and learning about syntax, but she is also learning from real-world inferences based on the semantic arguments of the verb and the deictic referents that co-occur with these interjectives. It would seem that this subject is using an inferential strategy based on syntactic, semantic, and pragmatic information and not simply the syntactic strategy Landau and Gleitman propose.

One simple way to further explore this is to consider how these syntactic frames would look in conversations with sighted children. One would not expect, in any scene with sighted children, that the use of "look" and "see" would be mainly constrained to referents that can be touched. In fact, one would expect to hear utterances such as "Look. See the bird/moon/sailboat" and so on. In other words, one would not expect to find these kinds of accommodations or co-occurrences with touchable objects that led the blind child to interpret *"look"* as meaning haptically explore. I think we cannot dismiss the possibility that learning meaning involves a complex interaction of many factors and cannot be explained by knowledge of grammar alone.

To return to the issue raised above, we are interested in learning more about how children begin to learn language when they do not have visual access to the world. The presence or absence of words and phrases tells us little about whether the blind children's use and knowledge of them is comparable to sighted children's. It also tells us nothing about how blind children go about learning these words. Since obviously different kinds of information are available to the two groups, what kinds of strategies are exploited by blind children? Can these suggest alternative strategies available to sighted children that will help us better understand the flexibility of the language learning system more generally? Since vision, or its absence, may also impact conceptual development, can this help inform us about the relationship between language and other aspects of cognitive development?

Chapter 3 introduces the methodology and subjects that will help us begin to examine these questions.

3 Methodology and introduction of subjects

The most crucial requirement for the study was to identify several congenitally blind children who were normally developing and who had no concomitant handicaps. This was imperative since the purpose of the investigation is not to describe blind children's language behavior but to examine the possible roles of vision in language development more generally and to try and understand better the impact of certain cognitive and social factors on language development.

The principal data base is media-recorded samples of spontaneous language produced in the familiar home environment. These are supplemented by parental records and individualized experiments. There are four major reasons for using this technique. First, experimental paradigms for gathering language data from infants and toddlers are not generally feasible. Secondly, we do not have adequate information about how blind children can be expected to respond in natural, much less experimental, situations. Thirdly, most of our understanding of early language acquisition is drawn from naturalistic studies of sighted children and this will provide an important basis for comparison. Fourthly, individualized experiments that are tailored to an individual child's vocabulary and experience maximize the possibility that a young child will comprehend and respond to experimental probes. These probes then are an important supplement to the spontaneous data that can illuminate findings and justify drawing certain conclusions.

This chapter describes each of the six subjects in some detail and then discusses the general methodology for data collection. Specific coding systems and analyses are described in the chapters presenting results.

In order to assess the role of visual information as a mechanism in normally progressing language development, it is essential to eliminate as many confounding factors as possible. Yet, the blind population is an exceedingly heterogeneous group who often share only their blindness. And even the degree of blindness varies.

Previous research has suffered considerably from a lack of controls that could differentiate the effects of blindness from other factors (e.g., premature birth, additional handicaps, and institutionalization) which can lead to developmental delays. Unfortunately, one factor can never be fully accommodated: the impact on families of having a severely handicapped child. Recent research has also suffered because comparable data for sighted children were not available.

3.1   Criteria for subject selection

In an effort to compensate for some of these problems, stringent criteria were identified for the selection of blind subjects. In addition, sighted children who were comparable in as many respects as possible to the blind children were included in the study. This served two functions. First, it ensured availability of wholly analogous data for blind and sighted children; and secondly, it provided a basis for comparing information gathered in the present study with results obtained in other investigations of early language acquisition. Methodological and time factors permitted the in-depth study of six children: four blind and two fully sighted.

The blind children who participated in the study all met the following rigid criteria:

(1) *Congenitally blind:*   Two children had to be totally blind from birth or have light perception only, and two had to have severely limited residual vision such as shadow perception or minimal form recognition (see table 2.1, Hierarchy of Visual Function). The rationale for including two children with relative rather than total blindness was that differences between the two would help identify those aspects of language which are most strongly associated with vision. If differences in certain aspects of language development could be observed, it would suggest that those areas are facilitated by even limited visual information. It was also hoped that a kind of continuum of communicative strategies could be identified rather than merely identifying absolute contrasts between blind and sighted children.

(2) *No concomitant handicaps:*   The ophthalmologic diagnosis had to indicate an ocular pathology that is not associated with complicating conditions. Certain disorders are associated with additional handicaps (e.g., cortical blindness is highly correlated with mental retardation) or other factors such as chronic pain (infantile glaucoma), recurrent hospitalizations, prematurity (RLF) and so on. Likely etiologies were genetic disorders that are generally only ocular in nature and structural anomalies that do not appear to be related to other disorders. The children had to be neurologically and physiologically intact apart from the blindness.

(3) *Monolingual English-speaking families:*   The complication of a bilingual home environment or of attempting to compare children acquiring different languages was unthinkable given the scope of the present study. Moreover, most existing research on child language is based on studies of children acquiring English in a monolingual setting.

(4) *Intact family with reasonable economic security* (i.e., middle class):   It was

important that the children benefit from an emotionally stable home where the parents are coming to accept their child's impairment and are providing a supportive environment to maximize the child's chances for "normal" development. (See Urwin's discussion of "Shaun" for analysis of an emotionally unstable home.) Economic security was desirable since it would eliminate a possible source of additional instability. In addition, many studies of language acquisition with sighted populations have gathered data from middle-class children, so this requirement increased comparability. All other things being equal, we also hoped to locate children with an older, normally developing sibling since this would provide the blind child with additional opportunities for social interaction and might help diffuse the parent's frustration and obsession with their blind child (see Lairy and Harrison-Covello, 1973).

(5) *Normally developing:* The children had to appear to be age-appropriate during the initial meeting and be beginning to acquire language (babbling, imitations, and ideally the emergence of two or three words). This was assessed through a maternal interview and through the subjective impression of the researchers (see the section on Referrals below).

(6) *Parents willing to participate and interested in the project:* Because the study would be longitudinal and because it would require that the parents keep a record of their child's early words, it was especially important that the parents be enthusiastic about the study.

The sighted children in the study satisfied all of the above criteria except the first.

Initial interviews

Potential subjects were located through several pediatric ophthalmologists and organizations servicing the blind. Each family was visited in their home shortly after the referral. The goals of the study were explained and the data collection and observation procedures were discussed with the parents. This also provided an opportunity for observing the child interacting with his/her parents or sibling and the researcher. In addition, I conducted a maternal interview and completed a check list for certain behaviors observed during the session. Many of the items were drawn from various infant development scales. This record then permitted more accurate evaluation of the child's general development. (See appendix 1 for the list of items on the interview questionnaire.) The entire interview session was audio recorded.

Most of the children contacted were not included in the study because they failed to satisfy one or more of the criteria. Only four blind children who satisfied the criteria were located and all of them participated in the present investigation.

The sighted children were located through advertisements placed in the local newspaper and posted around the university. Children who satisfied the criteria and whose families had similar backgrounds to the blind children were then visited exactly as the blind children had been. Two children who were just beginning to use language and who were most similar to the blind children in terms of development as revealed in the interview questionnaire were selected for the present study.

3.2   The children

Each of the children is briefly introduced below in the order of increasing visual acuity. All of the children are identified by pseudonyms.

Teddy

Teddy is the second-born child of an intact middle-class family and is totally blind from a genetic disorder known as Leber's Cognital Amaurosis, which affects the retina. His situation is a very special one because his older brother, Alex, is also blind due to Leber's. This is an autosomal recessive inheritance which means that the affected children receive an abnormal gene from each parent making the child homozygous at that particular gene locus. There is no prior history of visual disorders in the family and both parents are phenotypically normal but heterozygous. After Alex was born the parents had genetic counseling and learned that there was a 25% chance that the disorder would be transmitted to any future child. After much consideration, Teddy was born four-and-a-half years later. Blindness was diagnosed when he was two weeks old. The family is a remarkable one: very loving and supportive, and there are many caring relatives in the area. Teddy's parents are thoughtful and positive in their approach to the children and have provided an environment that stresses independence and responsibility. Teddy's father is a high school teacher and has completed a master's degree in English. His mother is a pre-school teacher with an early childhood education background and several years of experience working with underprivileged children. She has not worked since Alex was born. The family has been active at the Blind Children's Center, where the children have been enrolled in infant and pre-school programs and the mother has participated in various parent support groups. Both children are in excellent health and are socially rewarding and engaging.

Teddy was five months old at the first visit and was a happy infant who was just beginning to sit independently and to vocalize on waking in the morning. He rapidly developed communicative and mobility skills and at fifteen months he was walking independently and had a productive vocabulary of eight words. ("Productive" is used here to mean that the child spoke these words on his own initiative and that the words were contextually appropriate. Children typically comprehend more words than they produce themselves and many children can be prompted to imitate words that they would not spontaneously say.)

He has engaged in relatively few stereotypic behaviors, though he does sometimes press his eyes. There have been no developmental delays or problems of the sort often reported for blind children. Because he apparently does not have light perception his walking is slow and sometimes mis-directed, but he eventually finds his way to his destination. He has always been able to occupy himself with interesting activities (especially finding objects to make noise with!) and has searched for favorite toys and objects as soon as he became independently mobile.

During many of the observation sessions Alex was at school, but the children regularly play together in the afternoon and we have made periodic recordings of these interactions. The relationship between Alex and Teddy (and of Alex's language more generally) is not a focus of this study and is discussed only where it has direct bearing on Teddy's development.

Teddy's social quotient as measured by the Maxfield–Buchholz scale has ranged between 117 and 134 (see section 3.3 below).

Lisa

Lisa is the second born of two children in an intact upper-middle-class family. She is congenitally blind with light perception due to Leber's and like Teddy she is an especially attractive child. Her elder brother was almost five when she was born and is unaffected by the disorder. He is a bright enjoyable child, both cognitively and socially advanced for his age. Both parents are college educated. Lisa's father is a businessman and her mother a housewife. Several housekeepers have provided some custodial care, but the mother is the primary caregiver. Both maternal and paternal grandparents live in the Los Angeles area, as do several other relatives, and all are supportive.

Lisa's blindness was first diagnosed when she was approximately three months old and her devastated parents spent several months consulting leading ophthalmologists throughout the country. By the time Lisa was in the second half of her first year, her parents accepted the irreversibility of her condition.

When we first met Lisa, she was an active fifteen-month-old who was mobile in her walker and also enjoyed walking while holding her mother's fingers. She had an extensive receptive vocabulary for nursery games and familiar routines and a productive vocabulary of eight words; names for family members, food and routines. She had well-developed hand coordi-nation at the midline, was beginning to eat table food and actively engaged in both tactile and oral exploration of objects. Lisa and her mother participated in a local infant and toddler program for handicapped children and in the infant program at the Blind Children's Center. When she was two, Lisa began attending the Center's pre-school two days a week.

Her parents have now become involved in fund-raising programs for visually impaired children. They have a positive attitude about Lisa's future and have provided her with a stimulating environment and a variety of experiences. Lisa's mother describes her as demanding and strong-willed, and there are times when the mother is (as she readily admits) quite indulgent of her, but this does not seem to have seriously affected Lisa's development. Stereotypic behaviors are limited to fairly persistent eye pressing and to gazing at bright lights.

Lisa began walking independently at $17\frac{1}{2}$ months. She was obviously nervous at first, but when she was 18 months she spontaneously began using echolocation as a guide. As she moved about she would periodically stop and then stomp her feet or clap her hands. From this time on she was able to turn into various rooms and avoid obstacles with remarkable accuracy. Her social quotient as measured by the Maxfield–Buchholz scale has ranged between 121 and 127. Lisa's language has been followed from the emergence of her first words to an MLU of 3.20, making it the greatest span of linguistic development documented in this study.

Julie

We first met Julie when she was ten months old, but regular visits were not scheduled until her first birthday. Julie was a full term baby born with microphthalmia (underdeveloped eyes). The etiology is unknown, though sometimes this is the result of an autosomal dominant genetic disorder. Her right eye is totally blind, but her left eye has a very small amount of residual vision. Initially this was thought to be limited to light perception, but there are behavioral indications that she has shadow perception and possibly some vague form perception. When Julie became mobile, she began to move toward large brightly contrasting objects and she also held certain small objects about one or two inches in front of her left eye. However, she will not reach for objects held in front of her, or held at various places around her periphery, and she continues to depend on tactile and oral exploration. Just prior to her first birthday, Julie's right eye was fitted with a prosthesis, making it impossible to detect her blindness from her physical appearance. (The left eye, while unusually small, is neither unattractive nor obviously defective in appearance.)

Like Lisa, Julie has a normally developing older brother. He was two years old when Julie was born, and has been a particularly devoted and solicitous sibling, anxious to have Julie participate in his play and go to nursery school with him. The two are so close that their mother rearranged their rooms so that they share one room for sleeping, and the other for playing. The family is middle-class and the maternal grandparents live nearby and often visit or care for the children, as do several other maternal relatives. Julie's mother is a housewife and her father is a shipping supervisor.

When we first met Julie, she was a happy responsive child, but very chubby, weighing nearly 30 pounds. She was not yet mobile and was unable to support herself in a standing position, and there was some concern that she was hypotonic (reduced muscle tone) as a result of her excess weight. She was babbling a little, but had no words, though at as young as ten months she was performing body movements associated with "patty cake," and during the next few months she acquired a large number of nursery games. She actively explored objects using a wide variety of schemata including tapping, banging, sniffing, tasting, and shaking.

When Julie was 14 months old her parents became concerned that her frequent "shuddering" behaviors were seizures. She then weighed 40 pounds. A medical examination revealed a normal electroencephalagram (EEG), but epilepsy was suspected, and Julie began taking phenobarbital. A barbiturate, phenobarbital has a depressive effect on motor areas of the cerebral cortex, but in some young children, it is non-sedative. Apparently it affected Julie in this way. Although her "seizures" were controlled, she became increasingly active and we began observing steady developmental progress. Soon after, her mother enrolled Julie in swimming classes which resulted in dramatic weight loss.

By 20 months, Julie was crawling about the house and climbing on furniture, and her lexicon began to develop rapidly. At 19 months she had acquired only ten words, which she rarely used. Then during a two-week period in her twentieth month, Julie went on vacation with her family, and while away she began using seventeen new words. From this point on, Julie became an increasingly verbal child.

After her second birthday, Julie began attending a pre-school class at the Blind Children's Center twice per week. At about the same time, her phenobarbital was discontinued with no adverse effects, and it appears that Julie does not actually suffer from epilepsy. By this time, Julie's weight had become normal and during the next few months she developed into a pretty toddler. Independent walking remained a problem as a result of out-turned feet, and orthopedic intervention may be necessary just before her third birthday.

Administrations of the Maxfield–Buchholz scale reveal a social quotient range of 81–103, but it is consistently the mobility items which lower her score. She is in fact age-appropriate or precocious for all other items and the relatively low scores are clearly not indicative of her general progress and potential, particularly during her third year.

Lydia

Lydia was referred to us almost a year after the other blind children had been located. She was 15 months old at the time, but was already surprisingly verbal. She is partially blind due to hypoplasia of the optic nerve, with unknown etiology. There is no vision in her left eye, and no central vision in her right eye, but there is some peripheral form vision in that eye. Blindness was suspected during a pediatric examination when Lydia was four months old, and the diagnosis was confirmed when she was six months old. Her mother recalled that she was surprised by the finding, since Lydia had been "like a regular baby."

The family is monolingual English-speaking, but of Mexican-American heritage, and some Spanish borrowings are used (e.g., *miha* – "my daughter" as a term of endearment; *papita* – "food" [colloquial]). Like the other children, Lydia is a second-born child and has a normally developing brother who is three years her senior. Her father is a blue-collar worker. Her mother, who was at home when the study began, now has a clerical job. During the day, Lydia is cared for by her maternal grandmother, who sometimes also cares for Lydia's infant cousin. While Lydia's parents have had some financial difficulties, the grandparents have been able to help, and the family as a whole is quite stable. The grandmother has had some college education and is currently completing a teaching credential.

When we met Lydia, she was just beginning to take a few independent steps and participated in numerous nursery routines in which she clapped, attempted to "sing" phrases or pointed out her own body parts. During the interview visit, I recorded 14 different spontaneous words used productively, and her mother reported several others. It was evident that Lydia's lexicon was already too advanced to begin the diary study, so I do not have a full record of the range of use for her first 100 words.

Lydia is a sparkling, vivacious little girl who is unusually social – both initiating and responsive. At the time of the interview visit, her object explorations were oral rather than tactile, and her mother reported that she rarely enjoyed toys. During the visit several reciprocal exchanges in which Lydia offered objects to others were observed, but these were apparently new and relatively infrequent occurrences. At the time, Lydia would reach for objects on sound cue and on visual cue if the item was placed in the lower left periphery, on or near the floor, but she would not reach for objects held silently in front of her. There has been no change in her visual function during the study.

When she was 16 months old Lydia began walking independently, and often went to her room to "play" by herself (mainly to take all of the toys out of a toy chest or make noise). She sometimes stumbles when she walks because she regularly misjudges the position of objects visible in her left periphery. Her vocabulary has steadily expanded, though she tends to pick up phrases as often as individual words. Her social quotient measured on the Maxfield–Buchholz scales has ranged between 147 and 156. Because she has some useful vision, the Vineland Scale was also administered, and her social quotient ranged between 91 and 107. Neither scale is wholly suitable for evaluating Lydia's personal and social development, since her residual vision gives her an advantage on the scale that is normed for blind children, yet she is at a disadvantage on the scales designed for fully sighted children. During the course of this investigation, her actual social quotient probably fell midway between the ranges on the two scales.

Brett

Brett is a fully sighted normally developing child with no apparent health problems. His parents are both college educated; his father is a scientist and his mother is completing her master's degree. While Brett's parents have had more education than those of some of the other children, he was well matched with the blind children in terms of his scores on developmental scales. He is a very engaging child, socially responsive and inviting, but equally able to play by himself with a variety of toys and household objects. When we met Brett, he was 16 months old, fully mobile and just beginning to use words. He had seven productive lexemes and regularly imitated words in his mother's speech, which made his linguistic development comparable to Lisa's and Teddy's at a similar age. Unlike the other children, he rarely enjoys nursery routines, though his parents have introduced him to several such games.

Two or three mornings a week Brett was looked after at a registered child care home while his mother attended classes. This experience was somewhat comparable to the infant and pre-school programs the blind children attended. One potentially important difference between Brett and the blind children was that Brett was an only child. However, handicapped children generally receive a great deal of attention and typically have intensive contact with their mothers, making their situations in many respects similar to an only child's.

Like the other children, both sets of grandparents live in the area and the families visit frequently on weekends. Brett's social quotient as measured by the Vineland Social Maturity scale has ranged between 127 and 138, again similar to the scores Lisa and Teddy had on the Maxfield–Buchholz scale.

Bonnie

Bonnie, an alert, socially oriented child, is the second born of two children in an intact middle-class home. She is fully sighted and normally developing and, like the other girls in the study, she has an elder brother two-and-a-half years her senior. Bonnie's father is a businessman and her mother is a pre-school deaf teacher with nine years of classroom experience. Her training and work background is similar to Teddy's mother's. Like the other children, Bonnie's family lives near both sets of grandparents, and her maternal grandmother often cares for her when her parents are out.

When we met Bonnie she was 12 months old and had a fairly large receptive vocabulary. Like the blind children, she enjoyed nursery games and had a repertoire of familiar routines where her role mainly involved body movements. She babbled while playing and vocalized to draw attention to herself. Her mother reported five lexemes, but these were used very infrequently and a lexical diary was not begun until she was $15\frac{1}{2}$ months old. Her lexicon has developed less rapidly than some of the other children's and she had not yet acquired 50 stable words when the present study ended.

But, far more important, Bonnie had an unusually rich gestural repertoire and communicated extensively with a behavioral network that included pointing, offering, showing, reaching, refusing and so on. She exploited visual regard and co-orientation and regularly imitated the behaviors and play of others. This was important for several reasons. First, this provided an opportunity to document the communicative strategies of a child who depended almost exclusively on visually based strategies for early communication – the complete antithesis of the system the blind children could develop. Secondly, if there is an ontogenetic primacy of certain communicative acts, the kinds of messages conveyed by Bonnie through conventionalized gestures should bear a strong resemblance to the messages conveyed in the blind children's earliest utterances, since both are the first instances of conventional signals. Such a finding would provide evidence for postulating developmental universals.

Although Bonnie has walked unsupported since she was $11\frac{1}{2}$ months old, her feet rotate inwards and she occasionally stumbles as a result. This situation has been improved through special shoes, but like Julie, she may require further orthopedic intervention to correct the problem.

Bonnie's social quotient as measured by the Vineland Scale is in the range of 118–141.

3.3   Observation sessions and data collection

Each child was visited in the home at approximately monthly intervals. The data were drawn primarily from media recorded interactions that spontaneously occurred during these visits, together with information supplied by the parents in informal interviews and from lexical diaries each family kept. Periodically, individualized experiments were conducted to explore various hypotheses about a particular child's development and there were several controlled observation sessions where the mother was asked to try to elicit specified behaviors or to encourage the child to engage in a particular activity.

Description of home visits and participants

The home visits began as soon as a child was located who satisfied all of the criteria for the study. Because referrals came slowly over the period of one full year, not all of the children were followed for the same amount of time, though all of the children were observed during the one-word stage. Table 3.1 lists the age range, number of visits and MLU range for each child for the duration of the study.

The home visits lasted approximately $1\frac{1}{2}$ to 2 hours and both the child and mother (in Lydia's case often her grandmother) were present at all sessions. In addition, fathers, siblings, and other relatives were sometimes home.

Table 3.1. *Number of visits, age range and MLU range for each child*

Child	No. of visits	Age range	MLU range
Teddy	16[a]	0;9;29–2;1;13	few words – 2.50
Lisa	16[bc]	1;3;14–2;7;26	few words – 3.20
Julie	16[b]	1;0;0–2;4;5	0 – 1.29
Lydia	6[b]	1;2;27–1;8;18	1.30[d] – 1.60[e]
Brett	8[b]	1;4;4–2;0;19	few words – 1.86
Bonnie	7[b]	1;0;1–1;6;7	0 – 1.0

[a] There were 7 additional visits prior to 0;9;25 but these are not analyzed in the present investigation
[b] Includes initial interview
[c] Plus data from 3 audio tapes recorded in a classroom or at home by parents
[d] Estimated MLU during interview visit
[e] Estimated MLU since portions of many utterances are unintelligible

There were two observers present at each session, primarily my colleague Linda Kekelis and myself.

Mothers were asked to do whatever they would normally do with their child and the families quickly became comfortable with the situation. It is important to note that the child was the center of attention throughout most of the session. Early in the visit, I discussed the lexical diary with the mother. The researchers informally elicited information about the child's development and recent achievements at convenient points during the visit – largely near the beginning and end of the session. Some visits were structured to include a specific activity such as having lunch, taking a bath or playing with toys so that the children were observed in a variety of similar situations at comparable ages.

During the sessions the researchers were largely quiet observers, but they responded normally if the child approached them and periodically engaged the child in a specific activity.

Media recordings

The home visits were audio recorded in their entirety using a battery powered Sony 142 portable cassette tape recorder and a portable omni-directional microphone. Throughout the period both researchers took extensive handwritten contextual notes to clarify the audio recording. When one researcher was actually interacting with the child, the other researcher took notes. Approximately 15 to 20 minutes of the observational period was also video recorded using a Panasonic portable video cassette recorder, model NV-8400, and a Quazar VK705RQ camera, modified with a specially fitted manually operated lens to permit filming in low light conditions. A Panasonic NV-8200 video recorder was used for data analysis. This non-portable unit has variable speed control and other features which permit a finer grained analysis than would be possible with a simpler portable model.

Lexical diaries

The mothers were instructed to keep a record of the child's productive vocabulary development. Each new word spontaneously used was entered on a special form, together with information about the situation of utterance and the referent involved. New uses of previously acquired words were also recorded so that the range of use could be documented and the bases for extensions could be identified. Because of the enormity of the task, the parents were not asked to record each instance of word use that duplicated a previous entry, but the mothers were regularly interviewed about recurrent usage in order to identify those meanings which were used only once or which were eventually extinguished and those meanings which eventually stabilized. The diary was kept for the first 100 words acquired by each child and some mothers continued the record until it became an impossible task to keep up with the child's rapidly developing lexicon. The diary methodology was based on similar studies previously reported in the literature (Nelson, 1973a; Braunwald and Brislin, 1979; Rescorla, 1981). The mothers were trained to use the form as soon as their child had acquired three stable lexemes and the records were discussed and collected at each home visit. Tasks relating to word comprehension were routinely conducted and comprehension was also specifically observed during home visits. (See also section 3.3.5.)

Developmental assessment

In addition to the collection of linguistic data, each child's motor, cognitive, and social skills were assessed at approximately six-monthly intervals. The Maxfield–Buchholz scales and the Bayley scales were used in order to provide comparability with previous research. Summary notes were written after each visit to describe progress in all areas and an extensive record of developmental milestones was kept for each child.

Individual experiments and controlled observational sessions

Experimental probes designed to explore a particular aspect of development in an individual child were administered at appropriate times throughout the course of the study. Many of these were comprehension tasks. Since each child had a unique lexicon, tasks were designed to elicit information specific to the child. Some of the tasks presented the child with appropriate and inappropriate exemplars of items for lexemes that appeared to be over- or underextended in the child's productive lexicon in order to determine if the same strategies prevailed in comprehension. At other times children were asked to identify unfamiliar exemplars of stable productive lexemes. Various other tasks were devised as the children's language skills matured. After a briefing, the mother sometimes helped administer these experiments. In addition to the individualized experiments, informal probes were conducted spontaneously to evaluate progress in numerous areas of language and cognitive development. For example, the child might be encouraged to engage in reciprocal exchanges, to search for displaced objects, or to follow directions in playing with a toy, and so on. The individualized experiments and developmental probes are discussed in detail at relevant points in the analysis.

3.4 Transcription techniques

Each audio recording was listened to within two days of the home visit and approximately 45 minutes of the tape were selected to be transcribed. This generally included all or most of the first side of the tape, when the children were generally "fresher," plus selected portions of the second side containing lengthy verbal interactions or particularly interesting verbal behavior. The segment of the audio tape corresponding to the video record was always transcribed in its entirety.

The written transcripts were made according to the format described by Ochs (1979). Certain modifications were introduced to accommodate the special status of the blind children. For example, eye gaze was irrelevant for these children, but a notation for facial orientation was introduced, since sighted interlocutors typically watch facial expressions even in blind children, and it was possible that the child's orientation may have inadvertently affected the interaction (Fraiberg, 1977; Urwin, 1978a). Since blind children don't use gestures, these could not be recorded, but the child's object explorations and hand movements were noted in more detail than would be usual for sighted children. The children's utterances were transcribed exclusively in the International Phonetic Alphabet (IPA), with terminal intonation contours marked, until the final sessions when the children regularly produced utterances of three or more stable words. At this point, their speech was written in standard orthography unless the interpretation was uncertain. However, after the children had acquired 50 words or more, many of the phonetically transcribed utterances were also glossed in standard orthography to facilitate analysis, yet at the same time to allow for alternative interpretations and the future investigation of phonological development.

The initial transcript of the audio tape took an average of 20 hours and was completed by carefully trained research assistants, who were graduate or advanced undergraduate students in linguistics or psychology. This initial transcript was then checked by either Kekelis or myself and differences in interpretation, especially those affecting the interpretation of meaning, were resolved between the two researchers involved. In a few instances, both interpretations were included in the final transcript. Each researcher added contextual information based on hand-written notes.

The transcript of the audio record was then supplemented with information from the video recording. This enabled us to check the accuracy of our handwritten contextual notes and provided very rich and precise detail about the non-verbal aspects of the interactions for a significant portion of the transcript. The entire transcription process took between 30 and 35 hours for each home visit. The completed transcript was then typed. A sample page from a typed transcript is presented in appendix 2.

3.5   Coding

Details of the coding and classification systems used are presented in the relevant chapters, that is, those relating to lexical acquisition are discussed in chapter 4, to the emergence of semantic structures in chapter 5, and to developments in the use of illocutionary force in chapter 6.

4   First words

4.1   The emergence of words

Children's ability to interact with others and to engage in rudimentary forms of communication emerges during their first year when they participate in reciprocal interchanges with their caregivers. Children usually exploit various sorts of vocal and gestural strategies which take the form of increasingly conventionalized signals during the last quarter of the first year (see Bates *et al.*, 1979 for review). Such signals are neither symbolic nor linguistic in any standard sense of these notions. Typical examples in the repertoires of most sighted children are instances of communicative reaching, pointing, and offering. Parallel signals from blind children appear to involve the use of ritualized hand movements associated with specific nursery routines (Urwin, 1978a, b). A significant qualitative change in children's communicative strategies occurs when they begin to acquire and use words.

The first instances of word-like vocalizations occur when children consistently use a relatively stable sound pattern in a particular situation. Such patterns differ from prelinguistic babbling in that they represent a stable sequence and they are used with a consistent communicative (or simply interactional) function, but these patterns differ from actual words in that they need not share meaning or form with any word in the target language. Hence, they seem to form a bridge between non-linguistic and linguistic vocalization. Many of the early diary studies indicate that these patterns originate in children's imitating various environmental sounds, including their own spontaneous noises (see Guillaume, 1978; Leopold, 1939–49; Stern and Stern, 1928). Researchers have referred to these stable patterns with a variety of terms including "phonetically consistent forms" or "PCFs" (Dore, 1975); "proto-language" (Halliday, 1975); "vocal gestures" (Bates, Camaioni and Volterra, 1975); "proto-words" (Menyuk and Menn, 1979) and "pre-words" (Ferguson, 1976).

The movement from "pre-words" to true words involves development along three dimensions: (1) true words represent an attempt to phonetically reproduce an actual word in the target language; (2) true words share some aspect of reference with the standard (adult) meaning for that word; and (3) true words are moved from their original context and are used in a variety of situations. Development does not necessarily progress simultaneously across all three dimensions.

There is considerable evidence that early "words," including those which are derived from adult forms, are associated with just one particular context and that the term designates an event in its entirety, rather than being associated with some specific aspect of the event. These have been called "global reference" (Piaget, 1952a; Werner and Kaplan, 1963) or, when used in certain ritualized contexts, "pure performatives" (Greenfield and Smith, 1976). (See also Barrett, 1983; Bates *et al.*, 1979; Ferguson and Slobin, 1973.) For instance, Werner and Kaplan cite an example in which a child appears to use the form "mammam" to refer to a cluster of events related to eating and to people involved in feeding the child. Such forms are differentiated from their original context fairly soon and come to refer to some specific element in a variety of different situations. However, there are times when a term becomes associated with the appropriate element in an event, but remains context-bound for a longer time. This may be especially true of words related to actions (see Barrett, 1983). Most researchers infer that terms become symbolic vehicles, and therefore true words, when the child uses them to designate a particular aspect of an event in a variety of situations (including identifying objects), even though the child's meaning for a word may not correspond completely to the adult meaning.

Evaluating early word acquisition involves documenting both the kinds of things, actions and concepts for which a child acquires some stable expression and examining the way in which meaning is attached to these expressions.

4.1.1   Content of early lexicons

There is a fair consistency in the kinds of words that are reported in the emerging lexicons of young children. A large proportion of most children's first 50 or so words consist of object words, but there are also words related to familiar routines, actions, relations and words involved in social expressions such as greetings. Most object words refer to familiar items of food, clothing, animals, vehicles, toys, and people. Some individual variation in the kinds of words acquired by different children has been observed, particularly the referential and expressive styles identified by Nelson (1973a). Expressive children show a largely self-oriented language use and typically learn nominals functioning at the personal-social level, such as words for feelings and needs, while referential children have an object-oriented use of language and center on names of objects and actions.

After several months of gradually accumulating 10 or 20 terms, a burst in the rate of acquisition is often observed when a child is around 18 to 20 months old. At this time the vocabulary may double or triple and rapid acquisition of new words continues for three or four years. This acceleration in vocabulary may be coincident with the child's discovery that words are symbolic referential expressions. This discovery has been called the "designation hypothesis" (Dore, 1978) and the "naming insight" (McShane, 1979). Bloom (1973) hypothesized that this development reflects the emergence of representational object permanence (Piaget's substage VI) toward the end of the sensori-motor period. She observed that the period was marked by an increasing frequency in the use of object words (which she calls "substantives"). Partly in response to this suggestion other researchers sought to find a correlation between object permanence and the emergence of object words, but failed (see Bates *et al.*, 1979 for review; McCune-Nicolich, 1981). It is important to recognize though that these researchers were seeking a relationship between object permanence and *first* object words and their findings do not refute Bloom's hypothesis that the later vocabulary burst and referential insight relate to an emerging conceptual capacity for mental representation.

4.1.2   The meaning of early words

Tracing the ways in which meanings evolve in children's early lexicons is crucial to understanding emerging conceptual and linguistic organization. Studies of children's early word use indicate that the domain of application for early words may be quite different from adult usage of the same word. Moreover, early meanings for words may vary significantly among individual children. These differences occur because children construct hypotheses about word meanings based on their own unique experiences, their understanding of the world in general, and the way in which their vocabularies are structured at a given point in time. Lexical development involves much more than merely establishing a set of one-to-one correspondences between a term and a referent. Children must abstract information associated with early instances of word use and use this information as a basis for generalizing the domain of application to new situations. This process is essential if a term is to move from functioning as a specific "name" to denoting a heterogeneous class of referents.

The principal evidence about the kinds of information that are attached to early words comes from investigations of overextension, or the misapplication of a word by using it to refer to a broader range of referents than is appropriate in the adult language (e.g., applying "doggie" to all animals). Explicit in most of this research is the assumption that overextension reflects certain principled strategies including some form of classification, though different researchers credit young children with varying degrees of sophistication in terms of the strategies that are inferred (Bloom, 1973; Bowerman, 1976, 1977, 1978; Clark, 1973, 1975; Kuczaj and Barrett, 1986; Nelson,

1973b, 1974, 1979; Piaget, 1951; Vygotsky, 1962; Werner and Kaplan, 1963). Of course, overextension is only a highly visible, and often amusing, aspect of the more basic process of "extension" in which early words are abstracted from their original context and applied to new situations. The failure to generalize a term to its full range of use is "underextension," a prevalent but far less visible phenomenon (see Anglin, 1977; Bloom, 1973).

There is some indication that words that are overextended in production may correspond somewhat more closely to standard use in comprehension (Benedict, 1979; Thomason and Chapman, 1975; Huttenlocher, 1974; Labov and Labov, 1974).

Much was written during the 1970s about how children acquire lexical meanings. The major ideas are summarized below. (For more detailed discussions see Bates *et al.*, 1979; Bowerman, 1978; Dunlea, 1982 and for a theoretical critique, Carey, 1982.)

Most analyses of lexical development point to a conceptual basis for word meaning and suggest that perceptual information constitutes the fundamental building blocks in the development of meaning. This is true of theories that explain acquisition in terms of increasing the number of meaning components (e.g., Clark's (1973) Semantic Features Hypothesis) and of theories holding that concepts, and hence meanings, are built on a family resemblance to prototype model (e.g., Rosch, 1978) and also to investigations which suggest an interaction between these two (e.g., Andersen, 1975; Bowerman, 1977). The notion that perceptual concepts are the primitives in constructing lexical meaning is held by the empiricist view of semantics more generally (see J. Fodor *et al.*, 1982).

The pioneering work of Clark (1973, 1975) and Nelson (1973b) assumes that children build word meanings on the basis of one or two stable elements of meaning. Clark's theory of semantic feature acquisition, based on analysis of numerous diary records, proposes that children begin by associating only one or two features with a word and gradually add additional criterial features until the child's understanding of the term corresponds to adult usage. The child's first hypotheses about what words mean stem from the conceptual organization of non-linguistic information, particularly the perceptually based features of shape, movement, size, texture, sound, and taste. For any given word, children initially command a limited number of features and may overextend the word to cover other referents which share one or more of the features. The following example based on shape is illustrative:

Lexical item:	mooi (child acquiring English)
First referent:	moon
Domain of application:	cakes, round marks on windows, and in books, round shapes in books, tooling on leather book covers, round post marks, letter 'O'

Note: based on Clark (1973), p. 80

There are also instances of "partial overextension" where a term is extended to new referents which have just one of two dominant features (e.g., the features of movement and roughness associated with a toy goat are the basis of one child's extending his name for that toy to all moving objects and also to all rough surfaces).

According to the semantic feature hypothesis, children eventually narrow down the meaning of overextended lexemes as new words are added within a single domain (e.g., animals, food) and some of the criterial features serve to differentiate one term from a related term. Thus, for example, the feature "horn" or "large" might differentiate cows from dogs when a young child who has used the word "dog" for all animals first acquires the word "cow," yet both terms may be overextended in comparison with adult usage.

Traditionally, Clark's view is seen as contrasting with that of Nelson (1973b) who proposes that functional rather than perceptual characteristics form the core of children's early object concepts. However, the debate spawned by the two views is in part the result of their interpreters. Nelson's purpose was not so much to develop a theory of lexical extension as it was to explore whether or not children in their second year exhibit categorization strategies. Although organizational strategies are thought to underlie early lexical development, many psychologists hold that young children are incapable of classifying (see Inhelder and Piaget, 1964; Vygotsky, 1962), while others hold that intensive classification does originate during the sensorimotor period (Cohen and Strauss, 1979).

Nelson's investigation of spontaneous sorting in infants between the ages of 12 and 24 months indicates that children engage in consistent sorting and grouping activities prior to the acquisition of relevant language and that the sorting criteria are generally functional in nature, that is, they are based on the child's understanding of how an item is used and of the dynamic states of objects. In this view, objects are initially viewed in terms of their "functional cores" from the child's perspective. Subsequent researchers have interpreted Nelson's position to be that lexical meaning is based on the extension of this functional information (see Barrett, 1978; Gentner, 1978; Press, 1974; Thomson and Chapman, 1977). In fact, Nelson proposed that while functional criteria are initially defining, extensions may also proceed on the basis of perceptual criteria.

The notion that children build word meanings on the basis of one or two stable elements of meaning contrasts with the more traditional view in psychology that early word meanings are used as "complexive" groupings. That is, a word is extended on the basis of some recognized similarity between two referents, then may be extended to a third referent on the basis of some feature shared with a preceding referent, but the various referents do not all share the same features. Vygotsky's (1962) classic example is of a child who extends the word "quah" from a duck swimming in a pond, to all liquids, then to a coin with an eagle on it, and finally to all round coin-like objects. In fact, there are reports of both categorical and complexive uses of early words and neither strategy seems to have ontogenetic priority over the other.

An alternative to the feature component model of lexical development draws on the prototype model of category structure (see Rosch, 1973, 1975a, 1977; Rosch and Mervis, 1975). The crucial insight is that categories for both adults and children may consist of a core meaning, or a focal exemplar, which is surrounded by other category members of progressively decreasing similarity to the core meaning. Category boundaries are by definition vague, since peripheral members may exhibit a fairly high degree of fluidity: they may shift category membership in response to circumstances prevailing at a given time. A good exemplar of the category "bird" is a robin, while a penguin is a more peripheral member. An implication of this theory for child development is that rather than focusing only on the child's acquisition of criterial attributes, researchers should also consider the role of core meaning in children's initial lexical classifications.

Application of the theory reveals that the complexive strategies used in early categorization are not necessarily the primitive "chained complexes" proposed by Vygotsky that reflect unstable categories, but rather that category membership is a matter of degree of variation from a prototype (see Bowerman, 1976, 1977, 1978, 1979 and for slightly older children Andersen, 1975 and Anglin, 1977). All referents share something, but not necessarily the same thing, with a prototype referent. This is of course similar to Clark's notion of partial extension.

In child language, several factors contribute to the formation of a prototype including high saliency, frequency of input, and first referent, though typically firstness correlates with prototype.

Bowerman's (1977) application of the family resemblance model suggests a logical strategy on the part of children that might otherwise appear whimsical, as illustrated in the following example for the word "kick."

Kick

Prototype: kicking a ball with the foot so that it is propelled forward.

Features: (a) waving limb (b) sudden sharp contact (especially between body part and the object), (c) an object propelled.

Selected examples: 18th month: (first use) as kicks a floor fan with her foot (Features a, b); looking at a picture of a kitten with ball near its paw (all features, in anticipated event?); watching moth fluttering on a table (a); watching row of cartoon turtles on TV doing can-can (a). 19th month: just before throwing something (a, c); "kick bottle" after pushing bottle with her feet, making it roll (all features). 21st month: as makes ball roll by bumping it with front wheel of kiddicar (b, c); pushing teddy bear's stomach against [sister's] chest (b); pushing her stomach against a mirror (b); pushing her chest against a sink (b), etc.

Bowerman, 1977; table 2

Children seem to analyze prototypes, at least to some extent, since young children extract and recognize attributes of the original referent when they occur in different configurations in new referents. Further, some aspects of a prototypical referent may be more criterial than others. Hence, there is a complementary relationship between representation in terms of prototypes and feature analysis.

The difference between Vygotsky's chained complexes and the analysis based on family resemblance to a prototype lies in the degree of organization researchers are willing to impute to children. Prototype theory credits the child with a category concept where the process for inclusion of instances is similar to adult application of prototype groupings, though specific features may not correspond to adult criteria for the same category. The psychological construct of chained complexes ascribes a more primitive process to children than to adults which yields less stable classifications.

Extensions, whether viewed in terms of featural analysis of a prototype or a more traditional categorical analysis, show a predominance of perceptual attributes, but clearly there is a multiplicity of information that contributes to the construction of meaning components, including perceptual and functional features and to a lesser extent affective information (e.g., "hot" for non-hot forbidden items) and association through contiguity (e.g., "night night" for blanket). Underlying the process of extension is the children's propensity to construct hypotheses about the essential components of meaning for various words.

4.1.3   Classification as a process

It is the cognitive process of categorization, or classification, that permits the grouping of entities and events that are distinguishable from one another. Hence, an underlying mechanism in lexical development is assumed to be categorization schemata. The classifications that are inferred from children's lexical extensions are not the same as adult classifications. In particular, naturalness of classes is not necessarily preserved. Naturalness would predict that attributes such as 'animal' or 'liquid' or 'toy' are inherently defining. Nevertheless, children do seem to recognize similarities and operate on them. Although Nelson and others (Riciutti, 1965; Starkey, 1981) have demonstrated that infants under two years do engage in consistent non-linguistic sorting behavior, ascribing classification abilities to very young children remains controversial. Sugarman (1983) suggests that class-consistent constructions in one year olds can result from the child's simply first selecting items that stand out in an array. (All instances of one item stand out relative to all instances of another.) Sugarman's investigation of object manipulations by 40 children between 12 and 36 months indicates that even 12 month old children perform class-consistent selection of objects and group identical objects. However, the nature of the constructions and the cognitive organization that appears to underlie them suggests developmental differences. Sugarman talks of "constructions" rather than groups since class-consistent behaviour may be revealed in a variety of ways including such rudimentary behaviors as successively banging on objects of one class (usually the youngest group); serially manipulating objects in a class (1 to $1\frac{1}{2}$ years); spatially grouping objects of one class ($1\frac{1}{2}$ to 2 years); and among older children, arranging objects so that members of one group correspond to members of another (e.g., putting spoons into cups) or creating symmetrical arrays of objects. Most constructions from the 12 and 18 month old subjects involved objects from only one class and Sugarman argues that their behavior may be an artifact of picking out salient or interesting objects. For our purposes, the crucial finding is that even one year olds respond to similar objects in similar ways and that during the second year there is increasing evidence of more analytic behavior. The emergence of this behavior is coincident with the acceleration of vocabulary acquisition and the emerging processes of lexical development.

4.2   Hypotheses about lexical development in blind children

There is evidence that the content of blind children's vocabularies is similar to sighted children's (Urwin, 1978a; Landau, 1981; Landau and Gleitman, 1985). In fact, Landau's research led her to conclude that "blind children do talk about objects and their locations in space, actions, and events and do so in just the same way as sighted children at the same linguistic level" (1983, p. 66). But previous studies have not sought to document the domain of application of blind children's first words or to analyse the children's hypotheses about the meanings of these words.

Even if blind children use the same lexical forms as sighted children, it is probable that the referents to which they extend the original word will differ from sighted children's. This is because lexical constructions must be based on the features that are salient or criterial from the blind child's perspective. Hence, categorical arrangements may differ from sighted children's *and* may vary from adult usage to a greater extent than is the case for sighted children, since different features may dominate. If perceptual features are most criterial they are likely to involve texture, weight, taste, and audible sounds, rather than peripheral shape and movement. As a result, as blind children's meanings are refined in terms of the target language, they face the additional task of trying to learn sighted criteria for categorization and then discovering ways of reconciling their own information about objects and events with those which predominate in the sighted world.

In the light of this discussion, two hypotheses relating to lexical acquisition in blind children are advanced:

Hypothesis 1: Blind children will extend the domain of application for first acquired lexemes as the result of the same process which motivates sighted children's lexical extensions, but the extraction of criterial information will reflect the blind children's organizational principles and the relative salience of tactile, kinesthetic, auditory, and oral features. This predicts that overextensions will be equally frequent in the blind and sighted children's data, but that the blind children will disproportionately rely on features such as textures and sound.

Hypothesis 2: Blind children will misapply terms for a longer period of time and will have greater difficulty than sighted children in bringing their meanings in line with standard adult usage.

4.3   Method

Five children participated in this portion of the study: Teddy, Lisa, Julie and Brett and Bonnie (in order of increasing vision). Bonnie, somewhat younger than the other children, was using only 20 or so words when the study ended and her lexical records are used only to explore earliest strategies. Lydia was excluded from the lexical study since she had already learned a large number of words when she joined the project.

The primary sources of data were diary records kept by each of the mothers, documenting the emergence and use of their child's first 100 productive words. The record started as soon as the child began to use words. Records were collected during each session and reviewed by the mother and me to clarify information and to elicit the parents' impressions about their child's use of words. Mothers were given photocopies of the records after each collection. Diary records were augmented by information obtained during home visits and from the media recorded samples. The diary required the mother to record each use of a new word, and each use of an already acquired word unless it was produced in an identical situation to an already recorded use. (The mothers found it impossible to record every use of every word.) The diary included data on the actual word produced; the date of use; whether or not the word was an imitation of something said by someone else; the approximate adult gloss; the mother's interpretation of the child's message; whether or not the word had been used before, and if it had, whether the meaning was the same. A word was considered productive if the child used it spontaneously on three occasions.

There are of course drawbacks to the diary method (Nelson, 1973a; Rescorla, 1980), but in the absence of a suitable alternative, this is the only

Table 4.1. *Object group, salient features in order of presentation in sorting task*

	Object group	Salient features
1	3 pieces fabric (4″ × 4″) 3 pieces cardboard (4″ × 4″)	texture, weight
2	3 metal eating utensils 3 metal cars	function, shape
3	2 wooden cylinders 2 wooden blocks 2 plastic cylinders 2 plastic blocks	form, texture, function
4	3 round plastic rattles 3 plastic balls	form, function, sound

way to obtain the necessary data. Moreover, because parents are particularly interested in their children's first words, especially when the child has special problems, a large proportion of novel development is recognized (Braunwald and Brislin, 1979). The parents were trained thoroughly, and the recorded data was corroborated by observations during the visits.

In addition to recording word use, individualized experiments were introduced to supplement information and to explore differences in production and comprehension.

Sorting Task: Following the procedures reported in Nelson (1973b) and Sugarman (1983) children were presented with collections of items that could be grouped on the basis of various criteria; all items were selected for saliency of non-visual attributes. The items, salient features, and order of presentation are listed in table 4.1.

The coding system

Classification of word type Each word was classified into one of ten mutually exclusive categories based on the meaning encoded in the child's initial productive use. In principle, it was possible that a term could shift from one category to another in the process of extension, though in fact this rarely occurred, except when expressions originally associated with routines were extended to new kinds of activities.

Classification of word types

Objects: Concrete substantive items which can be directly manipulated by the child, in whole or in part (e.g., food, clothing, body parts, vehicles).

People and family pets: Important animate beings, usually referred to by a specific name (e.g., mama, dada, rover).

Sounds: Referents which are known on the basis of the sounds they emit. As it turned out, this category was useful only for the blind children and at all times inferences about the blind children's perspective were used to classify these terms, thus birds are known only on the basis of chirping sounds to most blind children, although sighted children have access to additional information.

Actions and states: Principally used to classify the activity or conditions of people (jump, sing) and objects (roll, bounce).

Relational terms: Terms used to express the functions of existence, non-existence, recurrence, negation and possession. All such terms refer to elements of situations and behaviors that extend across activities and objects. By definition, relational meaning is interpreted only through the context of the utterance (e.g., there, all gone, more, mine, no).

Quality: The expression of a trait or characteristic of some event or entity (e.g., big, cold, fast).

Routines: Term extracted from a ritualized game or nursery rhyme, including rote memorization of animal sounds (e.g., patty-cake, so big, (kitty says) meow).

Social expressions: Use of "courteous" expressions and greetings (e.g., thank you, bye, hi).

Deictics: Expressions used to draw attention, or verbally "point to" places, events, entities and even temporal locations (e.g., this, that, here, "da").

Miscellaneous: Used for words whose meaning was too vague to permit assignment to one of the other categories.

Classification of bases for extension: Each instance of a child initiated extension in the domain of application of a word was classified as one of five mutually exclusive categories: *perceptual similarity, functional similarity, contextual association, affective similarity,* and a *combination of criteria.* Contextual associations were used to describe the application of a word for a referent normally found in contiguity with the usual referent for the word (e.g., "doggie" for dog's bed, "teeth" for toothbrush).[1] The combined category was included because features often cluster together and it is impossible to

---

[1] Towards the end of the single word period, children may use such utterances as "predicational statements" (Bloom, 1973; Greenfield and Smith, 1976; Rescorla, 1980). If the child in the example had an expression for both "dog" and "dog's bed," use of the word "doggie" might be predicational. It is difficult to distinguish between these functions. At the time a child is acquiring his or her first words, many researchers view these as kinds of overextensions. (see also Nelson, 1977.)

distinguish what is criterial for the child (e.g., several of the children extended the term "bath" to swimming pools, but these have many features in common, both functional and perceptual).

Some extensions were actually initiated by the parents. These are tallied separately and are not classified according to the criteria for application.

4.4   Results

4.4.1   Composition of the children's lexicons

There is a fair amount of consistency in the types of words acquired by the different children. Object words predominated for all of them (accounting for 35–51 per cent of the total lexicon for each child), followed by action words (17–24 per cent). Terms derived from routines were more frequent in the blind children's diaries (10–14 per cent of their total lexicons) than in the sighted child's diary (5 per cent of total). In contrast, deictic expressions are virtually unattested for the blind group, while they account for 6 per cent of Brett's early lexicon. Names for specific people and pets were well attested, except in Brett's vocabulary, though this is almost certainly an idiosyncratic pattern rather than an effect of vision, since it contrasts with reports of other sighted children (Bloom, 1973; Nelson, 1973a; Rescorla, 1980). Table 4.2 presents the various word types acquired by each child expressed as a percentage of the first 100 words. In general, the pattern is consistent with other reports of vocabulary in blind children (see Bigelow, 1986; Landau, 1981; Landau and Gleitman, 1985; Mulford, 1986).

As should be clear from the discussion above about the processes involved in lexical development, this striking uniformity in the content of early vocabularies does not warrant the conclusion that the lexical development of blind and sighted toddlers is wholly comparable, as is suggested by Landau and Gleitman (1985). Only a careful analysis of word use and of evidence about how the children understand the symbolic nature of words can yield the information necessary for evaluating the similarities and differences between these two populations.

Individual differences, rather than degree of visual impairment, explain variation in the rate of acquisition and the age at which words first emerged. Teddy, the totally blind child, began to use eight terms when he was twelve months old, though there was initially some articulatory overlap among forms and considerable phonological simplification. His "lexicon" at that point consisted of two specific names (for his father and his brother), four object words (cookie, apple, bottle, doggie), one greeting term ("hi" said on hearing someone enter the house), and one term associated with a routine ([doggie says] "woof woof"). Just prior to the emergence of words, Teddy developed a large repertoire of behavioral responses to numerous routines, especially body part games (e.g., pointing to his nose when asked "Where's

Table 4.2. *Proportion of word types in first 100 lexemes*[a]

	Sounds	Objects	People	Actions	Relational	Qualities	Routines	Social	Deictic	Misc.
Teddy	6	43	13	17	2	2	14	3	0	0
Lisa	2	51	11	17	4	0	10	2	0	3
Julie	2	35	10	24	7	2	13	2	1	4
Brett	0	49	4	23	4	1	5	5	6	3

⟵ Vision ⟶

[a] Since the total number of lexemes analyzed is 100, words are both proportions and actual counts.

Teddy's nose?"). From the time he was 12 to 14 months old, Teddy gradually acquired a few additional object words (e.g., ball, baby, paper, [teddy]bear) plus a word for the sound produced by car horns (beep beep). Then, in his sixteenth and seventeenth months, he began using words to identify his own actions (e.g., "down" for getting off furniture; "rock" for rocking and swaying motions; "oh-oh" as he bumped into objects). At the same time, he began to use "no" as a negative response to offers and as a protest, and also to use "cold" to refer to ice and later cold drinks. Several additional routines were added at this time. Beginning when he was 18 months old, his vocabulary roughly doubled in a four week period and he had acquired 100 lexemes by the time he was $19\frac{1}{2}$ months old, seven-and-one-half months after the first words emerged. The basic pattern, particularly the rapid increase in vocabulary around 18 months, is characteristic of many children's early lexical development (see Bloom, 1973; Greenfield and Smith, 1976; Nelson, 1973a; Rescorla, 1980). The appearance of interactive routines prior to the onset of language has been observed for sighted children and is one of the principal interactive strategies documented for blind children and their families (Urwin, 1978a, b).

Lisa, the child with light perception, acquired 100 words in six-and-one-quarter months, beginning when she was 15 months old. At the time of our first visit, she was just beginning to use eight words: three specific names (for her mother, father and brother), two words for food items (cookie, apple) and three words associated with ritualized games ("so big," "up-and-down," and "cold," used only when her mother invited her to feel the contents of her glass of milk, an event which evolved into a game). Action words began to appear when she was 17 months old (e.g., "up" as she stood up, "walk" as she walked about house). When Lisa was $19\frac{1}{2}$ months old she began to use "no" or "noway" as a protest. She also acquired the last of her words derived from ritualized games at this time ("laydown"). By $21\frac{1}{4}$ months, she had a lexicon of 100 terms. Unlike Teddy, Lisa's early vocabulary development was characterized by a steady and consistent increase in the number of words used, rather than by a sudden and rapid spurt of growth.

Julie, the child with minimal residual vision, began to acquire words when she was 17 months old and it was nine months later that she reached the criterion 100 words. When she was 13 months old, Julie began to participate in a large number of nursery routines and ritualized games. Her mother reported at least 19 different kinds of games during a two month period in which Julie provided behavioral responses (e.g., throwing kisses, pointing to body parts, performing hand movements associated with various nursery rhymes). The pattern was similar to Teddy's, but much more robust. During her sixteenth month, Julie began to produce several "pure performatives" including waving and saying "hi" or "bye" (the wave was not directed toward anyone, it was simply a learned behavior) and saying "boo" in the game of peek-a-boo. Within the next two months, she began to use two specific names (for her mother and father) and a few object words (ball, book, and "kaka," which was used for soiled diapers). At this point the diary record was started but Julie's lexicon was building very slowly and few new words were reported. Then, when she was $19\frac{1}{2}$ months old, Julie went on a two week camping holiday with her family during which she acquired 17 new lexemes representing a variety of word types: action words (e.g., "up-down" for her own squatting and stooping movements, "num-num" for eating, "oh-oh" for dropping things); object words (e.g., shoe, mitt, paper); a social expression ("thank you," used when she was given something to hold) and so on. She also used "no" as a protest, and used "yes" as a response to most questions, though this appeared to be more a routine than an understanding of the affirmative meaning encoded by the term. Slowly but steadily over the course of the next six months, Julie's vocabulary expanded, reaching 100 lexemes when she was 26 months old. As with Lisa, there was no real "spurt" of growth, other than the camping trip which probably marks the beginning of Julie's interest in talking.

Brett, the sighted child, began to use words when he was 16 months old, and his vocabulary grew to 100 lexemes in just $5\frac{1}{2}$ months. Routines were of little interest to him and were not clear antecedents to the use of words. However, he did exploit gestures (pointing and reaching) prior to language and he created a general deictic "proto-word" at 15 months [∧ gwa] which he used to draw his parents' attention to objects and activities. His first words mainly identified objects (doggie, hat, eye) and performed greetings (hi, bye). During the next three months he acquired new object words and a few routines (e.g., (doggie says) "ruff-ruff"; (the monster says) "roar"). When he was 20 months old, Brett's vocabulary began to expand very rapidly. The number of object words doubled in three weeks; more action words began to emerge (e.g., push, back, walk, throw, jump, knock); and relational words and deictic expressions appeared. By the time he was $21\frac{1}{2}$ months old his lexicon exceeded 100 words. The sudden increase in lexemes and the later emergence of action words is very similar to the pattern of Teddy's development, suggesting that vision has little affect on rate and order of lexical acquisition.

While the children acquired similar types of words, there are qualitative differences in the nature of the words themselves. First, none of the blind children created idiosyncratic terms at any point, while the sighted child invented several expressions. His use of a general idiosyncratic deictic term prior to the onset of language is typical of other sighted children and its form, [∧ gwa], is his own innovation. Early on, he created the term [bi] for kisses and [gai] for his grandfather's hat. Several months later, he appeared to make a hybrid of "hand" and "fingers" in the form of [hænerz], which he used to refer to arms. These innovations, plus three other early words, later disappeared from Brett's vocabulary. In contrast, there was a zero mortality rate for the blind children's first 100 lexemes (except in terms of articulatory refinement). The failure to observe word mortality and idiosyncratic inventions in the blind children's lexicons distinguishes them from most sighted children (see Bates *et al.*, 1979; Bloom, 1973; Bowerman, 1976; Braunwald, 1978; Clark, 1973; Ferrier, 1978).

Mulford (1986) suggests these findings may not be generalizable to blind children as a whole since both Urwin (1978a) and Wilson (1985 and personal communication) report instances of child creations and word mortality in their blind subjects. However, these correlate with degree of vision. Wilson has been carefully documenting his blind son Seth's language development. Three of Seth's first 10 words were child created and he continued to invent forms throughout the early word period. Wilson also noted forms falling into disuse. But Seth does have partial vision, probably similar in amount to our subject Lydia. Similarly it is only Steven, Urwin's subject who has some residual vision, who created words. While Urwin's purpose was not to conduct a detailed lexical study, she does record the children's early words. Of the 168 words she reports for Steven, 5 appear to be child created. In contrast there appear to be no idiosyncratic terms among the 143 terms Urwin mentions from her totally blind subject, Jerry. Further, 7 of Steven's words fell into disuse while only 3 of Jerry's did. These three words were initially part of ritualized games and the fact that they fell into disuse, perhaps as the game became uninteresting, is not quite the same as the disappearance of more *bona fide* words of the sort reported for sighted children and seen in our own sighted subject.

Mulford observes, I think correctly, that we do not yet know the significance of such inventions in children's early language. But it is striking that the children without useful vision fail to show this kind of creativity and it suggests that children with little or no useful vision take a less active role in determining the contents of their vocabularies.

Returning to the present analysis, there are also qualitative differences within some of the categories of word types, in particular action and relational words, that distinguish the blind and sighted subjects.

Action words: While action words were well attested in all of the children's lexicons, the blind children used them exclusively to refer to their own movements (e.g., "dance" while the child was dancing, "walk" while walking, "rock" while swaying or being rocked), whereas Brett not only had a variety of expressions for his own movements, but for actions of other people, animals, and objects as well (e.g., "go" on seeing someone leave the house, "fall" when something falls independent of his acting on it, "bite" when the family dog grabs something in its mouth). The limited use of action expressions on the part of the blind subjects is consistent with Urwin's report that the totally blind children in her study primarily encoded their own movements.

Relational words: Relational words emerged at about the same time that the number of action words began to increase in each child's vocabulary, after the child had acquired at least 20 words. As with action words, the blind children's use of relational terms tended to be restricted to their own activities; they were rarely used to actually encode information about the dynamic states of entities.

Lisa's use of relational terms was particularly restricted. While she had four forms, they were actually two pairs of synonyms: no/noway and all-gone/all-finished. Throughout the duration of the diary study, the former were used exclusively as protests and rejections and the latter were used to indicate when she had finished eating.[2]

Julie had six relational forms: all-gone, again, don't, finished, more, and no. Most of these were tied to specific situations (eating, protesting) and there were several sets of synonyms (all gone/finished/done; again/more; don't/no). There is no principled explanation for the use of synonyms for either Julie or Lisa, and they appear to be distributed randomly within the restricted contexts of use.

Teddy used two relational expressions, "mine" and "no." "Mine" was used only when he was trying to extract something from someone's grasp. However, he clearly explored a variety of meanings associated with the form "no." It was initially used as a protest and to reject offers when he was $16\frac{1}{2}$ months old. At 18 months he began using it to encode disappearance, as when he said "no banana" on failing to find additional pieces of a banana he was eating. Two weeks later he began to use it to express the absence of some desired object (e.g., "no top" while hunting for a favorite toy spinning top). At the same time, "No + Noun" constructions appeared in his word play and he also repeated his mother's admonishments (e.g., "No stove," meaning "Don't touch the stove"). Thus, by the time he was 19 months old, Teddy was using "no" to express a variety of meanings and he had at least a rudimentary notion that the term could be used to express information about transformations involving objects on which he was acting. In this respect, his development was significantly different from the other blind children and from the totally blind subjects of Urwin's study.

Brett's four relational terms were "gone," "mine," "more," and "no." Within two weeks of its emergence each of the terms was extracted from its original context and was used to identify the dynamic states of entities in a variety of situations. "Gone" was somewhat more limited than the other expressions and was mainly used in connection with eating, but it occasionally occurred in other situations (e.g., on seeing a ball roll under the couch). "Mine" initially overlapped in articulation with "me" and may have been used for self-reference as well as for indicating things in his immediate possession. Soon after, it was applied to objects he wanted, objects he often used, and to demand possession of something. "More" was

[2] One month after the diary ended, Lisa began to use "all finished" as a request to terminate an activity.

used to request or describe additional instances of something (e.g., "more milk" as a request, "more" + pointing on finding unexpected books in his toybox after having already looked through several other books) and to request continuation of pleasurable activities. "No" was used to encode the absence of something expected (e.g., "no poopoo" on being surprised to find the toilet empty after he'd been sitting on it), to encode errors (e.g., "no" as he tries unsuccessfully to insert a block into a container) as well as to reject and protest.

To summarize, the blind children used relational terms largely as a means of satisfying their own needs rather than in connection with the dynamic states of entities. Thus, while some of the forms that correspond to relational terms in the adult language are present in the blind children's lexicons, they do not really function as relational expressions for these children. The single exception to this generalization is Teddy's use of the word "no." In contrast, the sighted child's use of these forms reflects an awareness of some of the transformations encoded by them in standard usage.

The picture that emerges with respect to the types of early words that are present in the children's lexicons suggests that the general distribution across category types is similar for all subjects. In fact, many of the actual tokens are common to all four subjects. But, for the blind children, the meanings associated with the terms depend largely on their own activities, particularly with respect to action and relational words. The distribution of the words among the various categories, with the predominance of object and people words (comprising 50 per cent or more of the first 100 words), suggests that all of the children are motivated by referential rather than expressive strategies as defined by Nelson (1973a).

4.4.2   Extensions

Overextensions

The reader is reminded that "overextension" is simply the very salient aspect of the more general process of lexical extension. It is relatively easy for parents and researchers to observe. Because they have received much attention in the literature we will first consider overextensions here and will then move on to evaluate the overall extension process.

Only 8–13 per cent of the blind children's first 100 words were overextended, whereas Brett, who has full vision, overextended 41 per cent of his early lexicon, somewhat more than the average of 33 per cent reported for sighted children (Rescorla, 1980). Teddy and Lisa each overextended 13 words, all but four of them object terms. The others involved actions (3 words) or sound (1 word). Half of Julie's eight overextensions referred to actions, two were object words and there was one instance each of a person and a social word being overextended. Object words accounted for 65.8 per

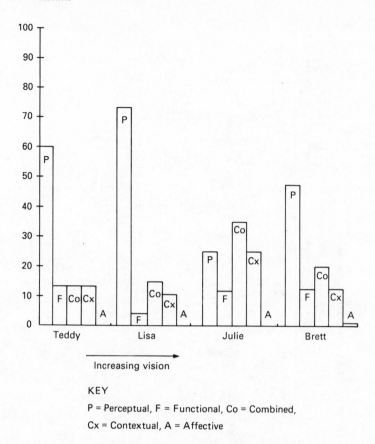

Figure 4.1 Proportion of overextensions based on perceptual, functional, combined, contextual and affective criteria for each child.

cent of Brett's overextensions, 19.5 per cent involved actions, 7.3 per cent were names for people, 4.9 per cent were terms associated with routines and 2.4 per cent were social terms.

Perceptual similarities were inferred as the basis for the majority of overgeneralizations produced by Teddy, Lisa, and Brett, while Julie's strategies were somewhat more evenly distributed, with combined features accounting for 37.5 per cent of her applications, and perceptual and contextual information accounting for 25 per cent each. The difference between Julie and the other subjects is probably the result of the predominance of action words among her overextended lexemes. Unconfounded extensions based on abstraction of functional similarities were infrequent in the data from all subjects. Figure 4.1 indicates the basis of overextensions for each child as a percentage of the total number of overextensions they produced.

Table 4.3. *Perceptual criteria expressed as percentage of total unconfounded perceptual overextensions*

	Shape	Size	Movement	Color	Sound	Taste	Texture	Olfactory
Teddy	27				27	9	36	
Lisa	25		17		17		33	
Julie[a]	33	33					33	
Brett	63	12	8	8	3		3	8

[a] Based on only three perceptual extensions.

Tactile information, including both texture and shape (i.e., three dimensional surface contour) were the dominant perceptual criteria used by the blind children in overgeneralizations based on unconfounded perceptual similarities. Sound and movement were also used, but extensions based on olfactory information, taste, and size were infrequent. Consistent with other research, visual perception of shape was the predominant perceptual strategy used by Brett. Table 4.3 indicates the relative importance of various perceptual criteria in overextensions for each subject.

The overextensions produced by the two most blind children, Teddy and Lisa, typically occurred within four to six weeks of the emergence of a word. In contrast, most of Julie's overextensions occurred when she was between 23 and 26 months old, nearing the 100 lexeme point. Brett's overextensions also occurred later, and they were coincident with the rapid increase in vocabulary observed when he was 20 months old. The later emergence of overgeneralizations has also been reported by Rescorla.

With two exceptions, the overgeneralizations produced by the blind children were categorical overinclusions rather than associative complexes, whereas associative complexes accounted for all of Brett's overgeneralized action words and 30 per cent of his other overextensions. In addition, overgeneralized words were typically extended to only one or two referents in the blind children's word use (e.g., "dance" used for rhythmic body movement performed while sitting in mother's lap). Most of the sighted child's overextended words were applied to many different referents (e.g., "chair" for steps in a swimming pool, toilet seat in an outhouse, bench in a park, picture of a dining table seen in a book, pillows propped against the wall, seats in a car).

The two associative complexes produced by the blind children are summarized below. The criterial attributes are derived from the kinds of sensorimotor information that are predominant for the blind infants: tactile, audible and olfactory information plus the child's own actions.

(1) Teddy: *Table*
   Prototype: Pounding on surface of kitchen table while sitting at it
   Features: (a) extensive flat surface
            (b) pounding action
            (c) dull thud or knocking sound
   All recorded examples: 17th month: (first use) walking around kitchen table and pounding it (features a, b, c,); sitting at table and pounding it (many instances, features a,b,c,); banging on wall (a,b,c,); when M knocks on door (c); as knocks on a glass door (a,b,c); when toy falls to floor (c); on touching large wooden gym toy (a). 18th month: as pounds door of oven (a,b,c); as feels front of refrigerator (a); as taps toy against hand (b); as hears empty cup fall to floor (c)

(2) Lisa: *Cookie*
     Prototype: Eating cookie or cracker
     Features: (a) placing small object in mouth
                  (b) feeling small rough surfaces
                  (c) sweet fragrance
     All recorded examples: 16th month: (first use) eating cookie, many
     instances (a,b,c). 17th month: feeding self small bits of food (a); as
     tries to put loquat leaf in mouth (a,b); as touches piece of paper (b).
     18th month: as sniffs pine tree (c).

The extension process as it is represented in these two examples is similar
to what is reported for sighted children and to what was observed in many of
Brett's overgeneralizations. What is unusual is that there are so few instances
of these and that the examples of non-associative categorical overinclusions
consist of a term being overgeneralized to only one or two inappropriate
exemplars, rather than its being applied to a broad domain of referents
which share certain attributes with the prototype referent.

Thus, the bases of overgeneralizations for these blind children are not
"abnormal," as Landau and Gleitman (1985, p. 31) have inferred from
earlier reports of this study. Rather, they reflect the relative salience of non-
visual sensory information. But they also reflect an unexpected constraint on
the part of the blind subjects.

Extensions within the standard domain of application

The extension process in general was unusually restricted among the blind
children; approximately half of their first 100 lexemes were never extended
beyond the original context during the diary study. In contrast, all but five
of Brett's words were generalized rather than being used to identify a single
unique referent or recurring event. Moreover, many of the words that were
used by the blind children to denote different contexts or different tokens of
similar referents were "names" for specific people or food, both marginal
uses that have been excluded in some investigations of extension (Rescorla,
1980). These terms accounted for 13–22 per cent of the blind children's
extensions. In addition, all of the subjects learned to extend a few terms as
the result of specific parental training (2–8 per cent of the total corpora).

Figure 4.2 presents the proportion of words that were extended,
overextended, and non-extended during the emergence of the first 100 words
in each child's lexicon.

If we collapse these categories together to identify the proportion of words
actually extended *by the child* to discriminably different referents, the picture
is even more dramatic. Figure 4.3 indicates the number of words extended
and overextended by each child, this time excluding the marginal instances
of food and specific people, and also indicates the number of words that the

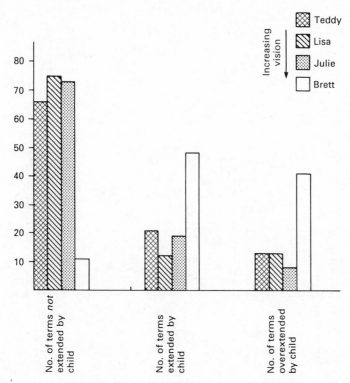

Figure 4.2 Number of words overextended, extended and nonextended (first
100 words)

child failed to extend at all. These data are most appropriate for comparison
with other reports of lexical developments, such as Rescorla (1980), Barrett
(1978) and Nelson *et al.* (1979).

While perceptual features account for most of the overextensions,
combinations of features served as the basis for most extensions that fell
within the normal range of use. However, functional criteria were equally
important as a basis of application for Lisa. For the other children,
perceptual criteria accounted for the least number of extensions within the
standard domain of application. Individual variation, rather than a specific
effect of vision, appears to account for the differences between subjects. The
basis of normally extended word applications for each child is presented in
table 4.4.

Again, there is an important qualitative distinction in the kinds of
extensions produced by the blind children and those produced by the sighted
children. Brett extended each of his lexemes to a heterogeneous set of
referents. His applications were based on the abstraction of distinguishing
attributes which suggests that principled categorization strategies were in

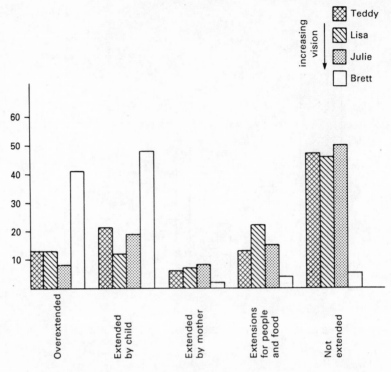

Figure 4.3 Instances of child initiated extensions and overextensions and of
terms the child did not extend (first 100 words).
Note: Terms *not* extended by child include terms which were
extended by the mother rather than the child, or that were used in
"marginal instances" of extension to identify specific people or food
in different situations. Such instances are not considered extensions
in other studies.

Table 4.4. *Bases for appropriate generalizations*
(expressed as percentage of total appropriate generalizations)

	Perceptual	Functional	Combination	Contextual
Teddy	28.6	23.8	47.6	0
Lisa	16.7	41.7	41.7	0
Julie	31.6	15.8	52.7	0
Brett	33.3	12.5	54.2	0

operation. Moreover, the rapid increase in his vocabulary, beginning when he was 20 months old, was paralleled by a change in his use of words. In particular, association and possession relationships were also encoded, as is typical of other children during the late single word period (see Bloom, 1973; Greenfield and Smith, 1976; Rescorla, 1980; Werner and Kaplan, 1963). In contrast, the "extensions" observed in the blind children were far more limited, often simply meaning that words were differentiated from their original context and were used in a variety of situations to request and recall absent objects, to identify them, and to anticipate them. As was the case with overextension, those lexemes that were actually extended to new referents on the basis of common attributes were applied to only one or two additional referents, rather than to a large set of items. This suggests that while some of the forms were applied to new referents, they remained underextended in terms of standard usage.

Another aspect of early lexical development is decentration, in which children move from referring to objects that they are acting on or which they encounter, to identifying the actions of others and the objects on which others act. (See Barrett, 1983 for a particularly clear discussion of this.) This progression is very evident in the diary data from Brett, but the process is incomplete for the blind children. The blind children move from the frozen, ritualized use of words to using words in different, though limited, contexts. But there is no evidence of decentration in word use.

Once again the present findings are suggested by a close analysis of Urwin's data. Her subject Jerry, who is totally blind, had highly egocentric speech. He broadens the use of action words to new contexts, but these terms remain tied to instances of his own activities. (There are no clear examples for noun classifications.) In contrast, Urwin's data for Steven, who does have some useful vision, clearly indicates decentered use of words toward the end of the second year.

To summarize the results thus far, the kinds of referents for which blind and sighted children have lexemes are remarkably similar in that object words and words for actions constitute the majority of terms. But, the way in which these lexemes are understood by the children is vastly different. For the most part, the blind children appear to treat words as a "name" for a specific referent, whereas sighted children construct hypotheses about word meanings and use words to denote generalized referent classes. Further, sighted children's use of words shows clear evidence of decentration whereas the blind children's language remains centered on themselves during this period. When words are extended by the blind children, perceptual attributes involving tactile features and combinations of features appear to be criterial.

However, it is inappropriate to draw a performance conclusion from the evidence without testing this through experimental probes, since it was possible that the blind subjects had not had the appropriate opportunity to generalize forms to new situations or entities.

Individualized experiments to elicit extension

When this investigation was originally conceived, I had intended to use these probes largely to determine whether terms that were overextended in production were similarly overextended in comprehension. But, as I began to gather data in the lexical diaries, it became clear that the crucial issue was to evaluate the extent to which blind children *underextend* lexemes. In particular, it was important to determine whether extensions could be elicited by presenting the children with new exemplars for terms that appeared to be underextended in their lexicons.

In the individualized experiments, the blind children were each presented with collections of objects that were unfamiliar exemplars of terms in their productive vocabularies. The child was encouraged to thoroughly explore the items. If the child did not spontaneously label the object, the mother or I requested an identification using a frame familiar to that particular child. If there was no response the child was encouraged to "find the X," once he or she had explored all of the various objects. In order to decrease task demand I presented no more than four objects at a time. Such tasks were administered on several occasions to each child, but at no particular point in the acquisition process. In all instances, Lisa refused to even explore the items and Teddy and Julie mouthed and banged the objects, but never identified any item other than a cookie. Moreover, the children failed to locate items when they were requested to, but it is impossible to determine whether this was due to the fact that they did not recognize the referent or whether they refused to participate in the activity. Evidence from the observation sessions indicates that the blind children disliked searching on request, though they were all capable of doing so. In contrast to their responses to unfamiliar exemplars, when I presented the children with their own familiar objects they *always* spontaneously identified them. As will be discussed below, this suggests an isomorphism between word and referent.

Sorting tasks

Unlike the children in Nelson's study who spontaneously sorted a variety of objects on the basis of perceived similarities, none of the blind children exhibited any evidence of organizational behavior in manipulating the objects presented in the sorting task. (These were enumerated in table 4.1 above.) Generally, they mouthed a few items or banged them and then threw them aside. The banging and manipulation could not be construed as class consistent behavior as described by Sugarman (1983). In fact, I was willing to consider time spent exploring one type of object over another or searching for one type of object as evidence of selection due to saliency but even this rudimentary strategy did not occur. Even when I reintroduced the items that had been explored and discarded, no classification behavior (or even preferential behavior) was observed. I was unable to elicit any sorting behavior in spontaneous probes using toys or household objects familiar to the children, and the mothers reported that it did not occur in day-to-day object manipulations.

4.5　Summary

The results of the lexical investigation indicate that blind children, like sighted children, begin to acquire stable vocal forms around the time of their first birthday and have acquired 100 or more words before they are two years old. The content of early vocabularies in terms of the kinds of words used (object words, action words and so on) appears to be similar for blind and sighted children, a finding consistent with other investigations of blind children (see especially Landau and Gleitman, 1985 and Mulford, 1986 for an excellent summary). Despite this similarity, there were several qualitative differences that distinguish the blind subjects in the study from both the sighted subject and the sighted population as generally described by other researchers. For example, no words acquired by the blind children were dropped from their lexicons whereas sighted children often discard terms which no longer serve their needs. Also, there were no idiosyncratic, or child created forms, in the blind children's lexicons. Such forms were observed in the sighted subject and are well documented in other diary studies. Both of these findings also appear to be characteristic of the totally blind subject described in Urwin's (1978a) investigation but not of her partially sighted subject.

An especially significant difference between the blind and sighted children is that the blind children's words seem to be tied to their original context for a protracted period of time and there is little evidence of decentration. The blind children's use of words for actions and their "functional" or "relational" words (e.g., more, again, no) describe their own activities or satisfy their own needs. They do not refer to the activities of others or encode information about the dynamic states of entities. While self-orientation is typical of sighted children's earliest action expressions (Huttenlocher, Smiley, and Charney, 1983), sighted children soon refer to the activities of others or the objects others act on (e.g. saying "milk" while watching another drink or "down" as a parent comes down stairs). This absence of decentration was also observed by Urwin, and was especially evident in her totally blind subject. Similarly, sighted children's use of relational terms reflects their growing knowledge of the transformations encoded by these words in adult language. This knowledge is less accessible to blind children.

Finally, we observed that the process of lexical extension was very restricted in the blind children: 50–60 per cent of their first 100 words were not extended during the period of the study. In contrast the sighted subject extended (or overextended) 93 per cent of his first 100 words during this period. This is consistent with other investigations. Overextensions were rare in the blind children's lexicons (8–13 per cent), whereas sighted children overextend around one third of their first words (Rescorla, 1980). The sighted subject in the present study overextended 41 per cent of his first 100 terms.

Individualized experiments were used in an effort to elicit extensions. In these, the children were presented with new referents for words that were non-extended in their vocabularies and were asked to identify them. The children were successful only when presented with already familiar tokens. Similarly, comprehension tasks designed to allow the blind subjects to select unfamiliar referents for familiar words from small arrays of objects failed to elicit evidence of extension. Finally, no forms of class-consistent constructions or sorting behavior were observed in either spontaneous play or structured classification tasks for the blind children. Consistent with other investigations of sighted children these were clearly present for the sighted subject.

Taken together, the findings indicate that while both blind and sighted children seem to be motivated to acquire words during their second year, the mechanisms that allow sighted children to take an active creative role in vocabulary development and the processes that enable them to recognize and extract information as a basis for deriving word meanings are not functioning at the same level for blind children at the onset of language.

4.6   Discussion

Prior to the onset of language, sighted children acquire a great deal of information about entities within the environment: information about the functions and actions of objects, about the relationships between objects and people, about the sequence and organization of events, and about the qualities of a wide variety of near and distant things. The elements of meaning that these children associate with words that are used to identify these familiar referents are extracted from the child's encounters with these referents. Much of this experience is lost to children who have no access to visual information. Because very young blind children have limited information about events and objects in their environment, they are presumably less able to identify the common elements shared by different events, with the result that words associated with one context are often not applied to a new context or to new referents on the basis of perceived similarities.

Blind children in their second year produce "words" on encountering an object, a person, or a sound, and as they perform a familiar action or a ritualized routine. Their behavior suggests that the vocalization is a component of the referent itself, that the children have failed to objectify the word–referent relationship. A word symbolizes a referent, can stand for it, but it is not part of the referent. It is not clear that the blind children recognized this distinction during the period in which they learned their first 100 terms.

This kind of isomorphism between vocal forms and referents is not qualitatively different from the first responses of sighted children to words. For example, Bloom (1973) suggests that in describing the earliest stages of word acquisition, prior to the acceleration in vocabulary around 18 to 20 months, one cannot talk about the development of meaning or comment on the incompleteness of meaning in terms of features because the child does not yet have a full representation of the objects or activities being encoded. She suggests that the child's meaning for a word may be isomorphic with his or her representation of the object or activity. What is remarkable and unexpected in the present data is that severely visually impaired children continue in this pattern for a protracted period of time.

At the same time that words fail to be extended, the blind children also fail to engage in the kinds of classification strategies that have been inferred to underlie the process of extension for sighted children. Thus, behavioral and linguistic evidence from the blind children corroborate each other to suggest that the sensorimotor schemata for sorting elements of the environment by abstracting or at least responding differentially to various features is not functioning at the same level for blind children as it is for sighted children at the onset of lexical development. The blind children have difficulty in precisely those areas of lexical development where visual information can provide input about the world and can be a stimulus for forming hypotheses about the nature and meaning of words as symbolic vehicles.

When this study began, I assumed that the process of lexical acquisition would progress in much the same way for blind children as it does for sighted children, that the differences between them would be important mainly as clues to the kinds of information that are most salient in a world perceived without the aid of vision, and that the findings might help clarify how children in general construct lexical meanings. In light of this assumption two hypotheses were advanced. Neither is confirmed by that analysis. Hypothesis One suggested that blind children would extend the domain of application for early lexemes as the result of the same process that motivates sighted children, but that the extraction of salient information would reflect tactile, kinesthetic, auditory, and oral information. To the extent that blind children do extend their early lexemes, tactile and other non-visually based perceptual information seems to be important, but the hypothesis is only weakly supported since it is not clear that the same underlying process is operating. Hypothesis Two proposed that blind children would extend terms for a longer period of time and would have greater difficulty in bringing their meanings into line with standard adult usage. This is not supported by the analysis, though the second portion of the hypothesis cannot be evaluated from the available data.

Can factors other than severe visual impairment account for what appear to be delays or deficiencies in the lexical acquisition process of blind children? One obvious consideration is the issue of whether word meanings evolve largely from children's conceptual development or result more from consistencies in input language and its influence on children's conceptual organization. As with other handicapped children, maternal input may provide less information when directed to blind children than does input directed to normally developing sighted children. This is well documented for the present subjects by Kekelis (1981), Andersen and Kekelis (1982) and Kekelis and Andersen (1984). See also chapters 5 and 6 of this book. In particular, Anderson and Kekelis found that mothers' speech to blind children is more directive and the content of their utterances less elaborate and informative than mothers' speech to sighted subjects.

To evaluate the influence of input on lexical development we would need to document the full range and frequency of use in the input language for each child's first 100 words. This is beyond the scope of the present investigation but it is a topic worthy of future research. Three possibilities would need to be considered (see Huttenlocher *et al.*, 1983 for similar discussion): (1) Children's conceptual limitation could be inferred if a word is used with high frequency and in a variety of situations in the input language but these uses are not included in the child's repertoire; (2) conceptual development could be inferred to underline lexical development if the order of acquisition of words does not correlate with frequency of use in the input language; and similarly (3) conceptual development could be inferred if the child's meanings for words extend beyond the range of use in the input language. This third possibility includes the appearance of child initiated overextensions and it is on the basis of such well documented creative applications in sighted children that I think we must conclude that the child's conceptual capacity accounts for at least some aspects of lexical acquisition.

There is some evidence from other research that impoverished input does not *necessarily* imply lack of creativity in children's language. Of particular interest are investigations of deaf children. Deaf children of hearing parents typically receive exceedingly impoverished input during their first few years since they must cope with a vocal language that is barely perceptible and they are generally not exposed to a conventional manual language until somewhat later (see Klima and Bellugi, 1979; Newport, 1979). Cross *et al.* (1980) found that maternal input to five year old deaf subjects resembled input usually given to hearing babies of 3 to 6 months, despite linguistic competence in these deaf children equal to that of the two year old hearing children. Moreover, parents of deaf children are confronted with the same kinds of grieving and emotional trauma as parents of blind children so we may expect a high degree of comparability in the way they come to accept their 'imperfect' babies and the way this influences the course of development.

Goldin-Meadow and Mylander (1983, 1984; see also Feldman, Goldin-Meadow and Gleitman, 1978) report that deaf children learning only oral language spontaneously create gestural signs, or lexemes, and then go on to develop structured communication systems that share many features with linguistic codes. Their analysis indicates that the children's structures are not induced by their parent's spontaneous gestures, (including gestural accompaniments to oral language), but are largely the children's own innovations. Although Goldin-Meadow and her colleagues focused mainly on two-sign constructions, their data reveal linguistic and lexical creativity among deaf children beginning around 18 months. Furthermore, deaf children learning English as a first language appear to overextend early words in the same way that sighted children do, though they may be over 2 years old when words emerge (McGinnis, personal communication). For example, McGinnis reports a $2\frac{1}{2}$-year-old deaf girl extending the term "mommy" to all adult females and using "open" as a general request for action. These reports contrast rather vividly with the apparent lack of creativity among blind children.

Not only is there evidence of lexical creativity in young deaf children, but it also appears that deafness does not hinder the development of classification strategies. Sugarman (in collaboration with S. L. McCoy, see Sugarman, 1983, appendix 1) observed manipulatory classification in six deaf children using the same procedures Sugarman developed for hearing children. The children were 25 to 50 months old, but even the youngest subject performed spontaneous class groupings and class-consistent correspondences in a way that was comparable to sighted peers. I was unable to induce any form of class-consistent behaviors in the blind subjects, even when they were $2\frac{1}{2}$ years old. Sugarman and McCoy infer that patterns of classification behavior in deaf and hearing children result from the same cognitive organization occurring at the same age.

Taken together, these studies imply that, although deaf and blind children receive similarly impoverished language input relative to intact children, the strategies these children bring to the task of word learning are not comparable. Overly simplistic maternal input, then, cannot adequately account for blind children's difficulty in recognizing the nature of words. Moreover, the fact that two-year-old deaf children are able to perform class consistent behaviors while two-year-old blind children are not suggests that constraints on blind children's early lexical development may be conceptual in nature, since class consistent behavior is a prerequisite for constructing basic word meaning.

Finally, there is evidence from another area of research that suggests that lexical extensions may be more dependent on general conceptual processes than on specifically linguistic ones. Studies of non-human primates reveal that at least some aspects of human language can be learned and used communicatively by chimpanzees and gorillas. The actual capacity of these apes for language is somewhat unclear and there is no question that they are greatly impoverished compared to humans. In particular, there is little evidence that apes are sensitive to constituent structure and grammar (see Seboek and Umiker-Seboek, 1980, for detailed reviews from various perspectives). Even fairly generous accounts of language learning in non-human primates do not credit apes with the ability to use real grammatical rules. The least equivocal capacities credited to apes are elementary lexical ones. It appears that apes do have some capacity to learn arbitrary human words or symbols and to use these correctly to identify objects and activities (Limber, 1980; Greenfield and Savage-Rumbaugh, 1984; Savage-Rumbaugh, 1986).

Of particular interest to the present study are the reports that non-human primates are capable of using 100 or so words and may spontaneously generalize or extend word use along the lines that human children do. Several overextensions have been reported by researchers. For example, the chimpanzee Washoe apparently extended the sign "hurt" from scratches and bruises to red stains, a decal on the back of a person's hand, and a person's navel (Bronowski and Bellugi, 1980). Koko, a gorilla, is reported to have generalized "straw" to plastic tubing, hoses, cigarettes and radio antennae (Patterson, 1977). These, and other examples of overextensions by apes, seem to be based on perceptual information.

Apes do not appear to make up idiosyncratic words or signs, but they may combine pre-existing words or signs to identify new things. Some examples from Fouts (1974) are illustrative: Washoe reportedly produced "water bird" for duck and "rock berry" for brazil nut; another chimp, Lucy, called watermelon "drink fruit" and radishes "cry hurt food." Furthermore, there is some evidence that these primates have the cognitive capacity to adopt arbitrary conceptual codes and use them to classify or describe real-world perceptions. Experiments demonstrate that the chimpanzee Lana can reliably assign 350 Munsell color chips to one of eight color categories (Rumbaugh, 1980).

Some of the more important differences between apes and children with respect to language learning are that apes mainly seem to use language as an instrument to achieve certain things (mainly from humans), whereas children delight in language and use it as an expressive tool, and that apes use language only when they are deliberately taught it, whereas children discover much of language on their own.

Apes are most successful in those areas of language that directly relate to other conceptual processing strategies. In particular, it appears that non-human primates do have the requisite conceptual capacity and experience to construct at least rudimentary perceptual classifications and to learn arbitrary terms to refer to these.

Young blind children's relatively constrained performance in this area may then be largely due to the fact that they are denied access to very basic information that provides insight into the classifiability of real-world objects and experiences. I am not suggesting here that non-human primates are cognitively more advanced than blind babies. I am however proposing that vision may stimulate the intellectual mechanisms of integration and differentiation that permit classification. Further, classificatory behavior is a general conceptual product even when it is applied to language data. This assumption implies that lexical acquisition, at least in terms of building word meaning for non-grammatical morphemes, though not necessarily in terms of organizing lexical entries into grammatical categories, may be cognitive in nature and not an ability specific to language learning.

Drawing together the findings from investigations of blind, deaf, and sighted children, of apes and of various classification tasks we can infer the following (1) that conceptual classification is necessary for extension (2) that ascribing meaning to words may be more dependent on non-linguistic mental processes than on specifically linguistic ones, and (3) that visual information normally helps trigger these behaviors during the second year.

Although blind children have a limited understanding of word meaning, they are able to exploit the terms they have to convey a variety of messages – they label, request, protest and so on. Moreover, they are able to combine their early "words" to create multi-word utterances. The next chapter explores the nature of early word combinations and provides an opportunity to re-evaluate the conditions that seem to be necessary and sufficient to permit the development of multi-word utterances. Then, chapter 6 considers the development of communicative strategies at a pragmatic level by examining the illocutionary function of the children's early utterances.

5   First multi-word utterances

This chapter explores the content of the children's utterances once they have acquired 100 terms and in particular analyzes the first ways in which early words are combined. The chapter begins at the most rudimentary level of combinatorial language, where sequences of single-word utterances can be viewed as larger structures by virtue of the fact that they refer to different elements of the same event. The discussion proceeds to the examination of *bona fide* multi-term utterances, where the expression of various semantic roles suggests the emergence of basic propositional structures. Along the way, some of the special characteristics of blind children's language are considered, in particular their use of "stereotypic speech."

5.1   Sequential use of single words

5.1.1   Previous research

Many investigators have observed that children produce sequences of single-word utterances that are related to an event before they begin to construct two-word utterances (Atkinson, 1979; Bloom, 1973; Greenfield and Smith, 1976; Gruber, 1967; Leopold, 1949; Ochs, Schieffelin and Platt, 1979; Scollon, 1976, 1979). Most of these analyses view such sequences as early attempts to build propositions, in the minimal sense of expressing some argument and predicate or of establishing a reference and commenting on it.

Bloom (1973) observes that sequential single-word utterances emerge during the second half of the second year. Some of these are simply sequences of "naming behavior" whereas others are instances of single words said in succession which are somehow related. Of these, Bloom isolated two possible event structures: (1) *chained* successive utterances in which successive movements are encoded; and (2) *holistic* successive utterances in which the entire situation appears to be defined from the onset rather than being tied to the child's sequence of movement. Two examples from Bloom are illustrative:

> I Chained Utterances: Alison (19, 2)
> (A pushes truck past M, off rug; stands up)   uh!/

(A pulling truck back on to rug)	back/
Back.	
(A struggling to pull truck onto rug)	up/
Off?	
(A getting truck onto rug)	there/up/
On?	
(A pulling truck closer)	on/
(A standing up)	there!/
	(Bloom, 1973, p. 49)

II Holistic Utterances: Alison (19,2)

(A picking up blanket;	blanket/
handing blanket to M)	cover/
Blanket? Cover?	
(A touches doll's hand)	
(A touches doll's head, lifting doll	
to her own head)	head/
(A touching doll's head in front of her)	head/head/
Head?	
	cover/
	(Bloom, 1973, p. 50)

In the first example, the child's utterances accompany the performance of her own action schemes as they occur. In contrast, the second example suggests that Alison actually had some goal in mind from the onset (i.e., covering the doll's head) and she conveys this through a series of utterances, many of which are dependent on her mother's comprehension of (or failure to comprehend) prior utterances. Bloom proposes that the child has a mental representation of the whole event from the outset when holistic utterance sequences are produced. Moreover, there appears to be a developmental progression from chained to holistic utterance sequences. Bloom's analysis indicates that vocabulary size is not related to frequency in producing single-word sequences.

Single-word sequences may take a variety of forms. Often they are interrupted by an interlocutor eliciting further information and at times the child may repeat one or both utterances, sometimes several times. Scollon (1976, 1979) introduced the term "vertical constructions" to refer to sequences of utterances related to one topic, almost all of which correspond to Bloom's holistic sequences. He distinguishes between four basic types of vertical constructions, for which the presence or absence of repetitions and interruptions is criterial. In Type A constructions the child produces two words in succession that are linked by a context-appropriate semantic connection; in type B the child repeats at least one of the words one or more times; type C differs from type A in that the interlocutor interrupts the sequence and type D constructions are characterized by both interruption and repetition. Types D and B are developmentally prior to types C and A, respectively, with type A the last to develop and the most similar to horizontal constructions (utterances of two or more words). Scollon's data also indicate that a young child will persevere in trying to communicate an idea despite considerable problems in being understood and will even substitute closely related words (near synonyms) in trying to relate a message.

Although word order appears to be more variable in vertical constructions than in horizontal ones, Scollon found that most of his data is in a topic–comment format, where children persist in trying to establish some topic and then go on to predicate something about this topic. Similarly, Atkinson (1979) interprets such utterances in terms of illocutionary acts, where the first act functions to make sure the hearer is attending to the appropriate event and the second act has the force of a statement. He calls the attention-drawing function "quasi-reference." Bloom finds the topic–comment account inadequate for describing successive single-word utterances since utterances such as "juice/more" and "more/juice" both occur. In fact, the discrepancy between researchers is not quite as significant as it first appears, since Bloom is considering all sequences of single words, whereas Scollon and Atkinson limit their discussions to those utterances which are semantically related. Bloom's utterances do not all conform to a topic–comment format, but some of the examples she lists to illustrate the variable order are not sequences of utterances that together form a single proposition. (See Bloom, 1973, p. 47; compare the expanded form in the appendix, p. 195 and see Dunlea, 1982 for detailed discussion). While it is true that word order is variable in sequential constructions, when the utterances are clearly semantically related there seems to be a tendency to first establish a topic or referent and then to comment on it.

Atkinson's analysis deals not only with semantically related single-word sequences, but also with what have been called "replacement sequences." In such utterance strings the element(s) of the first utterance are contained in a subsequent longer construction as in the following examples: "house/elephant house/," "Kristin/Kristin sit chair/." For most such instances Atkinson suggests that the first utterance manipulates the addressee's attention and the second predicates something of the referent. Apparent counter-examples of the form "noise/man noisy/" can be interpreted as efforts to draw attention to some abstract property rather than to an entity. The role of attention-drawing strategies in the ontogenesis of propositional structures that are encoded across two or more utterances is also important for Ochs, Schieffelin and Platt (1979). While there is a unity of observation across these investigations, Ochs *et al.* differ from other researchers in that they permit a sequence of utterances to count as a proposition, regardless of whether the original speaker or the original addressee provides the predicating information. There are natural language situations in which a proposition can result from collaboration and where such a proposition would still be amenable to logical (truth conditional) analysis. However, in terms of development, I think propositional structures cannot be viewed as emerging unless the child is capable of expressing rudimentary predicate–argument forms. Hearer elicitations may operate to help the child develop propositional structures, but such instances are evidence of emerging propositions only if the child speaker is the one who provides further information. Structures which result from hearer elicitations should probably be viewed as antecedent to true propositional structures.

It is evident from various studies that children express and explore relationships through sequences of utterances before they are able to control explicit horizontal constructions and at least some of these "vertical" constructions appear to express rudimentary propositions. The emergence of such sequences is of some significance since it is the first *observable* aspect of language that expresses something about the child's understanding of associations obtaining between elements in the environment and it is a further clue to the child's conceptualization of that environment.

Most of the issues discussed raise questions about the role of visual information in stimulating the development of vertical constructions. If the emergence of such sequences is a necessary antecedent to the construction of multi-word utterances, it can be assumed that similar development will prevail for all populations, though the content of these may vary depending upon available sensory information. The kinds of information noticed and encoded by sighted children most often involve visual input. The information encoded by visually impaired children should reflect the relative importance of other sensory modalities. This is of particular interest given the problems in extension discussed in chapter 4. Another area of interest involves the blind children's ability to ascertain the focus of a hearer's attention and to draw it to some referent when necessary. Evidence from early lexical development in blind children indicates that the deictic particles that frequently function as attention-drawing devices in sighted children (see Atkinson, 1979) are virtually unattested in the blind children (see chapter 4). Similarly, visual and gestural strategies for reference (see Pechman and Deutsch, 1980) are unavailable. Thus, examining early utterance sequences provides us with the first indications of how blind children attempt to establish reference, how they perceive their interlocutors and how they conceptualize the environment.

5.1.2   Single word sequences in the present study

In order to evaluate how vertical sequences are used, all instances of "semantically" related single-word sequences were identified for each child, using transcripts for sessions when the children's mean length of utterance

(MLU) ranged between 1.0 and 1.5. Most vertical sequences that occurred after MLU 1.5 involved build-up sequences resulting in two- and three-word utterances and these are included in the discussion of horizontal constructions in section 5.3. There is little information available on the frequency with which young children produce single-word sequences. Greenfield and Smith (1976) report that sequences account for an increasingly large proportion of children's total utterances (up to nearly 50 per cent of the corpora) as they approach the two word stage, and then begin to decline. However, I know of no report indicating the number of semantically related sequences that are produced. The present data suggest that, while they do typically occur prior to two-word speech, less than 5 per cent of the children's utterances are involved in single-word sequences that form proposition-like structures. Holistic utterances were more common than chained utterances, though sequences of "naming" behavior were observed in early sessions for all children. (These were not included in the analysis.) A preliminary overview indicated that many of the blind children's single-word sequences seemed to occur in requests, so holistic utterances were further coded to indicate whether they constituted a request or an assertion. Assertions were subdivided into those that describe some event caused by or directly involving the child, and those that encode information not directly related to the child. The distinction between descriptions of the child's own actions and of information not specifically related to self action was included in order to capture evidence of decentration during this period of development. (Evidence from the lexical study indicated delays in decentration for the visually impaired children, as discussed in chapter 4.) Table 5.1 indicates how single-word sequences that formed proposition-like units were distributed in the data from Teddy, Lisa, Julie, and Brett. (Lydia's language was already at an MLU of 1.5 during the first recording session and no sequences were observed in Bonnie's data.)

The more primitive chained sequences encoded self actions for all of the children, reflecting egocentricity in their first utterance sequences. Holistic constructions did indeed emerge in request strategies, rather than assertions, for the blind subjects. While each child used holistic sequences for a variety of purposes other than to encode self actions, there are important qualitative differences which correlate with access to visual information.

Both Lisa and Teddy began to produce vertical constructions during their seventeenth month when their MLUs were approximately 1.05. For Teddy, the first recorded instance occurred at the end of a stream of babbling when he said "do:ggie/bye:/Do:ggie/"[1] as he began to move toward the porch where he typically plays with the family dog. His mother interpreted the utterance as a request and proceeded to bring in the dog.

---

[1] The children's speech is written in standard orthography unless articulation is highly deviant. All utterances have falling terminal intonation unless otherwise marked.

Table 5.1. *Single word sequences forming proposition-like structures*

Child	M.L.U. Range	No. of Sessions	Chained	Holistic		
					Act of	
				Rq[a]	Self[b]	Other[c]
Teddy	1.03–1.53	4	2	5	3	5
Lisa	1.02–1.11	8	1	12	2	2
Julie	1.00–1.29	5	2	7	1	11
Brett	1.00–1.30	4	3	0	2	8

[a] Holistic sequences that are requests.
[b] Holistic sequences that refer to the child's own actions or activities.
[c] Holistic sequences that refer to another person's actions or activities or to events in the environment that do not involve child.

A vertical-type construction first occurred within an episode of babbling for Lisa, but most of Lisa's subsequent sequences were requests. The first clear vertical request produced by Lisa occurred when she (1;8;18). It is striking for several reasons: it is one of the first instances in which Lisa actually sought her mother's attention before requesting something, it was not dependent on dialogue with another, and it was the first recorded instance of a request with two components. The speed with which the event occurred suggests that Lisa had the final goal in mind from the beginning:

1 Lisa   (1;8;18)   (M and Rs are sitting at breakfast table
                     and L is standing near M)
   L: Mommy/
            What?/
   L: up/
            (M puts L in her lap)
   L: rosie/
            (M begins to sing "Ring around the
            Rosie")

Dialogue with the mother characteristically facilitates the children's building of vertical requests. Thus the majority of vertical constructions produced by Teddy and Lisa are Scollon's C type, that is they involve discourse but not utterance repetition. The non-request strategies in Lisa's and Teddy's samples typically involve their re-creating familiar word patterns (e.g., doggie/out/) or result from dialogues in which the children incorporate words from their mother's preceding utterances in order to build a proposition. For example, the first recorded instance of Teddy's encoding possession appears in a vertical sequence which utilizes his mother's previous utterance. (Note that the concept of possession was first encoded by his mother.)

    2 Teddy   (1;6;8)   (M and T are playing with a cup, each
                               trying to get total possession of it).
             M: (LF)) I got the cup./
             T: cup/
             M: Mine./ (3.) Mine./
             T: teddy/
                  mine ≠ teddy/

Conspicuously absent in the transcripts of both Lisa and Teddy are instances in which the children draw attention to something in the environment and then comment on it. In one instance, presented below as example 3, Teddy seems to provide information about some object, but he is holding the object and acting on it at the time, and it is possible that he is encoding information about his own experience rather than about the object. Notice too, that his mother establishes the referent and then remains in immediate proximity:

    3 Teddy   (1;6;8)   (T is in his highchair and M is next to
                               T. There is a glass of milk on the tray
                               table)
          M: Glass./   (as T lifts glass of milk from tray)
          T: (2.) glass/   (as begins to drink)
               (5.) cold/   (removing glass from mouth)

Surprisingly, both Teddy and Lisa *do* attempt to establish reference in recalling a past event. In these cases the interaction is remarkably similar to what has been described for sighted children in "here and now" situations where the child establishes reference, the caregiver acknowledges the referent and/or elicits further information and the child "comments." The following examples are illustrative.

    4 Teddy   (1;6;8)   (Several hours ago T had refused to "say
                               goodbye to Laura," a secretary at school,
                               despite much prodding from M)
             T: laura/
             M: What?/
             T: say/
                  laura/
             M: ((LF))
    5 Lisa   (1;8;18)   (M and L are talking; "Zadie" refers to
                               L's grandfather and "Bubbie" to her
                               grandmother)

M: Can you say Zadie?/
L: bubbie/
M: Bubbie./ (1.) And Zadie./
L: apple/
⌣ M: That's right!/ (To Researchers) Bubbie and Zadie always give her apples./

In example 4, Teddy produced a completely spontaneous referent and it appears that he interpreted his mother's "What?" as acknowledgement of that referent, though it is equally probable that his mother's intention was to elicit a repetition of Teddy's utterance. It is interesting to note that Kekelis (1981) found that 80 per cent of the topics shared by Teddy and his mother at this age were introduced by the mother and very few topics related to "abstract" (i.e., absent) events. Thus, this construction is unusual in that it is both child-initiated and abstract. In example 5 Lisa introduced a referent, but it is one typically associated with the referent in her mother's preceding utterance (i.e., Zadie and Bubbie are often used together since these are the family's words for grandfather and grandmother). While this could be interpreted as word association, I think it is fair to credit Lisa with using the utterance to build a larger structure. The example is not propositional in the usual sense, since it appears to present two arguments rather than expressing a clear predicate and argument, but it can be rather loosely interpreted as a referent and comment, possibly with an argument such as "have" or "give" understood; i.e., "Zadie and Bubbie have apples" or "Zadie and Bubbie give Lisa apples". As with Teddy, Kekelis' analysis indicates that abstract topics are very rare in Lisa's data and that the mother typically dominates the conversation.

Sequences produced by Teddy and Lisa that comment on the "here and now" always encode the child's own actions (e.g., "teddy/pee" as Teddy urinates during a bath or "spank/blanket" as the child hits a blanket). In a few instances they encode the result of the child's own actions as in example 6, one of Lisa's first assertions. (Note that the referent is established by the interlocutor.)

6 Lisa   (1;9;11)   (L and Anne are playing with a doll).
                    (L fingers doll's hair)
          AD: Dolly's hair./
          L: (3.0) dolly/
          AD: Dolly/
          L: (4.0) (L drops doll onto floor) go down/

To summarize then, the vertical sequences which form cohesive structures in Teddy's and Lisa's language first emerge in request strategies. Later, there are a few instances which encode the child's actions or the result of the child's action. Other sequences involve the production of familiar word patterns.

More productive uses occur when the referent is established by someone else. The only clear examples of reference–comment structures involve the children's recalling a past experience.

As with Teddy and Lisa, Julie's vertical sequences emerge in request strategies, but she soon begins to encode other kinds of information as well. From their onset at 22 months, Julie's request sequences encode her desires very explicitly, as the following examples illustrate.

7 Julie	(2;1;23)	(J and M are taking toys out of a toy chest when J touches a toy drum)
	J:	[b ∧ :m] 'drum'
	M:	The bum. /
	J:	hit it/

8 Julie	(2;2;30)	(J is eating lunch; She wants milk but M is offering her soup first; milk is on table out of J's reach)
	J:	see-it/ (extends arms out)
		milk/

9 Julie	(2;2;30)	(As above, J is eating lunch; this time trying to feed herself apple sauce)
	J:	sip-it/
		apple sauce/ (tapping spoon to bowl of
		mommy/ apple sauce)
	M:	(guides J's hand to get apple sauce on to spoon)

In example 7 Julie verbally encodes precise information about what she wants to do with the drum, but examples 8 and 9 are even more interesting, since they demonstrate how non-verbal information serves to enhance the communicative power of Julie's requests. The hand extension in 8 is not a "reach" in the usual sense, but rather Julie is positioning her hands expecting her mother to provide milk. Teddy and Lisa do not do this. (I have since observed this in Lisa around the time of her third birthday.) In the final example, the force of Julie's request for assistance in getting more apple sauce encodes three crucial pieces of information: the desired object (apple sauce); what she wants to do with it (sip it); and the fact that she needs help in achieving this goal (mommy). The message is enhanced by her tapping the bowl with her empty spoon. Julie rarely encodes her own actions, and there are a few instances when she makes assertions about other entities in which she first establishes the referent. However, most of the sequences involve the production of familiar patterns, as in example 10:

10 Julie	(1;10;13)	(Julie is holding a small toy puppy while talking with a researcher, EA)

J: puppy/
     puppy/
EA: [p ∧ :?pi::]/   Is that a little puppy?/
                       Huh?/ Is it soft?/
J: ruff/

Almost all of Julie's vertical sequences occur in dialogues with her mother, and often key words are extracted from her mother's contributions. In these dialogues there are three occasions in which Julie comments on past events. There are three principal differences between Julie's sequences and those of Teddy and Lisa: (1) desired goals of requests are more explicitly encoded, and are sometimes supplemented by non-verbal behavior (2) there is evidence that Julie will establish reference in the immediate situation, and (3) there is only one instance in which Julie encodes her own action. The strategies used by the three children are similar in that vertical constructions emerged in request strategies and later were used to recall past events.

Brett's use of single word sequences more closely approximates the developmental sequence reported in the literature. Vertical constructions emerge in chained sequences which encode the child's own movements as in example 11:

11 Brett   (1;7;11)   (B is pushing a block along couch, apparently pretending it is a car)
        B: go/   (pushing block)
             (3.5) a crash/   (as block falls to floor)

These are shortly followed by holistic utterances. In contrast, the chained sequences used by the blind children did not appear to have any particular developmental position but occurred randomly in the data.

In most of the examples Brett and his mother are playing together and he does not encode the referent, but there are four instances when he first draws his mother's attention to an object and then comments on it. In example 12 he uses a general attention drawing device ("see").[2]

12 Brett   (1;7;11)   (B is helping a researcher construct a man out of Bristle blocks; when the man's arm falls off, he turns to his mother)
        B: see/   (looking at M)
             see/
        M: (M smiles)
        B: fall down/

[2] Julie's use of "see-it" in example 8 above was not used to draw attention to a referent, since both parties were already attending to the object in question; rather it was a request to have the object.

Two months later, in example 13, Brett struggles to articulate a difficult word ("elephant") and then proceeds to comment on the referent ("roar"), an example very similar to some of Scollon's (1979) data.

13 Brett   (1;9;8)   (B points to a tiny picture of an elephant on a can of playdough; M is sitting next to B)

    B: [aːut(·)auːek]/
        ((GRUNT))

    M: You can say it ≠ What is it?/

    B: -h- [ʔaːːu]/

    M: (2.) That's an elephant, remember?/

    B: [əʔaː]/
        [ʔaːːlpʰɛ]/

    M: Yeah, I know ≠ That's a hard word for you./

    B: [ʔa | ʌ]/
        [aːː | ʌ mɛt]/

    M: That's right./

    B: [aːːʔa |əvɪt]/
        this a/
        [ɛʔaːːmɪ |ɛt]/   } = this a/ elephant/ roar
        roar/

In addition, Brett uses vertical sequences to reply to questions (e.g., when his mother asks "What are you gonna do?" Brett replies "gonna-do/ bubble/") and to ask questions (e.g., "where/ bubble/").

Except when Brett specifically draws attention to some referent, which typically requires an acknowledgement from the addressee, his vertical constructions are not generally embedded in dialogues, but instead tend to be instances of Scollon's type A constructions. Thus, Brett differs from the other children in four significant respects: (1) his single-word sequences emerge in descriptions of his own activities rather than in requests (2) he is more concerned with commenting about events occurring in the here and now (3) he is less dependent on dialogue with his mother to help him create vertical constructions, and (4) there are no references to past events.

The first three observations can be explained by the kinds of information that are available to the blind children and by their particular needs. The emergence of vertical constructions in acts of requesting seems unusual, but requests may be important in helping blind children gain greater access to their environment. (This is considered in greater detail in chapter 6). Thus sequential constructions may indeed form a bridge between the single word and two word periods, but they need not be assertions in order to accomplish this. If they do form such a bridge, it is surprising that semantically related single-word sequences comprise such a small portion of the data for all subjects. The blind children's greater reliance on dialogue formats to communicate coherent single-word sequences can also be explained by visual impairment. Lack of visual information makes these children more dependent on verbal interaction for feedback. A referent first encoded in their mother's speech is then known to be shared on the basis of the discourse context. In this respect, mothers, whether intentionally or not, appear to play an even more important scaffolding role with blind children than with sighted children. It is quite surprising that the children talked about past events since most researchers have found that early language is overwhelmingly dependent on the "here and now." This is considered more fully in section 5.3.

In general, once single-word sequences and the first instances of two-word utterances emerge, children rapidly begin to produce numerous two- and three-word utterances encoding a variety of semantic relations. While the blind children do indeed produce increasingly complex utterances during this period, there are a number of ways in which their language development progresses along a slightly different path and these are discussed in the following section.

5.2   The blind children's use of stereotypic speech

One of the outstanding characteristics of blind children's early language is that the children have a propensity to pick up and use utterance patterns that are typically produced by their mothers, or other familiar people, though the influence is principally from their mothers. This tendency emerges early on in sequences of language and sound play and is extended into communicative situations and appropriate contexts within a few months. On the one hand, the adoption of maternal speech patterns may contribute to certain confusions, particularly with respect to pronominal reference. Yet, at the same time, I believe this use eventually helps the children to grasp elements of fundamental event patterns about which they have little direct information. This section documents the emergence and development of this phenomenon and considers how it may affect various aspects of language and conceptual development. The analysis is based on transcripts from Teddy and Lisa, for whom the strategy is most prolific.

The use of stereotypic speech is of course not unique to blind children and chunks of maternal speech that are associated with a particular context are also reproduced by sighted children (see Peters, 1983 for extensive review and also MacWhinney, 1978; R. Clark, 1974). The chunks or phrases that are picked up seem to be single unanalyzed units of language for the child. They appear to be associated with an appropriate context and have meaning related to that context, though many are also extended to new situations. Gradually the units are analyzed and broken into their constituents. (The reader is referred to Peters, 1983 for an excellent discussion of the processes that might be involved in segmentation.)

5.2.1   Early re-creation of maternal speech by blind children

As will be discussed in chapter 6, the three children with severe visual impairments produced a relatively high proportion of non-interactive utterances, i.e., sound and language play that is not directed toward any hearer (see section 6.6.1). Such sequences averaged 8 to 9 utterances per episode. Many of the examples are instances of babbling with marked prosodic contour, but with no recognizable lexemes. Some of these resemble two-party dialogues with clear sentential melody. Most often they reproduce the prosodic patterns used in maternal speech as in the following example from Lisa:

14 Lisa   (1;8;18)   [k ʌ h̄ɪ]
                            [ωm:ba:k ʌ h̄ɪ]
                            (2.) [nōw?]
                                [də̄dωkāh̄ɪ]

What is striking about this is that it sounds exactly like her mother's speech, including a two second pause for a reply, except that the sequence is void of lexical content. Compare it to the hypothetical example below:

15 Hypothetical maternal speech: Cookie?/
                                        ((SLOW)) You want
                                        cookie?/
                                        [PAUSE]
                                        No?/
                                        Mm good cookie./

Such patterns are not unique to blind children and features of similar "prosodic envelopes" have been reported for sighted children (see Crystal, 1979; Peters, 1974, 1977). Peters has suggested children may learn tunes before words very early on. Moreover, children learning tone languages, such as Chinese, acquire tones very early suggesting that children generally are sensitive to both lexical and phrasal prosody.

Shortly after the prosodic patterns appeared, the blind children begin to produce whole chunks of their mother's speech in its appropriate context. In the following example, Lisa reproduces her mother's typical speech as she goes through the rather complicated procedure of climbing a ladder and then sliding down a slide. (There are actually six episodes spanning several pages in which various aspects of the activity are encoded.)

16 Lisa   (2;2;2)
               step/   (walking toward ladder)
               ladder/   (reaching out to ladder)
               step up ladder/   (putting one foot on first step)
               up/
               ⋮

       yeah lisa/   (as stands on top of platform)
       sit down/   (begins to sit)

Lenneberg (reported in Fraiberg, 1977) has suggested that the production of similar language sequences by one of Fraiberg's blind subjects functioned as a form of self regulation, and that would seem to explain example 16. However, a few minutes later Lisa again climbs the ladder and reproduces more of her mother's language, but in this case, it does not serve a regulatory function:

17 Lisa   (2;2;2)   (Climbing slide)
             no/   (steadily progressing up ladder)
   (1.)   no/
   (5.)   [(ωəsIplædai)]/('(   )ladder')
   (2.)   no no no lisa/
             you're silly/
             ((LF))
             no/
             no lisa/
             ⋮
             was that fun/   (as slides onto floor)

There are utterances in many of the passages which do in fact encode various behaviors as Lisa performs them, but these instances are not necessarily self regulatory since they rarely anticipate the activity. And there are equally many examples in which the language reproduced seems contextually appropriate but unrelated to the specific behaviors the child is performing. An alternative explanation is that the production of this language is part of the activity itself. In chapter 4 it is suggested that blind children generally fail to extend lexemes to new referents and that they characteristically show less objectification about vehicle–referent relationships. I suggested that term and referent may be isomorphic, together constituting the child's representation of something. If the analysis is carried forward, it suggests that the blind children conceive their mother's language as an inherent part of an activity. This possibility is supported by samples of Teddy's speech in which he re-creates typical maternal language associated with a specific familiar situation in circumstances that cannot be interpreted as self regulatory:

18 Teddy   (1;8;24)
   (a)   (on waking from a nap)
         did you have (.) nice nap/
   (b)   (on hearing water running in the tub)
         wanna take a bath/
   (c)   (as holding wash cloth and begins to wash face and chest)
         wanto wash face teddy/

(d)   (in tub, hunting for a toy frog that has slipped away)
       where's froggie teddy/

Stereotypic speech such as that in example 18 is also seen in sighted children. R. Clark (1974) provides several examples from her son's speech, reproduced here as example 19 (see also examples from Snow, 1981).

19 (a)   (Said whenever a hot meal was being brought on to the table)
          Wait for it to cool.
Several weeks later a different adjective was substituted for cool.
   (b)   (Hanging up on a towel rail a nappy that he had dropped in the bath)
          Wait for it to dry.

(R. Clark, 1974, p. 4)

Example 19a is the simple reproduction of maternal speech in a familiar recurring context; 19b differs from it in two ways: First, it appears that the phrase has become somewhat segmented and is now a frame-insert pattern where a particular type of word can be slotted into the chunk. Secondly, the context of 19b is less frozen than 19a since presumably nappies don't habitually fall into the bath (though of course they may have in the past and mother may have uttered similar words). If 19b is not a recurrent event, then the child is independently classifying this situation as one of several in which the frame can be suitably used.

Example 19a is similar to the blind children's stereotypic speech, as in the example in 18, but in the blind children's data, evidence of segmentation, as in 19b, does not follow a few weeks after a phrase is adopted.

5.2.2   Communicative use of stereotypic speech

At the same time that the blind children are producing large chunks of stereotypic speech in connection with familiar activities, they are beginning to construct two- and three-word horizontal constructions. Many of these are similar to what sighted children produce, as when Teddy (1;8;24) says "me take bath" after his mother had lifted him from the tub (see section 5.3 for discussion of semantic relations exploited by the various children). But the blind children also begin to use stereotypic speech to convey various messages.

Both Lisa and Teddy begin to use their mother's standard offers of the form "do you want X" in order to request X. A few examples are presented in example 20a–d:

20 (a)   (T requesting a record)
          Wanna hear a record /
   (b)   (T requesting a doll)
          Wan' go see baby /

(c)   (L requesting a ride in a large cardboard box in which
        her parents sometimes push her around; pronoun is
        reversed)
        You wanna go in a b͡ox /
(d)   (L requesting play on the slide; pronoun is reversed)
        You wanna step u͡p /

At the same time as these examples occur, the children are quite capable of producing well-formed requests, and it is not uncommon for both strategies to occur within one episode. And, both mothers, but particularly Teddy's, often require the child to ask correctly before the request is satisfied. The children also use "Let's" offers as requests, as in "Let's go on the slide." While these are not inappropriate, they are certainly unusual in children's speech, and they are clearly forms of stereotypic speech.

Use of stereotypic speech in somewhat inappropriate contexts is also observed in sighted children. Again, some examples from R. Clark are illustrative:

21 (a)   (Used when the child wanted to sit on adult's knee and
           probably copied from an adult saying "Sit on my knee")
           "Sit my knee"
    (b)   (Said when wanted to be carried and definitely copied in
           the first instance from his Father who said "I'll carry
           you")
           "I carry you"

Stereotypic speech in the blind children also occurs in other kinds of constructions, including in utterances which appear to encode the child's own actions. Such uses were more frequent in Teddy's data:

22 (a)   Teddy and LK are playing with a toy giraffe which T
           calls a "horsie"
           (T throws giraffe)
           LK: What did you do?/
             T: did you drop the horsi͡e /
    (b)   Teddy has been playing with a doll called "baby bolts"
           (T drops baby bolts)
             T: did you drop the baby bol͡ts /

Notice that the use of stereotypic speech contributes to the misuse of pronouns. This is also seen in sighted children's language as in 21a and b above, but pronominal errors are not long lasting in the speech of sighted children. In the early transcripts from the blind children pronominal errors are rare, but the vast majority of references to self occurring *after* the children have an MLU of 1.50 involve pronoun reversals. Almost all of Lisa's self references occur as "you" unless she specifically uses her proper name, which occurs with decreasing frequency. Approximately 75 per cent of Teddy's self references involve pronominal errors, but he does produce some utterances of the form "I want" or "gimme." Even the pronoun *me* has become reversed in productive use: Lisa regularly says "give it to me" when asking others to take things from her, and Teddy once produced "want me blow" in an effort to get a researcher to blow his toy horn.

The extent to which pronouns are reversed is revealed in the following incident between Teddy and his mother in which the mother instinctively responds to Teddy's intended meaning rather than what he actually says:

23 Teddy   (T is standing next to M, M is in a chair)
            M: Where's your teeth?/
                 (T correctly points to his own teeth)
            T: Where's my teeth/
                 (M leans over so T can touch *her* teeth!)

Interestingly the increase in pronoun errors closely parallels the increasing use of stereotypic speech. Moreover, the increasing frequency of errors in pronominal reference seen in the blind children is the opposite of the pattern for sighted children, where such errors are observed only briefly and quickly diminish (see Chiat, 1982; R. Clark, 1974).

5.2.3 Comprehension of pronouns

While the children's productive use of pronouns is inconsistent and often reversed, there is some evidence in the sessions that their comprehension of these forms is more accurate. To examine the differences between comprehension and production, an individualized probe was designed to measure the frequency with which first and second person pronouns, especially possessive forms, are comprehended. (None of the children use, or are regularly exposed to, third person pronoun forms.) Since the blind children continue to resist all structured tasks of this sort (see chapter 4), the probe sentences were presented by either the mother or myself at appropriate times throughout the course of a visit. All of the children were presented with the same sentences except that the objects referred to varied so that they were compatible with the child's individual experiences. The task was administered in the first session after the child achieved an MLU of 1.50. I tried unsuccessfully to administer it to Julie somewhat earlier.

The structures presented to the children are listed below using a hypothetical child's name, "Susie." Three examples of each type were presented whenever possible, but this varied somewhat across the children. Sentences were presented in random order. In the beginning of the session in which the task was administered, I gave the mother a complete list of all of the sentences, with precise objects and body parts indicated.

  1 Possession expressed with full noun
    (a) Body parts (inalienable possession)

    1 Where's Susie's (body part)?
    2 Where's Mommy's (body part)?
    3 Where's dolly's/Annie's/(body part)?
  (b) Objects (alienable possession)
    1 Where's Susie's (object name, both proximal such as
      shirt and distal, such as bed)?
    2 Where's Mommy (object, both distant and proximal)?
 2 Possession expressed with possessive pronouns
  (a) Body parts (inalienable possession)
    1 Susie, where's your (body part)?
    2 Susie, where's my (body part)?
    3 Where's your/Show me your (body part)
    4 Where's my/Show me my (body part)
  (b) Objects (question structures, alienable possession)
    1 Where's your (object)?
    2 Where's my (object)?
  (c) Objects (directive structures, alienable possession)
    1 Go get/find your (object)
    2 Go get/find my (object)
 3 Non-possessive pronouns
  (a) Directions to perform an activity, e.g., You go (do X)
  (b) Statements of intention to perform an activity e.g., I'm
    going to (do X); purpose is to determine whether or not
    child attempts to perform act.

All of the children responded correctly to the possessive structures containing proper nouns. Teddy, Lydia and Brett attempted to respond to such utterances when they involved distant objects, but Lisa did not, probably because she refuses to search for items on her own. Brett responded accurately to all sentences with possessive pronouns in group 2, and Lydia responded to 80 per cent correctly. Her errors all involved misinterpretation of "my." Lisa and Teddy interpreted "your" correctly, but responded to "my" as if it referred to themselves in 70 per cent of their responses. Moreover, sentences of the type "Susie, where's my X?" seemed more problematic than those in which the child's name was not used. This suggests that processing the proper name is a predominant strategy which leads the child to ignore or to misinterpret pronouns encoding reference to others within the same sentence. This was not observed in the responses from Brett and Lydia. The blind children had difficulty responding to directives to "go find X," with Lisa refusing to comply at all and Teddy responding to only two sentences, both of the form "Go find your X."

It is difficult to interpret the responses to the third group of sentences since Lydia and Lisa refused to perform most of the behaviors requested, while Brett and Teddy both attempted to comply with the requests. My impression is that the responses reveal more about the children's personalities than about their language facility. However, Teddy did attempt to perform some of the acts encoded in type 3b sentences, suggesting that the I/You distinction is not present.

The results of the individualized probes suggest that all of the children comprehend the basic concept of possession and can interpret possession encoded in sentences with proper names. But the children with no useful vision do not comprehend the distinction encoded in possessive pronouns and probably fail to understand pronominal deixis in general.

5.2.4   Discussion

In the present study, the use of language that is characteristic of their mothers seems to be uniquely limited to blind children. We should note here that when the current study ended, Julie, with an MLU of 1.29, was just beginning to use stereotypic speech, but more recent observations suggest that it occurs less frequently than for Teddy and Lisa.

Lydia uses many unanalyzed chunks of language but these appear to be the kinds of units reported in investigations of sighted children. She adopts them from a variety of sources, extends them to new contexts and, most importantly, the chunks seem to become segmented along the lines suggested by Peters (1983). In general, Lydia appears to have the characteristics of a gestalt language learner (Peters, 1977). When Lisa and Teddy use such units they sound exactly like their mothers, adopting intonation patterns, pauses and so on, and often reproducing *sequences* of utterances that are associated with an event. In contrast, Lydia, like the sighted children described by other researchers, extracts only a single utterance (or portion of an utterance) and uses it in an expanding variety of situations. It is interesting to note that Urwin (1978a) also observed a large number of "ready made phrases" in the language of her totally blind subject but found fewer such phrases in her subject with residual vision.

If the blind children's propensity for using stereotypic speech is a language learning strategy of the sort reported for sighted children, we would expect to see a large number of frame-insert patterns and other evidence of segmentation as the units are analyzed. In fact this is not the case. While stereotypic language accounts for an average of one third of their utterances, frame-inserts are virtually unseen. Frame-inserts account for 13 of 3,062 utterances analyzed for Lisa and 39 of 2,684 utterances for Teddy. If language learners store all units (morphemes, words and unanalyzed phrases) in their lexicons as Peters (1983) proposes, then the blind children's failure to begin to analyze these, at least during the period of the study, is in line with the findings of the lexical analysis which revealed a general lack of decentration and extension. Both suggest that blind children are having considerable difficulty in recognizing the symbolic nature of language and in learning enough about the environment and the way language encodes events in the environment to stimulate creative language use and analysis.

Nevertheless, the fact that totally blind children use stereotypic speech provides us with certain clues about how these children structure familiar events. It is possible that parental language helps the blind children to recognize the component behaviors which constitute a single event. In other words, it draws attention to part–whole relationships. And, the linguistic code may help the children to draw together the separate sensory and kinesthetic experiences that combine to form a larger unit of activity. In chapter 2, I summarized work which suggests that vision is unique in that it provides instant simultaneous access to information which is otherwise segmented by space and time. Without vision, most information is necessarily perceived sequentially through haptic exploration. Maternal speech may facilitate the cognitive task of comprehending the position of action sequences within a larger event. For example, the language produced by Lisa's mother may help Lisa to build a more accurate representation of the event "sliding." Although it is improbable that Lisa understands many of her mother's words and sentences, the intonation contours, pauses, and other clues can help indicate how the event is partitioned into component units. I also suggested above that early on the child may actually conceive of this language as an integral part of the event itself. In any case, I think it is quite possible that parental language plays an important role in helping blind children to more accurately conceptualize their environment and the events that occur within it. It also enables the children to develop and share a set of expectations about everyday activities. This suggests that language input may be more important to blind children than to sighted children.

The blind children's use of stereotypic language may be a general conceptual key for the emergence of representational thinking. In one year old sighted children the performance of familiar routines is often viewed as an active representation of familiar information (see Nelson, 1973a; Huttenlocher and Higgins, 1978; Zukow, 1984). Moreover, sighted children may also actively represent some event in terms of thought or action as they do when they perform doll caregiving scenes. It is not necessary to assume that the doll is symbolic or designates in any way the child or another baby. The child may simply be *actively* representing a familiar event. Recently a number of researchers have discussed the notion of an "event" as a basic representation for very young children (Barrett, 1983; Bates *et al.*, 1979; Bloom, 1973; McNeil, 1979; Nelson, 1983; Slobin, 1981). Nelson (1983) calls these event representations "scripts," which she defines as "a structured whole representing a sequential activity involving roles that people play and objects that they interact with in the course of the activity" (p. 180). Blind children do not play with objects (Fraiberg 1977; and corroborated by my own field notes). Their only way of overtly representing an event at this time is through reproducing the speech patterns associated with it. Interestingly,

Nelson (1983) proposes that concepts are derived from scripts via analysis or partitioning.

Thus, the blind children's use of stereotypic language may provide information about the environment and also provide a means of representing aspects of that environment. On the other hand, the use of stereotypic speech by the children provides an index to some basic misconceptions about the world, and about language. It provides evidence of, and presumably contributes to, their failure to understand the reciprocity encoded in pronominal deixis. It also indicates that the children have less understanding of the differences in the roles of various interlocutors. Despite considerable modeling, the blind children persisted in encoding things from their mother's perspective. Clearly, something about visual information enables sighted children to grasp their roles earlier and more clearly than blind children. (For a discussion of how the incorporation of this kind of language into discourse contexts causes problems in conveying messages when the children are older, see Andersen, Dunlea and Kekelis, 1984.)

It would seem that the blind children's unusual propensity to pick up and use their mother's characteristic speech is at once an index of some of their basic confusions and a vehicle through which they may come to better understand the invisible environment.

The appearance of vertical constructions is the first clear indication that a young child is moving toward the expression of rudimentary propositions. Furthermore, the blind child's exploitation of stereotypic speech indicates that the child is capable of articulating multi-word utterances with at least some awareness of contextual suitability. However, one of the most important and exciting developments in the ontogenesis of meaning occurs when the child begins to creatively express two or more different aspects of an event in a single utterance: when the child begins to combine meanings according to different semantic relations. This section analyzes the children's emerging two- and three-word constructions and considers how access to visual information affects the ways these roles are expressed.

5.3   Expressing semantic roles

Many researchers have used a modified case grammar approach to analyze the semantic roles that are expressed in children's early multi-word utterances (Arlman-Rupp, van Niekerk de Hann and van de Sandt-Koenderman, 1976; Bloom, 1970, 1973; Bowerman, 1973; Braine, 1976; Brown, 1973; Kernan, 1969; Leonard, 1976; Miller, 1979; Retherford, Schwartz and Chapman, 1981; Schlesinger, 1971). Case grammar identifies the role of the arguments in a proposition. Very simply, every proposition consists of a verbal unit and one or more nouns (arguments). The verbal unit expresses an action or state (run, be happy). The nouns may express a number of different roles, depending on their relationship to the verb. For example, they may perform the action, in which case they are agents (*Mary* hit the ball); they may receive the action, in which case they are recipient objects (Mary hit *the ball*); they may be used to perform the act, in which case they are instruments (Mary hit the ball with *the racket*) and so on. Case grammar is thus concerned with the thematic roles of the words in a proposition and captures the notion that not all nouns in the same structural role (e.g. subject, object) have the same function with respect to the verb.

The findings from case grammar analyses of child language suggest that there is an impressive consistency among children acquiring a variety of different languages in that most children begin by expressing combinatorial meaning principally through a group of eight semantic relations: Agent + Action; Action + Object; Agent + Object; Action + Locative; Entity + Locative; Possessor + Possession; Attributive + Entity;[3] and Demonstrative + Entity.

In addition to these, several grammatically defined structures appear early on including expressions of negation and recurrence. The relationships are further combined when children construct three-word combinations. Four constructions are most characteristic of early three-word utterances: Agent, Action, Object; Agent, Action, Location; Agent, Object, Location; and Action, Object, Location. Seven other semantic categories used in adult languages are reported to be much less frequent in children's early utterances: instruments, benefactives, indirect object datives, experiencers, comitatives, conjunctives, and classifications (e.g., mommy lady, apple fruit).

While the eight categories are prevalent across a wide range of data, there is some variation with respect to the order of their emergence and the relative frequency of their use within a given corpus. However, it appears that these eight relations constitute a universal core that may be actualized by the child's cognitive schemata for organizing and representing real-world physical and social relationships (Bloom, 1973; Brown, 1973; Golinkoff, 1981; Miller, 1979). Furthermore, some researchers have proposed that limitations of sensorimotor intelligence can account for the restricted set of roles that have been observed.

The investigation of relational meaning is not without its problems. To begin with there is no consensus in the field about where semantic roles come from (see Bloom, 1983 for discussion). Moreover, semantic relations are not overtly observable, but must be inferred (or simply hypothesized) on the basis of what the child says, the situational context in which the child speaks, the known past experience of the child, and the interpretation of what is said by interlocutors. In other words, analysis of early combinatorial meaning crucially depends on the acceptance and application of the method of "rich interpretation" or "interpretive analysis." Interpretive analysis has been

---

[3] Brown (1973) and others classify attribution among early semantic relations, though it is more correctly a grammatical category.

sharply criticized by Howe (1976, 1981) and Rogdon (1977) among others
(see Bloom, 1983). Howe's central arguments are that the semantic
categories overestimate the child's cognitive capacities and that a child's
conception of events is probably very different from an adult's. In particular,
she argues that children are incapable of conceptualizing the distinction
between agents, possessors, recipients and so on during the sensorimotor
period and she calls for evidence that such categories have validity in young
children. This position has sparked several point-by-point refutations which
reassert the suitability of interpretive analysis and the assignment of
semantic roles to children's early combinatorial language (Bloom, Capatides
and Tackeff, 1981; Golinkoff, 1981).

Some of the most convincing evidence comes from research which explores
non-linguistic concepts that parallel the concepts implied by the assignment
of semantic relations. For example, several researchers have used a
habituation paradigm to demonstrate that during the sensorimotor period
(0 to 2 years), children can distinguish action reversals that reflect changes in
agent and recipient roles occurring in carefully constructed films (Golinkoff
and Harding, 1978; Golinkoff, 1979; and see Golinkoff, 1981 for a review of
other research). McCune-Nicolich (1981) analyzed the early use of
relational words by five subjects and found continuity between the child's
meanings for terms and knowledge of relations established in sensorimotor
tasks, independent of language. Similarly, expansion in the meanings of
locative, negation, and recurrence terms each seem to correlate with the
ability to solve specific sensorimotor tasks (Gopnik, 1984; Gopnik and
Meltzoff, 1985, 1987; Gratch, 1975; Tomasello and Farrar, 1984). Taken
together, the evidence seems to support the view that children can and do
conceptualize the fundamental roles that are expressed by the eight core
semantic relations.

The research examining children's early expressions of semantic relations
raises an issue of considerable relevance in investigating the role of visual
information. Implicitly or explicitly, the research points to a core of relations
which appear to be ontogenetic universals that arise from the
cognitive–interpersonal matrix. If the way in which young children perceive
and categorize the world is expressed in the semantic relations they encode,
what happens when the child has limited access to certain perceptually
available information? If the various core relations are attested, will their
expression be limited by the extent of the child's direct experience? If the
claim is valid that semantic relations reflect the child's prior schematiciz-
ation of events perceived in the world, it should follow that children whose
conception of the world is necessarily different as the result of visual
impairment will express qualitatively different relationships in their early
utterances. No specific hypotheses are advanced about the emergence of
semantic relations in the blind children's language, rather their development is analyzed to determine whether or not those items which have been
postulated as universal actually occur, and to explore the relationship

between language and conceptual development as it is manifest in this particular aspect of the development of meaning.

5.3.1 Methodology

All of the children's spontaneous intelligible utterances that were used communicatively and that contained two or more words were analyzed and coded for the presence of eight semantic roles, and three additional semantic categories, supplemented by six grammatical categories. Build-ups or replacement sequences were analyzed once in their fullest form. The analysis follows the conventions developed in other research on the use of semantic relations by young children (see Retherford, Schwartz and Chapman, 1981). The classification system includes the categories involved in the eight core case relations. The rationale for excluding utterances which do not have a communicative force is that the interpretation of communicative utterances in the context in which they are uttered constitutes maximally interpretable data. We can only speculate about meaning when a child is babbling, playing with language or reconstructing past events to himself. It is often impossible to specify what information the child is consciously encoding in such circumstances. (Chapter 6 discusses the communicative function of the children's utterances and the coding system introduced there makes it possible to easily identify the utterances that did have communicative functions.)

The classification system and examples of each of the categories are presented below.

Case roles used in the analysis of semantic relations

Agent (Agt): The animate instigator of the action identified by the verb.
  Daddy laugh (as F laughs)
Object (O): A person or thing whose role is characterized by the interpretation of the verb itself, but which typically directly receives the force of the action.
  Me throw *the ball* (as child throws ball)
Locative (L): Indicates the location or spatial orientation of the state or action specified by the verb.
  Baby *here*
  Baby *in chair*
Instrument (I): The inanimate object or force causally involved in the action or state described by the verb.
  Mommy cut *knife* (As M slices food with knife)
Experiencer (E): The being affected by the action or psychological state specified by the verb.
  He wants bottle (child describing why cousin is crying)
  I hear it (child hears a cuckoo-clock sound)

Possessor (Poss): The person or thing belonging to or habitually associated
with another person or thing.

> *Dolly* hair (Touching doll's hair) The possessed item was
> indicated as *Possession* (Possn)

Recipient (or Dative) (Dat): The person or object who receives or was
intended to receive some object through the action specified by the
verb.

> Give *me* cookie (child requesting cookie)

Benefactive (B): The person or object which benefits from the action
specified by the verb.

> Do it for *me* (child requesting assistance in activating toy)

Comitative (Com): The animate being who participates with the agent in
carrying out the activity specified by the verb.

> I go *daddy* (child announcing she will accompany her father to
> work)

In addition, there are three other semantic categories:

Conjunctive (Conj): The specification of two or more co-occurring beings or
objects.

> *Daddy doggie* (on seeing F and dog enter room together)

Demonstrative (Dem): The specification of some particular referent through
the use of a demonstrative pronoun or adjective.

> *That* big (child specifying a toy)

Action/State (A/S): The activity or condition specified by the verb.

> I *combing* (child combing his hair)
> I *like* candy (child describing psychological state of self)
> Predicate adjectives were included in this category
> I *silly* (child commenting on self)

Classification of selected grammatical categories:

Negation (N): Any term used to express refusal, rejection, denial, disappearance, discontinuation, or non-existence with respect to some object,
person, activity, or state.

Entity (Ent): The identification of some object or being as an instance of a
class without action on that object or being.

> Its a *lion*
> That *froggie*

Recurrence (Rec): The specification of, or request for reappearance, or
further instance of beings, objects or activities.

> *More* candy (As M gives child another piece of candy)
> Tickle *again* (child requesting to be tickled again)

Attribute (Attr): The expression of some quality pertaining to an object or
person.

> *big* truck (child playing with large toy truck)
> *vanilla* candy (child eating vanilla flavored sweet)

Formulaic Requests (FR): Because of its prevalence among the blind
children, instances of "(I) – want x" were tallied separately.

Initially these were simply instances of identifying a desired object or activity (e.g., "I want cookie"). In time some of these became more complex statements. Many of the utterances seem to contain stereotypic units, but there is evidence of segmentation in the later sessions. Thus, these are probably midway between fully creative and merely formulaic utterances.

Question (Q): This was used for formulaic WH-questions requesting the "name" of an entity.

> *What* this (Picking up an unfamiliar toy)
> *Who* that (Seeing a new person in room)

Further considerations involving the coding system:

Uncoded morphemes: The decision was made not to code instances of determiners, quantifiers or prepositions since there were no instances in which the children seemed to use these productively, except in the final session with Lisa (2;7;26) which is not included in the tally. Similarly, combinations of verb + particle were counted as a single unit. Instances of such verbs included "fall down," "stand up" and "sit down." In addition the use of "take bath" and "make bed" were considered as one unit.

Agency: In standard usage agency refers to an animate being perceived as the instigator of an action (Filmore, 1968), though it has also been extended to inanimate forces as in "the *wind* opened the door" (see Chafe, 1970; Cruse, 1973). The convention was adopted to further extend the term to inanimate objects which seemed to function as animate beings in representational play, as in "*Dolly* drink."

Recurrence: Some researchers have differentiated the categories "recurrence" (more) from "repetition" (again) (Bloom, 1973). The two are combined here since they both express the predicative function of additional instance. In some situations the children requested recurrence of some thing or some event (e.g., demanding "more milk") whereas other times some event was described. This distinction was not coded.

Stereotypic speech: The semantic relations expressed in stereotypic speech were not analyzed, but the total number of instances in which such speech functioned communicatively in each session is included in the tallies. For example, Teddy's (1;8;24) saying "blow dry your hair Teddy" as an apparent request to have his hair dried is viewed as communicative as is Lisa's (2;4;3) saying "I pick you up" to request that her mother pick her up. Non-communicative uses, for example those which habitually occur with the performance of a familiar activity, are not included in the tally of communicative stereotypic speech.

Uninterpretable utterances: Utterances which contained unintelligible segments were not analyzed, but the total numbers of such speech are tallied. This was a particularly serious problem with Lydia's data.

Other excluded utterances: Politeness and greeting formulas ("thank you," "hi Annie") were not included in the analysis, nor were any instances of routines (see chapter 6). Similarly, formulaic offers of the form "here mommy" were not included so that no particular case would be artificially inflated. This was important in Lydia's data where offers were often prolific (see chapter 6).

Other: A few utterances which were difficult to classify are considered separately in the discussion.

Self versus other: As the analysis progressed it became important to distinguish between expressions which encoded information directly involving the child himself from utterances encoding information about others. The convention was adopted to use a "self" code to indicate agency, action, experience and so on which specifically involved the child, and to use an "other" code to indicate agency, action, and experience of another. Thus, "I

eat" was coded Agt   +   A/S and "Mommy eat" was coded Agt   +   A/S.
　　　　　　　　　 self   other

5.3.2   Results

The eight core relations, plus the four frequently occurring three-term constructions account for 68 per cent of Brett's intelligible utterances, well within the range of 60–70 per cent generally reported for these categories. Similarly, in Lydia's data they represent 64 per cent of the analyzable corpus and in Julie's, 72 per cent, though her sample is quite small. (Julie is only entering the two-word stage and the analysis of her data should be regarded as "suggestive.") In contrast, these key relations constitute only 31 per cent of Teddy's utterances and 34 per cent of Lisa's. This is in part explained by the effect of stereotypic speech in their corpora. If stereotypic utterances are excluded from the analysis the basic relations account for 50 per cent of each of their utterances. This is still lower than the norm largely because these children produced a greater number of "want statements." (Recall that such statements are midway between stereotypic and creative language.)

Tables 5.2 to 5.6 present the semantic relations encoded by each of the children, expressed as percentages of total multi-word utterance types satisfying the criteria specified above.

Core two-term relations: The first observation is that Brett is the only child who uses all eight of the core relations. Entity + Attribute is unattested in data from Lydia, and while instances of this occur in Teddy's and Lisa's speech, they tend to be common associations such as "nice bath" and "little horse" (Lisa has a "little" horse and a "big" horse). My impression is that these children have generally not abstracted attributional features from the items with which they were initially associated and that the phrases containing them are unanalyzed units. One exception to this is the cutaneously sensed feature, "cold," which occurs in single-word structures for all of the blind children. Attributes are not especially frequent in Brett's

Table 5.2
Teddy: Semantic relations expressed as percentages of total multi-word
utterances satisfying criteria*

MLU	1.03	1.25	1.47	1.53	2.13	2.50	≈2.49	1.95	
Total no. multi-word utts	4	16	20	58	53	60	42	93	
Agt + A/S						01			
(self)			(10)	(22)	(07)	(17)		(04)	
A/S + O				02ᵃ	02ᵃ			01	
(self)			(20)	(12)	(04)		(17)	(07)	
Agt + O		.							
A/S + L									
Ent + L				03ᵇ	02ᵇ		02ᵇ	02ᵇ	
Poss + Possn									
(self)		(06)	(05)		02				
Ent + Attr				02	02				
Dem + Ent			10	03				01	
Agt, A/S, O								01	
(self)					(13)	(03)	(07)	(11)	
Agt, A/S, L									
(self)									
Agt, O, L									
A/S, O, L									
Neg + A/S									
Neg + Ent	25	94		02	02				
Rec + Ent or									
A/S (self)				02ᵃ	04ᵃ	07ᵃ			
Q					02			05	
Formulaic									
Requests			20	08	04	07	07	23	
Expanded F R					02	22			
St Speech	75	0	20	37	45	36	67	24	
Unintell	0	0	15	03	04	07		05	
A/S, Poss, Possn					04ᵃ				
Dem, Poss, Possn					02				
Other									

[a]All non-self instances are requests   [b]All instances refer to past events
* May not total 100 due to rounding

Note: Parentheses indicate utterances that relate to the child himself.

Table 5.3
Lisa: Semantic relations expressed as percentages of total multi-word
utterances satisfying criteria*

MLU	≈1.11	1.05	1.11	1.10	1.20	1.30	1.86	1.85	2.01
Total no. multi-word utts	1	2	6	1	1	19	97	32	38
Agt + A/S (self)		(50)						(06)	(03)
A/S + O (self)	(100)		(17)				01ᵃ (04)	(15)	(10)
Agt + O						05ᶜ			
A/S + L									
Ent + L						10ᶜ	01ᶜ	05ᶜ	
Poss + Possn (self)									(05)
Ent + Attr				100		16	02		18
Dem + Ent							03		
Agt + A/S, O (self)							(04)	(03)	03ᶜ (03)
Agt, A/S, L (self)							(04)	03ᵃ	
Agt, O, L									
A/S, O, L									
Neg + A/S									
Neg + Ent						05ᵃ			08ᵃ
Rec + Ent or A/S (self)			50			05ᵃ	05ᵃ		(08)
Q									
Formulaic Requests		50	17				17	06	
Expanded F R							15	09	
St Speech			17		100	36	37	12	23
Unintell						10	06	40	08
Conj						10ᶜ			05
Conj & L						05ᶜ			
Other							02		

ᵃAll instances are requests   ᶜAll instances refer to past events
* May not total 100 due to rounding

Note: Parentheses indicate utterances that relate to self.

Table 5.4
Julie: Semantic relations expressed as percentages of total multi-word
utterances satisfying criteria*

MLU	1.04	1.10	1.29			
Total no. multi- word utts	3	9	22			
Agt + A/S (Self)			09[c]			
A/S + O (Self)		22[a] (55)				
Agt + O						
A/S + L						
Ent + L			36[e]			
Poss + Possn			04			
Ent + Attr						
Dem + Ent						
Agt, A/S, O						
Agt, A/S, L						
Agt, O, L						
A/S, O, L						
Neg + A/S						
Neg + Ent						
Rec + Ent						
Q	66					
Formulaic Requests						
Expanded F R						
St Speech			04			
Unintell.			40			
Conj.	33	22	04			

[a]All instances are requests   [c]All instances refer to past events
[e]Probably an habitual association
* May not total 100 due to rounding

Note: Parentheses indicate utterances that relate to self.

Table 5.5
Lydia: Semantic relations expressed as percentages of total multi-word
utterances satisfying criteria*

MLU	1.42	1.46	≈1.64	1.79	1.60	
Total no. multi-word utts	47	38	41	79	100	
Agt + A/S	13[a]			01	04[a]	
(Self)	(11)	02[a]	02	(04)	(03)	
A/S + O			02[a]	09[a]	11[a]	
(Self)		(13)	(04)	(10)	(03)	
Agt + O		08[d]				
(Self)	04[a]	(05)				
A/S + L						
(Self)			(01)			
Ent + L					(01)	
Poss & Possn						
(Self)		(13)	(12)	(08)		
Ent + Attr						
Dem + Ent	02	03	07	01	01	
Agt, A/S, O				02		
(Self)		(10)	(09)	(01)	(07)	
Agt, A/S, L						
(Self)				(01)		
Ag, O, L						
A/S, O, L						
Neg + A/S	15[a]			02[a]	01[a]	
Neg + Ent						
Rec + Ent				04[a]		
Q	19	08	07	01	09	
Formulaic Requests	02		15	04	02	
Expanded F R				01		
St Speech	06	05			02	
Unintell.	27	32	39	44	52	
Dem, Ent, Atr				01	01	
A/S, Poss, Possn						
(Self)				(01)		

[a]All instances are requests   [d]06 % are requests.
* May not total 100 due to rounding

Note: Parentheses indicate utterances that relate to self.

Table 5.6
Brett: Semantic relations expressed as percentages of total multi-word
utterances satisfying criteria*

MLU	1.15	1.30	1.33	1.86	1.62
Total no. multi-word utts	8	4	10	32	68
Agt + A/S	12		10	06	03
A/S + O		25		09	23
(Self)	(12)	(25)	(10)	(03)	(03)
Agt + O					01
A/S + L			10		
Ent + L		25			28
Poss & Possn		25		03	03
Ent + Attr			10		07
Dem + Ent	12		20	03	07
Agt, A/S, O (self)				(12)	(01)
Agt, A/S, L				19	
Agt, O, L					
Neg + A/S	50			16	01
Neg + Ent				03	01
Rec + Ent				03	
Q	12		30	03	
Formulaic Requests				03	
Expanded F R				06	
St Speech					
Unintell.			10	09	08
Neg, A/S, O					01
Ent (2 place)					06
Conj					01

* May not total 100 due to rounding

Note: Parentheses indicate utterances that relate to the child himself.

two-word utterances, but his single-word utterances indicate that he is generalizing this kind of information and has thus started to abstract the criterial features which define attributional terms. Other researchers have also found that attribution is relatively late to appear in multi-term utterances (see Bloom, Lightbown and Hood, 1975). Action/State + Location is unattested in data from Teddy, Lisa, and Julie. However, in an apparent paradox, these children do encode the location of entities. But, as the footnoted information in the table reveals, almost all uses are to ask a question about the location of something (e.g., "where ball") or to comment on past or habitual events (e.g., "doggie out"). Thus, *novel information concerning the location of objects or actions, and concerning qualities of objects is unattested in data from the blind children* and occurs infrequently in the language of Lydia, who has only limited vision.

The various combinations of Agent, Action, and Object occur in data from all of the children (except Julie). But there are significant differences in how these roles are used. For all of the children, Agt + A/S and A/S + O are relatively frequent, but Agt + O is very rare. A microanalysis of how these roles are used reveals variation across subjects that is influenced by degree of vision. Whenever Teddy and Lisa express Agt + A/S relations, they are encoding ongoing information about themselves. The single exception to this is when Teddy (1;11;9) said "Linda burp(ed)." (In fact it was Teddy who burped and it is difficult to know how to interpret the utterance.) In contrast, when Brett encodes the agentive role in two-term utterances it is *always* to refer to someone other than himself! As a rule, Lydia encodes her own agency in statements, but the agency of others in requests. Julie's only uses of this role were in reporting past events.

Altogether, only a quarter of Brett's A/S + O constructions involved activities of which he was the instigator. Yet, all four visually impaired children used this relationship to encode information about themselves, except when they made requests.

Not surprisingly, the visually impaired children typically encoded only those possessive relationships in which they were the possessor. A striking exception is when Teddy (1;10;8) said "your baby" on touching a doll his mother was holding.

Finally, Dem + Ent constructions are used by all children, generally to identify objects (to "name" them). There were predictable differences in the use of the demonstrative itself since the blind children used it only to refer to objects they were holding ("this dolly") or for audible objects ("that (a) motorcycle").[4]

Core three-term relations: Three-term relations are just evolving in the children's productive language and none of the samples encode Agt or A/S

---

[4] It would be fascinating to investigate how (whether) blind children interpret the distal/proximal contrast that distinguishes *this* and *that*, but there was insufficient data to even speculate about the issue here.

with both O and L. The blind children do use the other three-term constructions commonly reported in studies of child language (i.e. Agt + A/S + L and Agt + A/S + O). The pattern of use is similar to that of the two-term utterances with agent expressions generally encoding self agency except in requests and occasionally in talking about past events. Notice though that Brett's Agt, A/S, and O constructions also tend to be self agentive, which supports the position that there is a general developmental progression from "self" to "others" as children acquire various structures.

Negation and recurrence: Recurrence appears relatively infrequently, but follows a now predictable pattern: the blind children use recurrence only in making requests, whereas Brett uses recurrence to comment on or describe an event. Negations of both action/states and entities are more frequent than recurrence for all children. Again, Brett uses negation in assertions while Lydia and Lisa use it only to request the cessation of some event or to reject an offer. However, a very surprising difference is that all of Teddy's negations are assertions. Teddy uses negation principally to express disappearance or "all-goneness" as in "no banana" (on feeling his tray-table where pieces of banana had been after having eaten them all) and "no circle" (after dropping a lid that he calls a "circle"). The word "no" also appears in Teddy's stereotypic speech when he reproduces such admonitions as "no stove/hot." Constructions of "no + N" also appear as frame-insert structures. I can offer no explanation as to why Teddy produces negation constructions in many of the ways suggested for sighted children (see Bloom, 1970) while Lisa and Lydia do not, but it is very evident that he explored and extracted much of the meaning associated with "no" when he was 18 months old (see also chapter 4).

Formulaic requests: The reader is reminded that "formulaic requests" are coded as separate units because of their high frequency in the blind child's speech. Simple "want statements" are unanalyzed units which come to have frame + insert forms (I want + cookie/outside/milk). Some of the frames became more elaborate and I think they have a special status as the stereotypic forms that are first segmented in the blind child's speech. Thus, I could neither code them as fully productive forms nor did I want to lump them with other instances of unanalyzed speech (St Sp). These are very rare in Brett's corpora, but are frequent in the data from the blind children, especially for Lisa and Lydia. Of particular interest is the fact that Lisa begins to refer to both objects and locations in want statements, even though these roles are rare in other kinds of constructions. Examples of such utterances are "want ride the box" (box = special toy); "wanna go outside the car" and "want stand-up at the box" (this time, "box" refers to a toy chest on which Lisa wanted to stand so that she could touch some pictures on the wall above it).

Other: Isolated instances of other codable relations are entered in the tables for each child as appropriate. There are no particular trends to point out. The semantic roles which are infrequent in other studies of child language are virtually unattested in the present data. Instruments, benefactives, experiencers and comitatives do not appear at all; indirect object datives are limited to the construction "give me X." A few conjunctives are used.

Both Teddy and Lisa produced a few combinations which were difficult to analyze. Lisa (2;2;2) produced the following very long request in an effort to get her mother to push her along in a large empty box from the family room to the kitchen, L is in the box at the time: "you go riding mommy kitchen car" ("you" = Lisa). What is particularly problematic about the interpretation of this utterance is the status of the word *car*. Two possible interpretations are that it modifies "go riding" in some way or that there is an association of the box with a car. It is also unclear what status should be assigned to "mommy" (e.g., agent, instrument, attention getter).

When Teddy was 25 months old (2;1;13) he began to use question structures apparently to identify objects. For example, "is that spoon" (on picking up a spoon), "is it the glass" (on picking up an unfamiliar glass; determiner is incorrect). It is unclear whether these are further instances of stereotypic speech, an interactive strategy (someone always replied) or a genuine request for information.

To summarize, then, the results suggest that both the sighted child and the blind children produce many of the basic relations that have been identified in other studies of early combinational language, but there are several important differences that involve access to visual information. First, novel information about the locations of events or objects and about attributes of entities is virtually unattested in the language of very young blind children. Secondly, while many of the core relations are expressed by the blind children, the vast majority of these constructions encode events in which the child is the principal instigator or the possessor. Thirdly, when the blind children do encode roles of other people it is to request things of them and/or to discuss shared past events. There is a consistency between these findings and the results of the analysis of single-word sequences presented in section 5.1. In both instances, request strategies rather than assertions seemed to be important for the development of constructions by blind children and the blind children's most creative and advanced utterances referred to past events rather than to the here and now. Finally, we should note that Lydia, who has some useful residual vision, seems to pattern closer to the blind children in the expression of semantic roles, while the absence of stereotypic maternal speech in her data is more characteristic of sighted children.

5.3.3   Discussion

The differences between blind and sighted children probably result from two different kinds of factors. On the one hand, the constructions produced by the blind children reflect the considerable deficit of information they have about the world around them. On the other hand, the actualization of various kinds of semantic expressions and the use of increasingly complex requests and questions imply that certain adaptive strategies are in operation.

What the blind children express in their emerging propositional structures seem to reflect the elements of an event for which they have *direct* experiential information. For many events, blind children are at a considerable disadvantage in terms of the information available. For example, consider the event encoded by the adult sentence "George rolls the ball to Mary." A sighted child at the two-word stage commenting on this is likely to encode "ball," "ball roll" or even "George roll ball" (assuming that perception of an object undergoing a change of state is the likely element to be encoded: see Greenfield and Zukow, 1978). Now consider this from the blind child's perspective. If Mary is blind, she has immediate knowledge of her own existence and she can discover, after the ball has made contact with her, that the object in question is a ball. Note that she must explore her environment *after the event* has been completed in order to identify the ball. If a sighted child encodes "ball" in this situation, she seems to be encoding an object in change (or at least that is one possible interpretation). We can't say the same is true for the blind child – it seems to me "ball" is an identification of an object just encountered. The concept "roll (to)" is virtually meaningless for a blind child. Mary may come to recognize a contingency relationship between hearing a ball roll and the ball's bumping into her, but this is unreliable since the ball can miss its mark or be directed to someone other than herself. Clearly, Mary could never experience an object's rolling action or understand its trajectory. Finally, Mary can be *told* that George caused the ball to contact her, or she can infer it, but she cannot "know" it on her own. Moreover, her understanding of George's role is limited to her understanding of what she herself can do. She can then project this to George because she cannot witness George's action. Such projection does not occur at this stage of development even for sighted children (see for example Piaget, 1952).

My own observations of blind children suggest that even if the child is able to produce two- and three-word utterances, in the situation described above the child is likely to encode only "ball." This is because such children have experiential access to the ball. (It is also possible that they would encode possession as in "my ball.")

Based on this line of reasoning, we may infer that blind children's conceptions of events are at times different from sighted children's conceptions of them, and this is necessarily reflected in what blind children express linguistically. The agent and action relationships that young children can productively encode are those for which they have some kind of understanding through first-hand experience. As a result, most agents expressed by blind children are self agents and most actions are actions blind children can experience more or less in their entirety. This relative inaccessibility to certain basic information about objects and events can also help explain why blind children fail to encode locative and qualifying information.

Yet despite their sensory deprivation, young blind children do have access to a fair amount of first-hand information that seems to be unexploited as a basis for creative language. It is very surprising that novel information about the locations of events and objects, about the qualities of entities, and even about the activities of others is not encoded on the basis of available non-visual information. The qualities of sound, texture, taste, and odor are the basis of blind children's knowledge and these do provide information about objects and people in the environment. Curiously, this is rarely expressed. Moreover, this kind of information is almost never used as a basis for talking about the activities of others, even though the familiar sounds of a sibling's computer, a squeaking swing, or a pet dog's barking; the sounds and smells of a parent cooking; or even the sounds of laughing, coughing, and sneezing do provide blind children with information about the ongoing activities of others.

The fact that the blind children are not encoding novel locative or descriptive information, or for that matter constructing novel assertions, is reminiscent of the developmental delays observed in the lexical analysis presented in chapter 4. There we found that the blind children were slow to extract criterial features of referents and they tended to associate a term with a specific referent for an unusually long time. The same factors that kept the blind children from extracting and classifying information during the single-word period presumably prevent them from extracting and encoding information about things in their early multi-term speech. Both require the child to recognize and categorize attributes from encounters with entities and events. Similarly, we observed that almost all of the blind children's early word combinations relate to themselves and this parallels the striking lack of decentration observed in their single word utterances.

In commenting on an earlier report of some of this data, Snow (1984) suggests that the restricted nature of blind children's language is because their parents may not often tune into non-visual information, with the result that the linguistic environment provided by the caregivers does not match the child's cognitive capacities. Certainly, this could be a contributing factor, but it does not explain all of the facts. An exhaustive and detailed analysis of input is required to determine precisely how much it can explain. Such an analysis is not available, but an especially relevant aspect of language input in these data has been analyzed by Andersen and Kekelis (1982). Interestingly, it reveals that the egocentric nature of the blind children's language cannot be accounted for by the effect of input alone.

Andersen and Kekelis analyzed the types of topics expressed in the maternal input to the same blind and sighted subjects who participated in

Table 5.7. *Proportion of topic types initiated by caregivers*

Topic type	Blind		Sighted	
	16–18 months	19–22 months	16–18 months	19–22 months
Child centered	48%	46.3%	36%	28%
Environmental[a]	36%	35.3%	46%	53%
Abstract[b]	16%	18.2%	18%	18%

[a] Referring to things going on in the immediate environment.
[b] Referring to things not in the immediate here and now context.
Source: Based on Andersen and Kekelis (1982).

the present investigation. They examined the period when the children were 16 to 22 months old and classified each topic initiated by the mother as one of three types: child centered, environment related, or abstract – that is, not relating to the "here and now." The results are reproduced here as table 5.7.

The analysis completed by Andersen and Kekelis reveals that child centered topics did predominate in mothers' speech to blind children whereas environmental topics were most common in mothers' speech to sighted children. But in neither case was the tendency to the exclusion of other topics. In fact, more than half of the topics introduced to blind children had to do with things other than the children themselves: 52 per cent of the topics were environmental or abstract during the 16 to 18 month period and so were 50.5 per cent during the 19 to 22 month period. It is true that this is somewhat less than the proportion of non-child centered topics introduced by mothers of sighted children: 64 per cent of their topics during the 16 to 18 month period and 71 per cent during the 19 to 22 month period were abstract or environmental. The higher proportion of child centered topics used with blind children may contribute to the problems they had in decentering. It is also probable that the mothers use these topics to tune in to the child. Most importantly, though, the blind children were being exposed to hundreds of topics that were not related specifically to them. We should also note that the mothers of blind and sighted subjects produced just about the same number of abstract topics: 16 per cent for blind subjects and 18 per cent for sighted during the 16 to 18 month period and 18.2 per cent for blind and 18 per cent for sighted during the 19 to 22 month period. Therefore, maternal input cannot account for the surprising finding that blind children talked about past events – an abstract topic – while sighted children this age do not. This demonstrates the active role children have in constructing language and it suggests that the blind children are finding some ways to use language in order to solve problems they have in dealing with the sighted world.

While there are clearly conceptual deficits reflected in the blind children's early multi-term utterances, the fact that the children encode an increasing number of roles in their requests in order to indicate more precisely what activity, object or information they want may well be an adaptive strategy which increases their access to the environment. Similarly, talking about shared past events with their caregivers is one of the ways that blind children can maximize the possibility for drawing an interlocutor's attention to a new "topic." With limited access to the immediate environment, past events provide the blind child with greater certainty that the parent and child share similar information. (It is also possible that some of these events were previously encoded by the adult.) The tendency to discuss past events in fact emerges in some of the vertical constructions discussed in section 5.1. Taken together, the picture that emerges from the analysis of semantic roles lends support to the hypothesis that the expression of semantic relations reflects a child's underlying conceptual framework of the fundamental thematic relations obtaining in the world. The core relations that have been proposed as universal are expressed by the blind children within the confines of the information available to them. This suggests that the emergence of these is an intrinsic or natural progression in language development, but that they cannot be actualized without a supporting conceptual framework. Children's early productive word combinations are thus mediated by their own conceptual space and reflect information that is accessible and meaningful to them.

5.4   Theoretical implications

If we draw together the findings from chapters 4 and 5, we are in a position to consider the conditions that might be necessary and sufficient to permit early semantic development. Research to date has *described* the typical sequence of events in language acquisition from the onset of stable pre-words to early word combinations, but it hasn't adequately explained the conditions necessary for this development to occur. It has been assumed that the steps that are typically observed in language development for intact children are in fact the steps that are necessary to allow the normal pattern of development. The operating assumption is thus that development involves the following sequence of events:

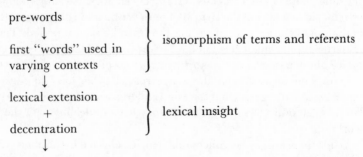

vertical constructions
↓
emerging multi-word
constructions

If each of these conditions is necessary in order to progress from pre-words and single-word utterances to multi-word expressions, then the blind children in this investigation should not have been able to make the move to combinational forms. Instead, we found that combinational speech evolved *prior* to lexical insight for these subjects, the implication being that two-word semantic constructions can emerge even when the terms involved do not have the full symbolic status of words. With this in mind, we need to identify the conditions that were present and that seem to have been sufficient to trigger development.

To quickly summarize, then, the blind children's language during *their* single-word period had the following principal characteristics: (1) a lack of creativity: there were few innovative applications of words and no evidence of child-created (idiosyncratic) forms (2) rigidity: terms were not generalized, that is, most words were referentially inflexible and initially contextually inflexible and there was a "zero-mortality rate," that is, words didn't fall into disuse when they stopped serving a purpose for the blind children. Some decontextualization gradually appeared as more terms were acquired, but most terms stayed referentially inflexible; (3) steady rate of acquisition: the sudden burst in vocabulary growth, which seems to correlate with a change in *use* of words for sighted children, was either not present for the blind subjects or, in Teddy's case, was simply a rapid increase in the number of terms with little change in their use.

The process of generalization, involving both decontextualization and extension, appears to be a necessary condition for the child's recognition of lexical forms as true words. Thus, generalization may be used by researchers to operationalize the parameters of word use and to help recognize the point when a child has achieved lexical insight. The blind children did *not* achieve this during the course of the present investigation. The blind children's language behavior during the single-word period consisted of an almost ritualistic recitation of terms on encountering objects or on performing actions associated with these terms. From this we inferred that there was a protracted period of isomorphism between "word" and "referent." These findings imply that vision is a catalyst for the process of generalization, at least if it is to occur during the single-word stage.

This was neither self-evident nor predictable since a wide variety of sensory modalities could, in principle, provide a basis for generalization, but they did not during this period of development. The problem for the blind child is a conceptual one in that vision, because it alone permits simultaneous access to an array of information, presumably encourages synthesis and classification of sensory data and is therefore a stimulus for constructing hypotheses about the nature and meaning of words as symbols.

Curiously, when the blind subjects had learned around 100 lexical terms, combinations of terms were observed in their language. The characteristics of these combinations were as follows:

(1) Most roles emerged in requests rather than assertions. This was viewed as an adaptive strategy increasing blind children's access to the environment, thus it was presumably motivated by a desire to achieve tangible goals more effectively.

(2) At the same time as words were rigid, the blind children began encoding more information about themselves by combining these rigid forms. Thus, the same lack of objectification about words is evident but the motivation for combining terms may be language *internal* since it has no obvious self-serving purpose in terms of the external environment.

(3) Greater contextual freedom is observed when the blind children begin talking about shared past events. I suggested that this was also an adaptive strategy since it increases the possibility of establishing a common focus of attention between speaker and hearer. The motivation for this unexpected finding is then both social and communicative.

Drawing this information together, we may conclude several things. First, the blind children were able to move from one "stage" of language development to another without capitalizing on the expressive power or completing the developmental tasks generally associated with the prior stage. This suggests that there may be an ontogenetic progression in language which functions somewhat independently of other aspects of the cognitive system, but which cannot be fully actualized in the absence of a supporting conceptual framework.

Secondly, expansion in the expressive power of single-word utterances along the lines normally reported is *not* a necessary condition for the emergence of multi-term utterances, though the evolution of multi-term constructions is limited along the same dimensions as single-word utterances. Decontextualization alone appears to be sufficient for the emergence of proposition-like structures, even though the terms used in these structures may be underspecified for a protracted period of time.

Thirdly, the analysis suggests that the early (creative) use of multi-term utterances does reflect the child's underlying cognitive schemata and points to a parallel between conceptual development and language development in this domain. The children's early productive word combinations were mediated by their own conceptual space, and appear to reflect information that is accessible and meaningful to them.

Thus, in looking closely at the ways blind children encode two-word relations, it becomes clear that development, despite certain conceptual deficits, is promoted by a combination of factors. There may be a language internal impetus to produce more complex utterances that is itself fostered by both personal and social needs. Moreover, the conditions that are necessary to promote this development are surprisingly minimal, compared to what has been inferred from observations of normally developing sighted children.

In the next chapter we will move from semantic to pragmatic concerns and consider the kinds of communicative functions that are expressed by the children.

6 Developments in the use of illocutionary force

I: The coding system

The way children come to attach meanings to sounds, to evolve symbols in the form of lexemes and then to combine these to express rudimentary propositions, is of course only one component of learning to mean. Very young children are capable of communicating far richer ideas than is indicated by their impotence in terms of such purely grammatical resources as syntax, semantics, and morphology. It is certainly the case that children in their second year do a good deal more than simply "label" entities and activities. At the same time that children are introduced to a speech community's shared meanings for words, they come to recognize that words can be used in different ways on different occasions, that utterances can be interpreted as assertions, requests, protests and so on.

Yet it is certainly not the case that young children seek to communicate a message every time they speak. Nor is it the case that children succeed in conveying a message every time they attempt to do so. Moreover, the intention to convey a message and success in conveying a message are not intrinsically correlated with the degree of the child's linguistic competence: a pre-verbal child may employ a reaching gesture to convey desire for some object; a verbal child may produce utterances too vague to achieve their goal or may use multi-word phrases in a soliloquy that is void of communicative intent. For these reasons, the analysis of the communicative force in young children's utterances must be sensitive to a variety of factors, including both the interactional status of the utterance and the kinds of signaling devices the child is able to exploit in order to convey the force of his utterance.

This chapter focuses on the kinds of messages very young children attempt to convey, on the strategies that are available to them for distinguishing various sorts of messages, and on the way their messages change and evolve over time. In short, it examines the communicative function of the children's utterances and it explores how access to visual information affects the way in

110

which children use language. Part I provides background information on the notion of speech acts and presents the utterance analysis system. Part II is the analysis and discussion of the data.

The theoretical perspective on which this chapter is based is that of speech act theory. In linguistics, the function of an utterance is frequently indexed through a component of speech act analysis; the illocutionary act. The concept of illocutionary acts is therefore briefly defined in the first section of this chapter and then some of the ways speech act theory has been applied to child language research are considered. Several other approaches to studying children's early language use are also summarized. Previous research has contributed to our understanding of the pragmatic functions of children's utterances and/or to the antecedents of these functions, but none of the investigations has documented developmental changes since the use of illocutionary force.

In order to consider the emergence and use of illocutionary force, and to evaluate the extent to which visual information influences early pragmatic strategies, it was necessary to design an analysis system that can distinguish between interactive and non-interactive utterances, and that can be used to classify utterances according to their communicative function. This system is introduced and discussed in section 6.3 and the method of analysis is presented in section 6.4.

The results of the analysis are presented in the second portion of the chapter, beginning with section 6.5. Several issues are considered, including the first appearance of utterances with communicative force, the order of emergence of illocutionary acts, and the relative frequencies with which various illocutionary acts are used by the different children. The final section presents a brief summary of the major findings.

6.1   The fundamental insights of speech act theory in linguistics and philosophy

The concept of "speech acts" originated in the work of Austin (1962) and has since been elaborated and modified, especially by Searle (1969). Crucially, Austin explicitly recognized the social and interpersonal aspects of language and provided a contextual theory of meaning which distinguished between *locutionary acts*, or the sounds, words and constructions of an utterance; the *illocutionary act* or what is performed *in* saying something (e.g. commanding, baptizing); and the *perlocutionary act*, the effect of the utterance on the hearer. Searle (1969, 1971, 1975) refined Austin's work, making a tripartite distinction between *utterance acts*, *propositional acts* and *illocutionary acts*. In uttering words, morphemes and sentences, one performs utterance acts; referring and predicating constitute performing propositional acts; and stating, commanding, questioning and so on are illocutionary acts. The consequences of the act are relegated to a different status since they are not part of the speaker's acts *per se*, however the effect of an act is considered among the various "conditions" on speech acts (Searle 1969, 1975).

Searle also articulates various function-indicating devices which specify what illocutionary force an utterance is to have. In English the devices used to convey this information are word order, stress, intonation, mood of the verb, and the set of performative verbs (e.g. baptize, pronounce [husband and wife], sentence [to prison]).

The illocutionary force of any given utterance is explicated by a set of criteria, originally called "conditions on speech acts" (Searle, 1969) which were further elaborated as twelve dimensions in Searle's (1975) taxonomy of speech acts. Some of these dimensions are used specifically to define an illocutionary act. Others elaborate various socio-linguistic considerations, such as status differences between speaker and hearer or the relation between the speech act and the rest of the discourse and still others specify extra-linguistic factors that have bearing on the performance of speech acts.

Speech act theory, then, provides a method for specifying the communicative function of an utterance as distinct from its propositional content, yet sees both components as essential to the meaning of an utterance. It also recognizes a set of conditions which are necessary for successful communication and considers these in terms of both speaker and hearer.

6.2   Children's ability to convey messages

6.2.1   Speech act theory and child language

Speech act theory has occasionally been applied to child language research. The majority of studies dealing with children's early language have been semantic (or syntactic); relatively few investigators have specifically considered the communicative function of children's early utterances. While some researchers have examined pragmatic issues in conjunction with semantic development, I will restrict the discussion here to work which is explicitly concerned with the ontogenesis of communicative force.

Developmentalists have tended to use speech act theory in three general ways: (1) in a metaphorical sense (e.g., Bates, 1976; Bates *et al.*, 1975); (2) as a communicative framework which may have antecedents in non-linguistic behavior (e.g., Bruner, 1975); and (3) as a basis for exploring the ontegenetic relationship between communicative intention and linguistic structure (e.g., Dore, 1975, 1979; and Halliday, 1975).

Bates *et al.* (1975) examined the hypothesis that certain performative structures develop prior to speech. The notion is based on work of Gruber (1975), Antinucci and Parisi (1971, 1973) and others who have proposed that children's single-word utterances perform such illocutionary acts as negating, commanding, and declaring, all marked by gesture and into-nation. In an attempt to document the development of performatives during the first year of life, Bates and her colleagues propose a stage theory that adapts Austin's notions to ontogenesis: (1) a perlocutionary stage, in which the child has a systematic effect on his listeners without having an intentional, aware control over that effect; (2) an illocutionary stage in which the child intentionally uses non-verbal signs to convey requests and to direct adult attention to objects and events; and (3) a locutionary stage in which the child constructs propositions and utters speech sounds within the same "performative" sequences that he previously expressed non-verbally.

Thus, Bates *et al.* suggest that perlocutionary acts and illocutionary acts have a developmental history prior to locutionary acts. The implication is that at stage two children use non-verbal means to convey messages and that at stage three the same kinds of messages are conveyed, the only difference being that words are substituted for gestures. To mark the distinction between verbal and pre-verbal acts they apply the terms "proto-declarative" and "proto-imperative" to the latter.

The use of speech act terminology is somewhat metaphorical and in the standard speech act model one of the acts, for example the perlocutionary act, cannot occur independent of the other acts. In addition, the analogy suggests that non-deliberate behavior is amenable to the same analysis as conventional behavior, particularly at the "perlocutionary stage." In linguistic theory, the components of speech acts are characterised by a set of constitutive rules which are inherently necessary and these cannot operate at the pre-conventional level. It is important to understand that Bates and her colleagues are not proposing that infants control perlocutionary, il-locutionary, and locutionary acts. Rather, they are looking for the roots of these acts in the infant's behavior. In doing so, their work suggests that the later development of conventional acts is a fairly natural consequence of these early behaviors.

Note as well that Bates and her colleagues consider only "(proto)-declarative" and "(proto)-imperative" acts. These represent only a small subset of possible performatives and are used in a far more restricted sense than is usual for the terms "declarative" and "imperative" in linguistic theory (cf. Lyons, 1977). A "proto-imperative" simply means "the child's use of the listener as an agent or tool in achieving some end" particularly in achieving some object (p. 208). A "proto-declarative" is an "effort to direct the adult's attention to some event or object in the world" (p. 208). Thus, their work is concerned with identifying the most primitive communicative functions; it is not a study of the emergence of the range of performatives that are exploited in adult language. What Bates, Camaioni and Volterra are actually documenting is the emergence of intentional communication. They also mark the distinction between an infant's intentionally using non-verbal signals and a young child's using verbal signals to convey communicative intention.

Bruner (1975, 1983) outlines some of the pre-linguistic processes which he suggests are antecedent to speech acts and which appear to foster their development. These include: (1) the evolution of mutual action sequences between the infant and the caregiver; (2) the construction of routines for gaining shared attention; (3) the development of a predictable order of events in action sequences which permits shared expectancies (e.g., object–name, object–act); and (4) the child's development of prosodic patterns into which morphemes will eventually fit. Bruner suggests that these prosodic contours correspond to interrogative, vocative/demand and possibly indicative contours. But, as he points out, there is little evidence that infants actually associate prosodic contours with illocutionary force during this pre-verbal period. What is important is that infants come to recognize and practice certain basic melodies that will shortly come to be used to convey basic communicative intentions.

Each of these processes is rooted in joint enterprise between the infant and its caregivers, the most crucial of which is play. Bruner proposes that play draws the child's attention to communication and to the structure of communicative acts. Bruner's basic argument is that linguistic concepts, which may be viewed in a speech act framework, are first realized in action, and particularly that language develops as a means of regulating mutual activity.

The most direct application of speech act theory to early language is the work of Dore, which is chiefly concerned with how children acquire the linguistic conventions to express their communicative intentions (Dore, 1974, 1975, 1978, 1979). Dore adapts the Searlian framework and proposes that early acts are "primitive speech acts" (PSAs) containing a "rudimentary referring expression" (a word) and a "primitive force" indicating device (principally intonation). PSAs do not contain predicating expressions, rather the meaning of an utterance is dependent upon the relation between the word and the context. Single word utterances, then, represent the child's intention with respect to a concept without having a propositional structure. Development progresses with the emergence of a "rudimentary proposition" consisting of a predicating expression and referring expression(s). Dore suggests that the notions of predication and reference are innate, but it is unclear why he believes one should be actualized before the other.

The primitive speech acts suggested for two children Dore studied during the single-word period are labeling, repeating, answering, requesting action, requesting answer, calling, greeting, protesting, and practicing (Dore, 1975). There are several problems with this analysis. First, Dore does not distinguish those utterances which have a communicative function from those which do not. Practicing and some labeling, for example, may be used by a child to explore language without serving any interactive purpose. Those utterances that are not intended to communicate lack illocutionary force and should not be counted as instances of speech acts.

Also, Dore conflates the distinction between an utterance itself and how that utterance is used. "Repeating" is not really a communicative act at all, rather it is an utterance that may or may not be used to convey communicative function. For example, a young child might repeat the utterance "hi" after it is produced by a sibling who has noticed his grandparents coming to visit. But, the repetition may also serve as a genuine greeting on the part of the younger child. Similarly, repetitions can function as answers and even labels, though in the latter instances, they are not informative in the sense of meaningful to the hearer. (See Keenan, 1977 for discussion of various functions served by repetition in children's discourse).

It should also be noted that some acts are inherently more dependent on discourse history than others (e.g., answering) and it would be useful to document how and when young children come to control these. Their inclusion in the analysis of developing speech acts seems warranted, but with the caveat that the complete picture can only emerge if the roles of discourse and input are also considered.

Thus, Dore's work provides some interesting insights into some of the things young children do with language, but it confuses two different phenomena (type of utterance and function of utterance) and it fails to distinguish between communicative and non-communicative language. Dore does not attempt to document the order of emergence of different types of communicative acts.

A few researchers have considered the function of early utterances outside a speech act framework. Carter (1978, 1979) for example identifies eight "communicative sensorimotor schemata" that account for over 90 per cent of her subjects' communicative acts during the period from 12 to 16 months. During this time, the child was basically pre-verbal and depended on a vocal/gesture complex to convey messages. His principal communicative acts served as requests for various kinds of environmental transformations (e.g., requesting objects, requesting help in removing an object, getting attention) or expressing affect.

The most extensive study of emerging communicative functions draws on a different framework. Halliday (1975) has characterized adult language in terms of a tripartite system of functions roughly corresponding to conceptual content, interaction, and the production of connected discourse. Based on observations of his son between the ages of 9 and 24 months, Halliday concludes that infants are not a party to any of these functions, but rather that their language undergoes several "restructurings" ultimately culminating in the adult pattern. By the end of the first year children use language for three purposes: instrumental (requesting objects), regulatory (requesting actions of other people), and interactional (greetings and attention getting). After children acquire a number of words, they begin to express three additional functions: heuristic (identifications and questions about the environment), personal (expressions about self), and imaginative (pretending). Last to emerge are informative functions. (It is unclear how and when these are "restructured" into Halliday's proposed adult system.) The work is especially important in that it points to a sequential development in the emergence of various communicative acts, but the criteria for classifying behaviors are not explicit. The system as a whole does not offer new insights into language use, rather it presents a new set of terms to describe these uses, making it difficult to compare to other descriptions of adult language functions.

6.2.2   Inference, interpretation and intention

Two reasons for children's early success in conveying messages have repeatedly been advanced in developmental literature. First, their language tends to be context dependent, and secondly, the contributions of the listener are crucial. The child is maximally successful in communicating when the addressee is well equipped to infer the meaning of the child's message based on available clues, which include not only contextual information, but also the relevant experiences shared by the interlocutors and the hearer's knowledge of the child's idiosyncratic lexical meaning.

Many researchers view linguistic communication in general as an inferential process in which the speaker (S) provides by what he says, a basis for the hearer (H) to infer what the S actually means. The consensus is that what is actually expressed linguistically underdetermines the message that S actually seeks to convey (Austin, 1962; Grice, 1975; Gordon and Lakoff, 1975; Searle, 1969, 1971, 1975). The basic insight is that while meaning (in terms of semantic representation) is generally regarded as invariant, the message that is intended may in fact be determined through extra-linguistic (i.e., extra-grammatical) means. The interpretation of messages appears to involve the hearer's ability to make inferences about the specific intention and meaning of the utterance, based on such information as world and shared knowledge, context, and crucially, the clues provided by the speaker. This is an important concept and it has especially interesting implications for child language since it means that the interpretive role of the hearer and the imprecision of the message component relative to the meaning component is *common* to both adult and child language.

The inference of meaning takes on additional importance in early child language since H's inferences must fill the gap between the child's non-conventional language use and the conventional linguistic system of the target language. The child "underdetermines" to a far greater extent than the competent speaker. If we adopt the view that the inferential process is crucial for the interpretation of messages in general, then it follows that the essential process of linguistic communication is fundamentally similar in interaction involving competent speakers and for adult–child communication. What differs is that the child is inexplicit and is not a party to language conventions, so that the burden for successful communication falls disproportionately on the adult. (We should note here that the listener's role in adult–child interaction is not simply to interpret the child's behavior, but also provides the child with important clues as to how language works.)

The notion of interpretation is intimately related to the notion of intention, a concept approached with both interest and apprehension in psychology and developmental linguistics. The basic problem is that intention is assumed to reflect some internal representation of a goal for which we have little direct evidence. That is, intention must be inferred. (For discussions, see Bruner, 1974–75; Greenfield, 1980; Ryan, 1974; Piaget, 1952a).

Greenfield (1980) has reasoned that there are three phenomena which can be drawn together to operationally establish intention. Her suggestion is that intention (I) exists when there is directionality of behavior (D) toward a specific goal (G) and a termination (T) of this behavior upon attainment of G. A crucial assumption is that because the component parts are interdependent, the consequences (D, G, T) can imply the antecedent (I). Based on recent work from Searle (1979), Greenfield further proposes that intention in the pre-representational infant need not involve prior (mental) representation of the conditions of satisfaction, but instead consists of "intention-in-action" where the conditions of satisfaction are implicitly present *during* the intentional action. Thus, while adults are capable of both prior intent and intention-in-action, the infant is capable of only the latter, but both are therefore capable of behavior which accomplishes goals (i.e., achieves "conditions of satisfaction").

After analyzing data from several sources, Greenfield concludes that parent–child interaction typically involves a process of negotiated interpretations where the child will reject the parent's interpretation of his intention if the conditions of satisfaction are not fulfilled by this interpretation. Early on, this may be accomplished either through overt rejection or through repeating the directed behavior. These negotiations then function as an index of intention.

This analysis provides the researcher with observable criteria for recognizing the child's communicative intention, or the illocutionary force of his interactive language. It also suggests that even before the infant is party to conversational conventions, and at a time when his lexical meaning is massively vague, he is capable at a rudimentary level of behavior which assists his interlocutors in the inferential process which seems to be inherent in the communication of messages.

Taken together, the research on children's early interactive behaviors suggests that toddlers are capable of intentionally expressing a variety of communicative functions at a time when they are just beginning to ascribe meaning to words.

6.2.3   Issues related to the emergence of communicative function

While it is certainly clear that very young children convey communicative intention, there has been little effort to explore developmental trends in their propensity and ability to do so. The key issue is not in evaluating how children express propositional meaning, but in how they use illocutionary force to communicate a message. None of the research discussed above has specifically considered the ontogenesis of illocutionary acts. Those researchers who have examined language acquisition within a speech act framework have generally focused on the antecedents to speech acts or have failed to make the crucial distinction between communicative and non-communicative language. Moreover, while some researchers have observed the use of declaratives, imperatives, and negatives in infants, there has been little effort to document details of the emergence of a broader range of illocutionary acts.

I became aware of the need to investigate this development in observing the blind children interact with their families, and with the researchers. Here were children who seemed to have a great deal of difficulty in understanding the nature of words, in sorting the elements of their environment, and in making hypotheses about lexical meaning. Yet, these children did seem to be communicating, and they were becoming increasingly proficient in conveying messages during each successive visit, as were the sighted children. In attempting to understand this development, the following factors were of particular concern:

(1) The extent to which the proportion of utterances with communicative force changes over time;

(2) The relative frequency with which different types of language behaviors are produced (e.g., imitations, spontaneous use of lexemes, sound play) and how these correlate with the use of illocutionary force; and

(3) The relative frequency with which various types of messages (i.e., illocutionary acts) are conveyed.

My particular interest in the present investigation is to identify the emergence of children's ability to encode meanings with the purpose of conveying a message.[1] A further dimension of the analysis is to identify developmental variation in the kinds of language-related behaviors that are used to convey communicative force. When we think of a contribution to an interaction, we typically conceptualize a spontaneous utterance comprising one or more stable morphemes. But, of course, it is not the case that only spontaneous utterances may be used to contribute to an interaction. In particular, repetitions and imitations have an important and diversified role

---

[1] In fact, the notion of meaning in the absence of a message is at odds with certain philosophical and linguistic views on the nature of meaning itself. Grice (1957), for example, analyzes meaning in terms of a speaker's intending to produce an effect in a hearer by getting him to recognize the intention to produce that effect. This distinction has been the source of some controversy, (Austin, 1962; Schiffer, 1972; Searle, 1969, 1971; Strawson, 1971), but a common thread in all of the discussions is that meaning is intrinsically linked to the conveyance of message.

in child language (see Bloom, Rocissano and Hood, 1976; Keenan, 1977; Shatz, 1978). Conventional gestures are certainly important, and even sound play may contribute to maintaining interactions. The list is infinite if we include the entire scope of non-verbal behaviors (facial expression, pantomime, etc.) which may potentially be exploited to convey messages, or contribute to their interpretation, but here we are concerned with the development of conventional linguistic signals. Of particular interest is whether certain kinds of turns are more highly correlated with discernible illocutionary force than others, and if so, whether or not they seem to facilitate the development of expressive power.

To accomplish this sort of analysis, it is necessary to design a coding system which is sensitive to a number of different dimensions, including the nature of the language behavior itself, the interactive status of the utterance, and the illocutionary force of the utterance. An implicit assumption is that subdividing standard "adult" illocutionary acts will reveal an ontogenetic progression which has not been previously examined. This system is presented in the next section.

6.3   The utterance analysis system

The present investigation introduces a procedure for classifying utterances and certain conventionalized gestures along two dimensions: the nature of the language behavior including its discourse status and the illocutionary force of the utterance. Two sets of contrastive categories are introduced to accomplish this task, each of which is presented in detail below. The first set (set 1) identifies the *type of utterance* and the second set (set 2) is a *taxonomy of fundamental illocutionary acts*. The two sets in combination comprise the *utterance analysis system*.

The categories used in the classification system were developed in the course of analyzing language samples from the present data and from other sources as well as from evaluating previous research on communicative functions of children's utterances.

Certain types of utterances, such as babbling or soliloquies, are clearly non-interactive and therefore cannot be assigned any illocutionary force. The coding system therefore also specifies interactional status as part of the criteria for evaluating the type of utterance. In identifying the interactional status of a child's utterance as one basis for assessing possible illocutionary force, I am not proposing that utterances without illocutionary force are wholly meaningless. In fact, the content of such utterances can be analyzed to reveal trends in children's emerging ability to encode concepts through a conventional linguistic form. However, the status of such utterances is crucially different from communicative utterances since the message component of the utterance is ostensibly absent. In other words, the child talking in a non-interactive situation may be encoding conceptual meaning without encoding messages except possibly in some meta-cognitive sense of self regulation or of vocalized inner speech (Vygotsky, 1962). Of course, the kinds of information so encoded, together with the form of such utterances, enables the child to practice formulating utterances which may be used to express explicit messages at some appropriate future time.

6.3.1   *Type of utterrance and its discourse status*

The children's utterances and conventionalized gestures were each categorized into one of the eleven mutually exclusive categories defined below.
    Potentially interactive utterance types are:

> *Interactive vocalizations* (IV):   A turn by a child engaged in a communicative interaction with someone else; or an attempt to contribute to an ongoing interaction involving others; or an attempt to initiate a conversation. Crucially, the turn is a vocal behavior that contains no identifiable lexemes, but which has clearly interactive status and is thus distinct from "babbling" (see below).

> *Turns using conventionalized gestures* (TG):   These have the same status and defining criteria as IVs except that the contribution is accomplished through the use of conventionalized gestures. The gestural complex consists primarily of reaching, pointing, and displaying (see also Bates *et al.*, 1979, p. 87). Also included were ritualized (hand) motions associated with specific nursery games (e.g., for patty cake, itsy-bitsy spider, round-and-round-the-garden) since these provide an especially important basis for interaction in young blind children (see Urwin, 1978a, b).[2]

> *Spontaneous language* (SpL):   A spontaneous interactive utterance containing at least one recognizable and stable lexical form that is not embedded in a long stretch of babbling. It may be preceded or followed by one or two syllables which are not stable lexemes. Thus [bal] "ball" and [wi? bal] "___ball" or [balwi] "ball___"

> *Reiteration* (R):   Child's reiteration of his own meaningful utterance, (i.e., SpL). These must be consecutive utterances on the part of the child, although there may be intervening turn(s) from another providing these turns do not repeat the child's utterance. If they do, the child's utterance is coded as an imitation (see below).

> *Imitation* (IM):   The spontaneous (non-prompted) reproduction of another's utterance, or portion thereof, within five utterances of

---

[2] Non-conventionalized gestures are also used to convey messages by both adults and children, but the purpose here is to document development of the conventional system.

the model which does not add to or change the model except by deletion or simplification (see also Bloom, Hood and Lightbown, 1974, p. 383).

Requested imitation (RIM): An imitation that has been elicited by another. These typically are prompted by the caregiver asking, "Can you say X?" or by prosodic prompts such as ((Exaggerated intonation)) "Shoe:::"

Frame-inserts (F-I): In this situation the child is combining various patterns of two or more words by systematically substituting one element for another. For example:

$$\text{little fish} \begin{cases} \nearrow \text{little book. ...} \\ \searrow \text{nice fish} \end{cases}$$

but not:

little fish →nice book

In some cases the frame-inserts are triggered by another's utterance; or sequences of frame-inserts are cooperatively built up by a parent and child taking turns.

Sound play (SP): Practicing sound patterns based on one or more real lexemes (e.g. [mɔm(·)bɔmmɔmidɔmitɔm] or repeating a word with various intonational contours, different pitches, different pronunciations, or different voice qualities.

The non-interactive utterance types consist of various forms of babbling and non-referential soliloquies.

Babbling (B): "Babbling" generally refers to the non-lexicalized sound patterns articulated by an infant. Here it particularly refers to isolated syllables or longer sequences which are not grouped under prosodic contour and which are non-interactive.

Babbling/expressive jargon (B+): Refers to non-lexicalized articulation with marked prosodic contours, sometimes called "late-babbling" or "expressive jargon" (see de Boysson-Baries, Sagart, and Bacri, 1981).

Babbling/jargon with words (BW): These emerge when children further mature, and we begin to see recognizable lexemes embedded in streams of babbling which often also include intonational contours. *A unifying characteristic of all types of "babbling" (B, B+, BW) is that they are exclusively non-interactive.* With children in their second or third year the B+ and BW indications may include lengthy passages or monologues. In such cases, each utterance (defined in terms of breath and terminal intonation contour) is coded separately. It is somewhat uncommon to include lexemes in a definition of "babbling", but it is by no means unique (e.g. Weir,

1962) and I believe the inclusion is justified since it permits us an important level of abstraction.[3]

By definition, most of the behaviors listed above occur in interactive situations and have the *potential* for conveying illocutionary force. Specifically excluded from this possibility are various forms of babbling including monologues with jargon and words. Note that sound play and frame inserts may be used both in interaction and in non-interactive situations. The remaining categories occur only as part of communicative interactions.

With this system it is possible to classify all of the language-related behavior in the transcripts. A few specifically excluded behaviors are crying, fussing, and laughing that are reflexive in nature (e.g., crying in response to pain). Also excluded is audible breathing.

In some instances gestures accompany other behaviors. Since each utterance is coded only once, the code signifying the highest level of symbolic (conventional) representation is assigned to the utterance. Compare the examples below:

	Child	Non-Verbal/Context
(a)	3. [∧]	3. Holds cup out to mother
(b)	4. here./	4. Holds cup out to mother

In (a) the child uses no recognizable lexeme, but a non-conventionalized vocalization co-occurs with an offer, thus the highest level of representation is turn using conventionalized gestures (TG). In (b), the gesture is seen as part of the communicative act, but the use of an appropriate lexeme is a higher level of representation and the utterance is coded as spontaneous language (SpL). In analyzing such examples, the gesture is viewed as part of the contextual information that supports the interpretation of the utterance.

6.3.2 *Taxonomy of fundamental illocutionary acts*

This section presents the principal kinds of illocutionary force with which young children may invest their utterances in order to communicate various kinds of messages. While it is possible to distinguish numerous dimensions along which adult illocutionary acts may vary, not all of these criteria are suitable for differentiating the kinds of acts that are exploited by young children. It is certainly not the case that children are party to the

---

[3] In our data there were also a few instances where the children engage in non-interactive speech consisting of real words and intonation contours, but which is also overtly referential in that the child is playing with some object and his or her utterances clearly refer to the toys and activities involving them. This is quite different from the situation Weir (1962) describes, where children's monologues are non-referential. The phenomenon is what many researchers have called egocentric speech (see Piaget, 1926). This pattern occurred only in children with vision and then only in a few of the later transcripts. I coded these utterances as BW, but it would be useful to introduce a separate code for this in the future.

conventions for use of all of the various function-indicating devices employed by competent speakers of English.

Two of the most important dimensions specified by Searle (1975) for differentiating illocutionary acts are the difference in point or purpose of the act and the direction of fit between words and the world. By the latter we mean that statements, assertions, and descriptions match the world whereas the intent of requests, promises, and commands are to have the world alter to match the words. These two actions were used in defining the essential conditions in the taxonomy of children's illocutionary acts. Rather than specifying the kind of propositional content associated with various acts or the complex set of beliefs and predictions associated with preparatory conditions, the taxonomy specifies the nature of the children's utterances and behaviors that are typically associated with various types of illocutionary acts. This avoids attributing semantic and grammatical structures to the children's utterances for which there is no manifest evidence and prevents speculating about the young children's emerging concept of their addressees.

Children are considerably impoverished in their ability to use conventional illocutionary force-indicating devices, and can generally only exploit context and, to a limited extent, employ terminal intonation contours and stress. Bloom (1970, 1973) did not find consistent or distinctive use of intonational contours until after syntax had developed, which corroborated earlier research by W. Miller and Ervin (1964) and Weir (1966). Other studies suggest that terminal intonation is a reliable indication of such contrasting illocutionary acts as asserting, requesting, and protesting (Dore, 1975; Lord, 1974; M. Miller, 1979). M. Miller (1979) and Menyuk (1974) found that adults can reliably recognize terminal intonation contours (falling, rising, and level) in children's single-word utterances when they are presented independent of their context. Such recognition, though, does not imply that specific communicative functions may be attributed to these contours. However, Miller's analysis of data from three children acquiring German indicates that each of the three types of terminal contours is routinely associated with specific types of illocutionary acts in the late single-word stage and during the transition period to two-word utterances (pp. 97–107). It has not been demonstrated that terminal intonation is used to mark *all* instances of a particular type of utterance. Taken together, the evidence suggests that when intonation is marked it typically is associated with a particular constellation of illocutionary force types but that it is not a *necessary* condition for an utterance to be classified as an instance of some particular illocutionary act. Moreover, any one of the basic types of terminal intonation is typically associated with several distinct types of illocutionary acts, indicating that it is not a *sufficient* condition for the assignment of illocutionary force.

This leaves the child (and his interpreters) largely dependent on context.

Through context, we appeal to two principal areas originally elucidated by Austin (1962): (1) accompaniments of the utterance and (2) circumstances of the utterance. Ryan (1974) has appealed to these two categories in specifying the criteria suitable for interpreting children's utterances:

> *Accompaniments of the utterances*, on the part of the child, such as pointing, searching, playing with specific objects, refusing; the physical state of the child.
>
> *Circumstances of the utterance*, such as the presence or absence of particular objects or people, the relation of these to the child, any immediately preceding events or speech, the relevant past experience of the child.
>
> (p. 201)

In the taxonomy presented below, the various specific features of context that are used in interpreting the children's utterances are made explicit for each classification. One further element of "context" is brought to bear in coding the utterances (in addition to those available to the interlocutor) and that is the caregivers' *response* to their children's utterances.

The taxonomy was applied to all behaviors coded as instances of a "type of utterance." However, the behaviors that were explicitly non-interactive (i.e., babbling) received a code of "no illocutionary force" as did non-interactive instances of sound play and frame-inserts.

The taxonomy

Types of fundamental illocutionary acts

Request: Counts as an attempt to get H to do A, which would bring about a change in the world. Sub-types vary with respect to nature of A.

Request for objects: (RqObj) Child's goal is to obtain an object (through an intermediary). This requires that H perform an action in order to provide object, though this action may be subsidiary to child's primary intent. At some level the child comprehends or comes to comprehend that H's performance of A is a consequence of the request, and child clearly addresses remark to H and expects H to provide object.

Child's utterance and behavior: Word and/or pointing or reaching gesture may be accompanied by grunting or prosodic pattern. May have rising terminal intonation.

Contextual clues: (Sighted) child attends to (looks at) object if it is present.
(Blind) child may engage in searching behavior.
Parent provides object.

Request for routine: (RqRout) Child's goal is to initiate a ritualized participatory activity with H such as playing patty-cake, row your boat, or some other nursery game.

Child's utterance and behavior: Singing/saying part of rhyme or its rhythmic or prosodic contour and/or performing hand or body routines associated with that nursery game.

Contextual clues: Child's performing routine gestures; laughing, etc. Parent participates in routine.

Request for action/activity: (RqAct) Child's goal is to obtain a physical response from H other than a nursery routine or other ritualized games. For example, child's requesting "down" (to be lifted down from chair) or "up" (to be picked up). This category also includes requests for familiar activities such as going to the store or school or doing various household tasks.

Child's utterance and behavior: Word sometimes accompanied by gesture or even struggling if child attempts to perform action on own.

Contextual clues: Child's attempting action on own. Parent performs actions which almost always results in change of state of child.

Question: (Q) Counts as an attempt to elicit information from H. These differ from requests in that requests attempt to get H to do something. Early on, the prototypical question is the child's holding or gazing at an object or in some other way directing H's attention to an object and asking for a name for it, frequently through uttering some variant of "this."

Child's utterance and behavior: Child attempting to direct H's attention to some object, activity or event. Often child's utterance will have formal function-indicating device in the form of rising terminal intonation. May gesture (point). Any WH-utterance, etc.

Contextual clue: Child waits for adult's verbal or vocal response. (Adult's response may be gestural in some instances. For example, if child wants to know where something or someone is, parent may point to relevant location.) Parent utters a response but there is no change in the situation.

Attention getting/calling: (AttnG) Counts as an attempt to get acknowledgment from H. Child addresses proximal or non-proximal H with intention of summoning H or engaging H in interaction.

Child's utterance and behavior: Addresses adult, generally by name, almost always with some increase in loudness and awaits adult response. Calling has marked prosodic contour and syllabic lengthening.

Contextual clues: Parent is typically not oriented to child or is some distance away prior to child's utterance. But this is not always the case with visually impaired children where it is common to find the parent attending to the child but the child unaware of this. H's orientation typically changes or H replies with an acknowledgment e.g., "Yes?" or "What?" or "I'm right here."

Social routine: (Soc) Counts as a "courteous" recognition of the presence of another person or the activity of another person (thanking). Prototypical examples are uttering "hi" when someone new enters room or environment; uttering "bye-bye" when someone departs and uttering "thank you" when being given something. These are frequently prompted by parent.[4]

Child's utterance and behavior: Uttering ritualized word and possibly performing accompanying gestures such as waving.

Contextual clues: Change in social situation.

Protest/refusal/rejection/denial: (P/R/R/D) Counts as an attempt by the child to get an activity discontinued, to remove an object, or to avoid getting involved in a prospective activity. Attempts to deny the truth of some utterance are also included in this category, though these typically emerge later than protesting, refusing, and rejecting.

Child's utterance and behavior: Word or marked prosodic pattern, may be accompanied by withdrawal, or pushing someone or something away.

Contextual clues: Generally undesired event is initiated by someone other than the child just prior to the child's utterance, though in some cases the child will have been enjoying an event and now wants it discontinued (child has "had enough" as it were). Frequently H terminates event, but not always (e.g., giving medicine, changing clothes).

No-response (N-Resp) If the entire event is verbal, it is coded as a "No" response. Such instances are segregated so that they can later be analyzed as either instances of "negation" or in terms of their role in the ontogenesis of response strategies.

Identification/description: (I/D) Counts as an attempt to assign an entity, event or activity as a member of a set or class by matching it with a lexeme from the child's current lexical inventory.

---

[4] This may overlap with attention getting in the blind subjects who often utter "hi" to get people to speak to them (sometimes in order to find out who is present and sometimes simply to get attention. Both such cases are coded as AttnG).

Comment: Descriptions correspond to the predicate, or part of the predicate, in adult language, whereas identifications correspond to the argument(s). But we cannot assume that a child in the early stages of language acquisition has made this distinction. One can identify a class of individuals independent of state or action, but one cannot "identify" action independent of the agent (or instrument or patient) that is intrinsically involved in that action. Hence, there is a kind of logical order that prevents one from "identifying" actions without implicitly or explicitly recognizing entities. In standard linguistic terminology one "describes" actions and states and these descriptions correspond to predicates in a semantic representation. They are realized as adjectives, verbs or predicate nominals in adult language. The crucial distinction between identification and description is essentially this: *description* involves the assignment of one or two place predicates to entities that have already been specified; whereas *identification* simultaneously involves description plus the selection of one or more specific individuals (all individuals in the case of universal quantifiers). Compare the two sentences below:

(a) This is a dog.
(b) This is the dog.

Sentence (a) indicates that (1) here is an object and (2) 'dog' is the class to which this object belongs. Sentence (b) accomplishes both 1 and 2 but further, it indicates co-referentiality to something that has been previously established, e.g., "our dog Fido."

Of course, we have no evidence that the young child controls this distinction. The categories may be collapsed for the child or the distinction may be indeterminate. What we want to achieve with the category identification/description is a means of recognizing that a child may sometimes identify instances of a class of entities and may sometimes zero in on a "predicate" as an instance of some action or state. Yet, we do not want to attribute a *bona fide* predicate–argument structure to such utterances, and we therefore want to avoid calling such utterances clear instances of *assertion* (see below). We are capturing a strategy which motivates the child to utter "doggie" on encountering an instance of DOG and to utter "down" on being lifted out of a highchair as an instance of DOWN. Even if the identification/description distinction is indeterminate for the child, the child is building a foundation that will permit future predicate–argument structures to be made more explicit.

Child's utterance and behavior: Utters lexeme as he encounters or notices an entity or event, including using an object or performing an action. Sometimes the child does this with no apparent communicative intent (e.g., as identifies toys while going through a toy chest), while at other times the identification appears to be communicative in nature.

Contextual clues: Child attends to object or event. Hearer may or may not respond. Utterance does not alter the situation in terms of world to word fit.

Elicited identification (Id +): Similar to I/D in all respects, except that they are elicited by someone else. Such utterances perform more than one act, for example, the child is asked an "exam question" of the form "What is this?" The child may utter something that is both an identification and a response.

Assertion (Asst): Counts as an attempt to convey information about a state of affairs. For single-word utterances knowledge of the child's lexicon as well as contextual information is used to separate assertions from overextensions. Thus a child who has terms for both "mommy" and "cup" and who says "mommy" while indicating a cup often used by mommy could be interpreted as making a comment about the cup whereas uttering "cup" in this situation would be an identification. Assertions are spontaneous (see subtype below for responses).

Child's utterance and behavior: May be interpreted as a "comment" that does not require or request a change in situation nor by definition does it elicit a behavior from H.

Contextual clues: Generally relates to ongoing or anticipated event. May also relate to a recalled event, but such utterances are generally elicited by parents in conversations with very young children and would therefore be coded as responses.

Response (Resp): (This would be subsumed under assertion for adults.) The utterance is elicited by interlocutor. Counts as an attempt to convey information about a state of affairs in response to a question.

Child's utterance and behavior: Child attends to interlocutor's utterance before uttering. Unmarked prosodic contour.

Contextual clues: Previous utterance of interlocutor-elicited information. Includes child's affirmative response to a yes-no question ("Do you want a cookie?" "Yes") "No" responses to yes–no question are coded separately as "No-response" (cf. P/R/R/D above). Similarly, elicited identifications (Id +) are also coded separately.

Routine (Rout): Counts as an attempt to produce all or part of a ritualized nursery game.

Child's utterance and behavior: Singing/saying part of a rhyme or its rhythmic or prosodic contour and/or performing hand or body routines.

Contextual clues: Parent or child has previously initiated routine. Parent and child participate in routine.

Draw attention (DrAttn): Counts as an attempt to get H to attend to some entity or activity, X, thereby bringing about change in world.

Child's utterance and behavior: Word and/or pointing gesture. May have falling terminal intonation.

Contextual clues: Parent attends to X and frequently acknowledges child verbally. The phenomenon of a child's urgently drawing attention to something occurs only when H is not attending when the child wants to "comment" (see Atkinson, 1979). When the research team is in the home, the child is generally being attended to.

Offer/show (Off/Sh): Counts as an attempt to give some object, O, to H or to display O to H.

Child's utterance and behavior: Word and/or gesture of extending item toward H.

Contextual clues: Child is in possession of O. Parent accepts O or comments about O.

Table 6.1 provides examples of the thirteen illocutionary acts.

The classification system is designed not only to identify specific communicative acts, but also to explicitly recognize that young children's utterances may be difficult to interpret in many respects – including in terms of communicative force. Moreover, not all utterances have communicative intent. For this reason, two further classes were included: unspecifiable illocutionary force (UIF) and no illocutionary force (NoIF).

UIF: To identify utterances which appear to have communicative force, but for which it is difficult to specify the *precise* intent of the utterance. This was generally used when it was impossible to determine which of two or more possible categories should be assigned to an utterance. Such vagueness typically resulted from a child's failure to use adequate force-indicating devices or where behavioral clues conflicted with a child's use of linguistic devices. This category was also used when the actual content of the utterance was uninterpretable to the extent that it was impossible to distinguish the exact message, but where behavioral evidence indicated that the utterance had communicative force. Thus, the use of this category reflects a problem in the interpretation of an utterance, though in theory no utterance is produced with an ambiguous status of this sort.

Table 6.1. *Examples of the thirteen fundamental illocutionary acts coded in the children's speech*[a]

Category	Utterance	Context
RqObj	cookie	C in highchair, searches tray table. In response, M gives C cookie.
RqRout	((SNG))[b] baker:man	C on floor, begins swaying and clapping hands. In response, M sings patty-cake.
RqAct	u:p	C standing next to M, pulls M's clothing. In response, M lifts up C.
Q	who's that?	C walking across room and bumps into one of the Rs. R identifies self.
AttnG	mo:mmy:	C on floor playing. M replies "I'm right here" and taps floor near child.
Soc	hi Annie.	C is playing. R has just arrived at house. R greets child.
P/R/R/D	((EI))[c] no::	C in highchair after eating. M begins to wipe C's face with washcloth. C moves back and tries to push cloth away.
N-Resp	M: shall we read 'Papa's Pizza'[d] C: No	M and C are sitting together on couch, and have just finished reading a story. M suggests another book.
I/D	Baby	C reaches hand into toy box and touches doll.
	Down	C climbing off couch on to floor.
Id+	M: What's this? C: Ball	M holds ball out to C. C explores ball and identifies it.
Asst	Daddy	C climbs into father's chair.
	Doggie bark	C hears dog barking outside.
Resp	M: What do you want for snack? C: Apple	C and M go to kitchen for a snack. M puts C in high chair.
Rout	((SNG)) M: patty cake M&C: patty cake	M singing song, C joins song and begins clapping hands.
DrAttn	(sighted child) [æ::]	C points to kitten playing in front yard. M looks at kitten and begins talking about it.
Off/Sh	Here	C has been playing with a book, holds it out to M. M takes book.

[a] Unless otherwise indicated, examples are from one of the blind children. As the children matured, their utterances of course became more complex; these are examples from the early sessions.

[b] Singing.

[c] Exaggerated intonation.

[d] Refers to one of child's "scratch and sniff" books which contains patches of treated material impregnated with various scents; some of the blind children enjoyed these.

NoIF: To identify utterances which do not appear to have any communicative force. This included utterances which were clearly not interactive, such as babbling, and also utterances which were interactive but whose function was limited to discourse maintenance. For example, a grunt in lieu of a turn. Devices such as grunts acknowledge another's contribution but they do not take the floor.

In addition to these two categories, each classification for a specific communicative force was coded to indicate the degree of certainty of the assignment. Thus, an utterance coded "RqObj" indicated that a particular behavior was judged to be a clear instance of "request object" whereas "RqObj?" indicated that an utterance was *probably* an instance of "request object." Throughout the analysis, the classification system was used very conservatively so that only those behaviors that matched the criteria for classification in every detail were coded as clear instances of a particular communicative act. Behaviors which were judged as instances of a particular type of act, but which failed to meet all criterial features for that act were coded as probable instances.

Summary of the utterance analysis system

The utterance analysis system as a whole, with its two components, provides us with a great deal of information about how it is young children come to convey messages. In particular, we can identify the types of utterance and the kinds of language behavior which are typically exploited to convey various kinds of communicative intents. The level of analysis for fundamental illocutionary acts was designed to capture the full range of communicative acts that have been reported in the literature. Note that there are considerably more categories than have been proposed for describing adult communicative acts. This permits us to examine more precisely how children use language and how language use changes over time. Various categories can be combined to yield a higher level of abstraction corresponding to standard adult illocutionary acts. For example, all responses, identifications, descriptions, assertions, and negations would be subsumed under the category "Representatives" in Searle's (1975) taxonomy. But if there are developmental differences in the various subclasses of "representatives," then it is important to recognize and document these. Moreover, this system permits us to examine variation among children and, in particular, to examine how access to visual information affects the ontogenesis of communicative force.

The coding system was specifically designed to be maximally flexible in what it permits us to analyze. Not only can the sub-classes be easily combined to form standard adult categories of illocutionary acts, but the various codes can be combined in a variety of ways to permit access to numerous other phenomena in child language. For example, the creation of the category "No-response" for a "no" answer to a yes–no question enables us to examine these acts in relation to the emergence of negation more generally or to the development of response strategies as a whole. Thus, the system enables us to group together all instances of negation, or of responding, and so on. Similarly, by combining information from the two component classification sets we can assess such things as whether or not conventionalized gestures in sighted children are used to perform the same kinds of acts as early words in blind children. The combined system also permits us to identify all turns which have a purely discourse-maintaining function. We noted above that the code "no illocutionary force" is used to indicate utterances which lack communicative force, including those whose "function" appears to be purely discourse maintenance. The combined system distinguishes between the two uses of this code since all instances of it that occur with interactive behaviors necessarily function as discourse devices. Thus, by isolating all such coding, it is possible to analyze in greater detail the development of discourse strategies. (Such an analysis is not included in the present study.)

To summarize, the principles of the Utterance Analysis System are as follows. The basic distinction is that an "utterance" (here stretched to cover a few conventionalized gestures) may be either interactive or non-interactive. If it is non-interactive, by definition, it has no intended communicative force. If an utterance is interactive in nature, it may function only to maintain discourse, or it may have further communicative force. Because young children are not party to the range of linguistic conventions used to indicate force, and because other factors, such as lexical inexplicitness or articulatory problems, may impede interpretation, utterances which appear to have communicative intent may succeed to different degrees in conveying specific communicative force.

6.4   Method of analysis

Each of the children's utterances and conventionalized gestures appearing in the transcripts of the home visits was classified according to the Utterance Analysis System. The corpus consisted of approximately 13,000 "utterances" each of which was assigned a category from both set 1 (type of utterances) and set 2 (illocutionary force of utterance) yielding 26,000 codes and 13,000 code-pairs. Table 6.2 indicates the number of coded utterances for each child.

Categories were assigned primarily on the basis of information contained in the typed transcripts. Material from the lexical study was used to help identify spontaneous use of words and to facilitate the interpretation of certain utterances. In some instances the audio recordings were used to clarify intonational contours and video recordings to explicate context.

Table 6.2. *The number of utterances analyzed for each child*

Child	Number of sessions	Number of utterances
Teddy	16	2,684
Lisa	18	3,062
Julie	15	2,862
Lydia	5	1,752
Brett	7	1,675
Bonnie	6	1,137

Approximately 40 per cent of the transcripts were analyzed solely by the author. A further 40 per cent were analyzed by a research assistant after a series of training sessions. These analyses were then carefully checked by the author. Differences were discussed and resolved at regular meetings. A reliability measure was based on the analysis of the remaining data.

Twenty per cent of the transcripts, drawn proportionally from the six subjects, were independently analyzed by the research assistant and myself. Interobserver agreement was calculated by Cohen's Kappa, an especially accurate measure which corrects for chance agreement (Sachet, 1979). Agreement was 92.1 per cent for type of utterance and 87.81 per cent for type of illocutionary act. This is one of the first times this type of system has been subjected to a reliability measure and the results indicate that these kinds of categories can be operationalized clearly. The high proportion of agreement was probably facilitated by carefully specifying the accompaniments of the utterance.

Tallying data

Frequency counts for each category in set 1 and set 2 were completed for every transcript. In addition, the frequency distribution of set 2 with respect to set 1 was calculated using a grid technique. Samples of the tally sheets appear in Appendix 3.

Calculation of MLU

The mean length of utterance (MLU) was calculated for each transcript following the procedure recommended by Brown (1973) with the following modifications. Only fully interpretable utterances were evaluated and all instances of imitation were explicitly excluded. If anything, the calculations tend to be conservative, since phrases were counted as single units (unanalyzed wholes) unless other evidence suggested that the child controlled component lexemes.

II: Analysis of developments in the use of illocutionary force

6.5   The emergence of utterances with some identifiable force

For all of the children there is a general progressive increase in the number of utterances which appear to have illocutionary force. In the earliest transcripts, when the children have an MLU of roughly 1.0 and generally produce far fewer than 100 utterances per session, the proportion of utterances with no illocutionary force seems to vary randomly: during some sessions the children attempt to convey messages, and in others, they do not, but there is no principled explanation to account for this variation.

At about the time a child begins producing a few two-word utterances this random variation seems to end and the proportion of language behaviors with no specifiable illocutionary force seems to steadily decrease over the remaining period of the study. The point at which this happens ranges from MLU 1.02 to MLU 1.64. It is not obvious why this should happen, but it could indicate increasing intentionality. In other words, at roughly the same time that words begin to be combined, children may have an emerging awareness of language as a communicative tool and therefore they may more deliberately use and explore various illocutionary functions. I have called this point the *communicative threshold* to indicate that communicative behaviors no longer seem to be a random feature of language. The only child who does not reach this threshold is Bonnie, who had an MLU of approximately 1.0 when the study ended (she does not actually meet the criterion 100 lexicalized utterances for calculating MLU) and had a vocabulary of only some twenty words at that time.

Across observation sessions, the total number of utterances with definite illocutionary force and the number having probable illocutionary force is positively correlated for all children except Bonnie ($P > 0.05$). Bonnie's data show no correlation between these two.

Tables 6.3 to 6.8 present the proportion of utterances with a definite illocutionary force, probable illocutionary force, and no illocutionary force during each session for each child. In each table, the apparent communicative threshold point is indicated by an arrow ($\leftarrow$).

The pattern of development is fairly consistent across all subjects (except Bonnie). The data for Teddy most closely match the general progression outlined above. At the onset of lexical acquisition his utterances show a randomly fluctuating pattern of no illocutionary force ranging from 57.1 to 90 per cent. For all children, the proportion of utterances containing no illocutionary force is greater than 50 per cent prior to the threshold point (mean for all children $\bar{X} = 71.7$ per cent). As Teddy begins to construct utterances with more than one lexeme (MLU 1.25) the data show a consistent increase in the number of utterances which have clearly identifiable illocutionary force, paralleled by a less dramatic but equally

Table 6.3. *Teddy: Proportion of utterances[a] conveying illocutionary force*

Child's age	Number of utterances	Percentage of utterances with certain IF	Percentage of utterances with probable IF	Percentage of utterances with no IF	MLU
0;9;29	7	28.5	14.3	57.1	1.0[b]
0;10;25	35	17.1	0	82.2	
0;11;17	30	10.0	0	90.0	
1;0;9	52	26.9	9.6	63.5	
1;1;14	88	13.6	0	86.3	
1;2;24	156	21.8	9.6	68.6	
1;3;28	166	12.6	11.4	75.9	
1;4;19	91	12.0	23.1	64.9	
1;5;8	347	20.7	17.6	61.7	1.03
1;6;8	304	21.0	9.9	69.1	1.25←[c]
1;7;5	249	30.9	9.6	59.4	1.47
1;8;24	357	40.9	17.0	42.0	1.53
1;10;8	170	40.6	20.4	38.8	2.13
1;11;9	173	41.6	20.8	37.6	2.50
2;0;8	111	60.4	23.4	16.2	2.49[b]
2;1;13	348	62.9	25.0	12.3	1.95[d]

[a] Including conventionalized gestures or routines
[b] MLU approximate since criterion 100 lexical utterances not produced
[c] Indicates communicative threshold point
[d] Teddy's MLU drops during this session because of the calculation criterion. In fact, he produces a large number of long utterances (e.g., "I get the dolly." "Here's your glass." "I want play basketball" and so on) but during the first 100 utterances many single-word utterances were produced. (Particularly greeting terms and "yes" responses to questions). The MLU calculated for the entire session was approximately 3.0.

Table 6.4. *Lisa: Proportion of utterances[a] conveying illocutionary force*

Child's age	Number of utterances	Percentage of utterances with certain IF	Percentage of utterances with probable IF	Percentage of utterances with no IF	MLU
1;3;30	37	8.1	2.7	89.2	1.00[b]
1;4;13	42	35.7	16.7	47.6	1.00[b]
1;5;3	75	33.3	14.6	52.0	1.00[b]
1;5;18	92	9.7	7.6	82.6	1.20[b]
1;6;7	101	18.8	2.9	78.2	1.03[b]
1;6;27	151	11.9	5.2	82.8	1.06[b]
1;7;17	146	27.4	6.2	66.4	1.03[b]
1;8;18	253	19.8	19.8	60.4	1.02[b]
1;9;11	164	36.0	13.4	50.6	1.11[b]
1;10;16	305	32.8	15.4	51.8	1.05
1;11;14	241	46.1	8.7	45.2	1.11←[c]
2;2;2	362	47.0	15.4	37.3	1.86
2;3;13	255	57.2	10.6	32.2	1.85

Table 6.4. (*cont.*)

Child's age	Number of utterances	Percentage of utterances with certain IF	Percentage of utterances with probable IF	Percentage of utterances with no IF	MLU
2;4;13	278	37.1	19.1	43.9	2.01
2;7;26	453	68.0	23.4	8.6	3.20
Supplemental data for Lisa[d]					
1;11;15	10	0	0	100	1.00[b]
2;0;0	68	8.0	1.4	89.7	1.10[b]
2;0;15	29	51.7	6.8	41.4	1.00[b]

[a] Including conventionalized gestures or routines
[b] MLU approximate since criterion 100 lexical utterances not produced
[c] Communicative threshold point
[d] Based on transcripts of tapes made in home by parents or in classroom; contextual information is incomplete

Table 6.5. *Julie: Proportion of utterances*[a] *conveying illocutionary force*

Child's age	Number of utterances	Percentages of utterances with certain IF	Percentage of utterances with probable IF	Percentage of utterances with no IF	MLU
1;0;17	68	36.8	2.9	60.3	0[bd]
1;1;14	27	25.9	3.7	70.4	0[c]
1;2;26	36	13.9	0	86.1	0[c]
1;3;21	69	18.8	1.4	79.7	0[c]
1;4;6	66	4.6	14.0	81.2	0[bf]
1;4;28	118	30.5	1.6	67.8	0[b]
1;6;0	257	5.0	0	95.0	0[bg]
1;7;27	159	13.8	1.9	84.3	1.00[b]
1;8;16	200	15.5	3.0	81.5	1.00[b]
1;9;13	175	21.7	3.4	74.8	1.00[b]
1;10;13	153	19.6	7.8	72.5	1.00[b]
2;0;9	488	31.3	15.4	53.3	1.02?[c]
2;1;23	189	45.0	8.9	46.0	1.04
2;2;30	452	36.3	13.4	50.2	1.10
2;4;5	405	36.8	29.1	34.1	1.29

[a] Including conventionalized gestures or routines
[b] MLU approximate since criterion 100 lexical utterances not produced
[c] Possible communicative threshold point
[d] Only three lexemes produced during session, all were part of a routine
[e] No lexemes
[f] Only lexeme is 'mama', which was produced eight times
[g] Only two lexemes produced during session, but associated with a routine.

Table 6.6. *Lydia: Proportion of utterances*[a] *conveying illocutionary force*

Child's age	Number of utterances	Percentage of utterances with certain IF	Percentage of utterances with probable IF	Percentage of utterances with no IF	MLU
1;4;8	286	18.2	17.8	64.0	1.42[c]
1;5;5	434	12.9	15.8	71.2	1.46[c]
1;6;7	254	26.4	25.2	48.4	1.64[c] ←[b]
1;7;8	334	27.5	22.5	60.0	1.79[c]
1;8;18	444	36.0	22.5	41.4	1.60[d]

[a] Including conventionalized gestures or routines
[b] Threshold (uncertain due to limited data)
[c] It is extremely difficult to evaluate how much Lydia understands of the component morphemes in phrases she uses. Lydia is clearly a "gestalt" language learner (cf. Peters, 1988). The MLU calculation is conservative, crediting her with structures only when there is evidence that Lydia substitutes components of various phrases for one another and/or uses the morphemes creatively. MLU may under-represent the level of her competence.
[d] Many of Lydia's phrases in this session contain uninterpretable sounds, therefore, it was not possible to include these utterances in the MLU calculation. The result is almost certainly that Lydia's facility with language is considerably under-represented by the MLU calculation. Her actual MLU is probably close to 3.0.

Table 6.7. *Brett: Proportion of utterances*[a] *conveying illocutionary force*

Child's age	Number of utterances	Percentage of utterances with certain IF	Percentage of utterances with probable IF	Percentage of utterances with no IF	MLU
1;5;10	33	12.1	6.0	81.8	1.00[c]
1;7;11	272	17.2	4.4	78.3	1.00[c]
1;8;10	254	13.4	7.5	79.1	1.05[c]
1;9;8	172	39.5	16.3	44.2	1.33 ←[b]
1;10;7	148	28.4	22.2	49.3	1.30[c]
1;11;10	258	23.2	16.3	60.4[d]	1.86
2;0;9	538	28.6	27.7	43.7	1.62

[a] Including conventionalized gestures or routines
[b] Threshold point
[c] MLU approximate since criterion 100 lexical utterances not produced
[d] See discussion: during this session there was a lengthy period of egocentric play

Table 6.8. *Bonnie: Proportion of utterances[a] conveying illocutionary force*

Child's age	Number of utterances	Percentage of utterances with certain IF	Percentage of utterances with probable IF	Percentage of utterances with no IF	MLU
1;0;25	189	17.5	0	82.5	
1;1;25	271	25.5	1.1	73.4	
1;2;25	166	18.1	1.8	80.1	
1;3;21	150	26.7	8.0	65.3	
1;4;26	123	35.0	3.2	61.8	1.00[b]
1;6;7	238	16.8	2.9	80.2	1.00

[a] Including conventionalized gestures or routines
[b] MLU approximate since criterion 100 lexical utterances not produced

consistent increase in utterances with probable illocutionary force. There is a corresponding decline in utterances with no illocutionary force, which fall steadily from 69.1 to 12.3 per cent.

The progression is not quite as perfect in the other subjects, but the basic trends are clear. Brett's pattern is quite consistent except at 1;11;10 when a lengthy period of individual play leads to an increased number of utterances with no illocutionary force. Lisa's pattern fluctuates somewhat more than the other children, and there is a slightly lower correlation between utterances with certain and probable illocutionary force. As soon as Julie begins to use lexemes, which occurs later for her than for the other subjects, we see a progressive increase in utterances with certain or probable illocutionary force. (This trend is corroborated by informal analysis of data from home visits after the present study ended.) Lydia appears to have reached the threshold point by the third observation session, but because the data are limited, this is difficult to access. In particular, it would be helpful to know how she used her utterances in the earliest portion of the single word period. More of Lydia's utterances have been assigned to the "probable" force category, reflecting the difficulty we have in understanding her long and rapidly produced utterances.

Bonnie uses virtually no language during any of the sessions and her attempts to convey messages are only assessed in terms of her use of conventionalized gestures. We should note though that she consistently uses actions and pantomimes to contribute to interactions and to involve others in her activities. For example, at 1;6;7 Bonnie wants her aunt D to brush her hair. Bonnie takes D's hand, turns it palm up, places a brush in it, then stands with her back to D. The use of such behaviors is frequent in Bonnie's data, but is entirely unseen in the data for the blind children. Such behavior is not part of a conventionalized system and it is not part of the illocutionary analysis.

Teddy and Lisa, the two children with no useful vision, have a slightly lower proportion of utterances with no illocutionary force after the threshold point is reached, averaging 39.3 and 33.4 per cent respectively. (When Lisa is 2;4;13 the proportion of utterances with no illocutionary force suddenly increases, but this is due to the fact that she engages in a long period of role play during this session.) Among the other children the average proportion of utterances with no illocutionary force after the threshold point is 45.9 per cent for Julie, 64.6 per cent for Lydia and 49.4 per cent for Brett. One possible explanation for this is that language provides the two most blind children with a means of keeping in touch with their families and their environment.

An important issue is whether or not there are qualitative differences in utterances which have no illocutionary force. As defined in the utterance analysis system, some utterances have a non-interactive status (e.g., babbling, expressive jabbering) while others may function to help maintain discourse; though in and of themselves, they do not communicate messages. Analysis of the data indicates that the *visually impaired children are much more likely to engage in non-interactive behaviors when they are in potentially interactive situations* (i.e., when family or friends are present and are not otherwise engaged) than are sighted children. This difference is even more pronounced if we only consider sessions after which the child has acquired 20 or more lexemes. For all subjects, the earliest sessions are marked by a high number of vocalizations which appear to be contributions to interactions. The fact that we recorded relatively few instances of babbling during these sessions is almost certainly due to the research setting – we rarely saw a child alone in his or her crib, and the mothers generally encouraged interactions, especially during the first few sessions with each child. In addition, even in these early sessions the proportion of non-interactive utterances, when they did occur, is higher for Teddy, Lisa and Julie (15 to 20 per cent of all utterances) than for Bonnie, Brett and Lydia (3 to 12 per cent of all utterances).

The picture that emerges from this initially appears somewhat contradictory, but I believe two principled strategies are co-occurring. First, the two children with no useful vision produce the fewest number of utterances with no illocutionary force. The probable explanation for this is that Lisa and Teddy use language to maintain contact with their families. Secondly, Teddy and Lisa, as well as Julie, who has only a small amount of vision, are more likely to engage in non-interactive language use when they do produce utterances which have no illocutionary force. That is, their utterances coded NoIF often do not have even discourse maintaining functions. These instances of non-interactive language use represent the emergence of play strategies, since verbal role play may take the place of object play for blind children (see chapter 2).

6.6   The order of emergence of illocutionary acts

The order of emergence of the 13 illocutionary acts shows a similar progression across all subjects, but an exact sequence of development cannot be identified. Instead, the ontogenesis of illocutionary force is best described by a set of implicational statements. These take the form: if a child has acquired some illocutionary act (or acts), A, then he will also have acquired some illocutionary act (or acts) B. Such "if A then B"[5] statements specify that the child must not have acquired act A without previously, or at the same time, having acquired act B (*A & -B). While A cannot be acquired prior to B, the opposite occurrence is permitted and B may be acquired prior to A (B & -A), or the child may have acquired neither A nor B (-A & -B). Thus, three possible co-occurrences are permitted in the acquisition of illocutionary acts and only one possible combination is prohibited (*-B & A). The implicational statements limit the co-occurrence patterns in the acquisition of specified illocutionary acts across all subjects. Hence, they define basic emergence patterns and constrain variation, while at the same time, permitting some individual differences. There is nothing explicit or implicit in the nature of implicational statements which expresses a causal relationship between the antecedent and consequent act. Once the implicational statements are presented, I will suggest some possible explanations to account for them.

The clearest picture of development is discerned when all "certain" instances of a particular act and all "probable" instances of that act are grouped together for any given session. Thus, in this portion of the analysis the distinction between, for example, "RqObj" and "RqObj?" is collapsed. Of course, the category UIF (unspecifiable illocutionary force) is retained for utterances which appear to have illocutionary force, but where it is difficult to assign some specific function to the utterance. Grouping together "certain" and "probable" instances of the various acts creates a picture which maximally portrays a child's illocutionary competence at a particular point in time, but I found that it did not distort the developmental picture in any way. (Notice that tables 6.3 to 6.8 above indicate that there are consistently more "certain" than "probable" instances of acts in any given session. Moreover, as a child begins to exploit a particular illocutionary strategy, both "certain" and "probable" instances were attested in the data.)

In analyzing the data, a particular illocutionary act was credited as having emerged when it was attested four or more times during one session. This criterion is somewhat arbitrary, but is motivated by the following

---

[5] Such statements are derived from propositional logic where the symbols "P" and "Q" are traditional. These typically represent some property (or properties) stated as propositions. Since I am considering acts rather than propositions, I have used the symbols "A" and "B" in place of "P" and "Q."

Table 6.9

Sequence for the emergence of illocutionary acts

Child	Req	Q	AttnG	Soc	P/R/R/D	N-Rsp	I/D	Id+	Asst	Rout	Resp	Off/Sh	DrAttn
Teddy	3 (1;2;24)	6 (1;7;5)	4 (1;4;19)	7[a] (1;11;9)	6 (1;7;5)	6 (1;7;5)	3 (1;2;24)	1 (1;0;9)	5 (1;6;8)	2 (1;1;4)	5 (1;6;8)		
Lisa	1 (1;4;13)	c	2 (1;5;3)	b	2 (1;5;3)	4 (1;8;18)	1 (1;4;13)	3 (1;6;7)	5 (2;0;18)	4[a] (1;8;18)	6 (2;3;13)		
Julie (verbal data)	1 (1;7;27)		4 (2;0;9)	4 (2;0;9)	2 (1;8;16)	4 (2;0;9)	1 (1;7;27)	3 (1;9;13)	4 (2;0;9)	1 (1;7;27)	4 (2;0;9)		
Lydia	1 (1;4;8)	1 (1;4;8)	1 (1;4;8)	2 (1;5;5)	1 (1;4;8)		1 (1;4;8)	1 (1;4;8)	1 (1;4;8)	2 (1;5;5)	3 (1;5;7)	1 (1;4;8)	
Brett	2 (1;7;11)	5 (2;0;9)	2 (1;7;11)				2 (1;7;11)	1 (1;5;0)	2 (1;7;11)	3 (1;8;10)	4 (1;10;7)	4 (1;10;7)	
Bonnie pre-verbal	1 (1;0;25)							3 (1;6;7)		1 (1;0;25)		1 (1;0;25)	2 (1;1;25)
Julie pre-verbal	2[d] (1;4;28)		1 (1;0;17)		1 (1;0;17)					1 (1;0;17)			

increasing vision →

(sighted)

(blind)

[a] Regular use occurred earlier, but not reaching criterion level of 4+ instances until age indicated
[b] Regular use, never reaching criterion
[c] May be emerging
[d] Credits searching and vocalizing as a convention for getting objects

considerations. First, if a particular act occurs only once or twice in a session, especially if it does not recur in the next few months, there is a high probability that the child's utterance was interpreted too "richly" by the parent and/or the researcher(s) – certainly the child is not really exploiting that act. Secondly, preliminary analysis indicated that if an act occurred four or more times during a particular session, it was likely to recur in subsequent sessions. (See Bloom, 1970; Bloom, Lightbown and Hood, 1975 for similar reasoning.)

The data from Bonnie reveal only a very few illocutionary acts, presumably because she was dependent on non-conventionalized, non-verbal strategies. In addition, the data from Julie's first seven sessions, during which time she too was non-verbal, reveals a similar limited number of functions. Some of these were different functions from those that emerged when Julie began to use language. I have therefore considered the non-verbal data separately, though I will compare and contrast it with the verbal data.

Table 6.9 presents the sequence for emergence of the various illocutionary acts for each child. The session during which a particular act is first used four or more times is indicated.

6.6.1   Implicational statements

The following implicational generalizations are derived from the sequence of acquisition in the data from all subjects except the non-verbal sessions from Bonnie and Julie. The implicational statements are empirical, but they tend to be corroborated by facts of language complexity.

(1) If the child has acquired request strategies, then the child has acquired identification/description strategies:

$$Rq \supset I/D$$

Explanation: Identification and description are consistently among the first illocutionary acts attested and they are perhaps the most basic to meaning since their rudimentary forms are simply the expression of recognition of a member of a class of entities, events or activities. It stands to reason that a child must be able to recognize and express such instances in order to request them.

(2) If the child has acquired assertion strategies, then the child has acquired identification/description, elicited identifications and requests:

$$Asst \supset I/D \ \& \ Id+ \ \& \ Rq$$

Explanation: The adult illocutionary act of "representatives" (Searle, 1975) subsumes several fundamental strategies including I/D and Asst. All members of this class "commit" the speaker to the truth of something. In the case of assertions S conveys information *about* something, which is cognitively more demanding than simply recognizing an instance *of* something. In fact, the one is logically prior to the other. There is probably no causal relationship between requests and assertions. However, in the earliest forms observed, requests merely served to gratify personal or biological needs and may be viewed as relatively simple.

(3) If the child has acquired negative responses, then the child has acquired at least some aspects of general negation, protest/ refusal/rejection/denial:

$$N\text{-}Resp \supset P/R/R/D$$

Explanation: The inclination and ability to express simple negation (basically protest, refusal, and rejection) is a necessary precursor to providing negative responses to questions. "No responses" are in fact refusals and rejections carried out at a higher level of representation since both the stimulus and response are necessarily verbal. Two other implicational statements are suggested by the data, but explanations for them are less evident.

(4) If the child has acquired questions, then the child has acquired assertions:

$$Q \supset Asst$$

(5) If the child has acquired responses, then the child has acquired assertions:

$$Resp \supset Asst$$

Explanation for 4 and 5: It may be the case that in order to ask about something or to respond about something the child must be able to spontaneously comment about things. However, other researchers have observed that parents typically encourage young children to comment on things by asking questions, and this would suggest that responses should precede assertions in development. This difference can be reconciled by considering the role of elicited identifications (Id +). These may be viewed as special instances of "response" and they do precede or co-occur with assertion as indicated in implication statement 2. I believe elicited identifications are more appropriately viewed as an interactive game than as true responses in the linguistic sense. Nevertheless, they may have a scaffolding effect which eventually helps children to construct full assertive structures. A related and more interesting causal relationship is also suggested by the data.

(6) If a child has acquired questions; then the child has acquired response strategies:

$$Q \supset Resp$$

This suggests that the ability to recognize and reply to questions is a prerequisite to the ability to ask questions of others. A limited exception to this implicational statement is seen in the data from Lydia. Early on, she requested the names of objects ("What is this?"), a commonly reported routine for many children. This routine did precede the emergence of responses in her data. Interestingly, elicited identifications, which I also regard as routines, appeared prior to the routine for requesting names, forming a more primitive parallel to implication statement 6:

6'. If a child has acquired requesting name routines (Rq Id), then the child has acquired elicited identifications (Id +):

$$Rq \ Id \supset Id +$$

Thus for both interactional routines and for more productive language it seems that children must be able to reply to queries in order to pose queries themselves.

Several of these implicational statements can be drawn together to suggest the following hierarchy for the sequence of acquisition for some of the principal illocutionary acts. The symbol ⩾ should be read "is acquired earlier than or at the same time as":

$$I/D \geqslant Rq \geqslant Asst \geqslant Resp \geqslant Q$$

This hierarchy corresponds in several respects to other reports of sequential developments in young children's early language that have been presented in a semantic rather than a pragmatic framework. For example, the early uses of "pure performatives" in which an utterance occurs as part of an activity (e.g., saying "bye" while waving) and of labeling or indication are reported prior to the use of volitional strategies (see especially Greenfield and Smith, 1976 for discussion). In turn, volitional strategies typically precede the use of complex representative statements which encode various case relations. Labeling is an instance of I/D in the illocutionary framework; volition is the semantic representation of the pragmatic act of requesting and these are ontogenetically prior to the various kinds of propositions encoded in the illocutionary act of asserting. Similarly, the illocutionary hierarchy is compatible with the observation that children's earliest utterances typically relate to their own desires and later begin to represent events occurring in the environment independent of the self, or to their wanting to change the environment in various ways. Although the illocutionary analysis says nothing about the *content* of assertive acts, the antecedent relationship of "identification/description" and "request" to "assertion" is in line with this kind of decentration. The later emergence of questions can be explained by the relative complexity of these messages since they require the speaker to instruct the hearer to represent relevant information. One aspect of language that is almost always reported among first utterances is negation, which is peculiarly underattested in the present data (see also chapter 5).

In summary, this investigation suggests that: (1) children are increasingly likely to use language communicatively as they progress through "stage I" (Brown, 1973), and (2) that there is a principled expansion in the number of illocutionary acts that children exploit during this period.

6.6.2 Non-verbal acts

The non-verbal data from Julie and Bonnie suggest that routines and requests are well attested during the pre-verbal period. Routines, in which the child's contribution is vocal, or gestural, or both, occur at the verbal level for all subjects, but are generally not found in the earliest verbal sessions. It may be that ritualized hand and body games are crucial early on (see Bruner, 1975), and then become less important as first words emerge. Later, more verbal routines may be of varying importance in parent–child dyads. The request behaviors in Julie's and Bonnie's pre-verbal data take the form of conventionalized gestures. While demand strategies appear to precede language, the use of linguistically conveyed requests clearly presupposes identification strategies. The differences between Bonnie and Julie appear to involve the role of visual information. Bonnie's behaviors are offering and attention-drawing strategies, which are socially motivated and reflect interest in the external environment. Julie's attention-getting strategies may reflect a similar desire to participate in social interaction, but she must overtly get attention through fussing and vocalizing (whereas Bonnie can accomplish this through eye gaze or approach behavior) and then she is dependent on others to provide a basis for shared activities. Kekelis (1981) reports that most of Julie's input during this period consisted of directives designed to encourage Julie to move or act on her environment. These strategies emerged in response to Julie's delayed gross motor development. Julie's protest/refusal strategy developed in response to these directives.

6.6.3 Overall pattern of development

The overall pattern of development is remarkably similar for the blind and sighted children. The principal differences involve the categories attention getting and offer/show, both of which can be explained in terms of the availability of visual information. Attention getting is clearly important to all four blind children and it consistently emerges prior to or contiguous with assertions in their data. Hence, a further implicational statement can be proposed for the blind subjects: Asst $\supset$ AttnG. In order to effectively communicate information about something, it is essential to obtain the hearer's attention. In the absence of vision it is difficult to be certain of another's attention without the use of overt strategies. Such strategies are generally unnecessary for the young sighted child (at least when the child is in the proximity of H and is the principal focus of attention) and they are unattested in the data from Brett and Bonnie. The implicational statement would probably also be true for sighted children in situations where their caregivers are not focusing attention on them.

The same logic entails that AttnG should occur prior to request strategies for the blind children, but this is not the case. One possible explanation is that requesting often inherently involves certain attention-getting devices, since it is typically marked with an exaggerated terminal intonation contour and since children generally will repeat their requests if they are not immediately satisfied.

The presence of offer/show strategies is highly correlated with the degree of residual vision, which corroborates Urwin's (1978a) findings. They are completely unattested in the data from Teddy and Lisa and appear only twice in Julie's data, even though both parents and researchers regularly encouraged reciprocal exchanges.[6] In contrast, offering and showing are well exploited by Lydia and Brett and are even an important basis of interaction for Bonnie during the pre-verbal period.

The absence of attention-drawing strategies from all corpora except Bonnie's indicates that this category functions principally as a non-verbal strategy. Its function may have been subsumed by I/D, Rq and Q strategies in the older children.

6.7   Relative frequency of use for the different illocutionary acts

While the basic order for the emergence of different illocutionary acts is similar for all of the children, the extent to which each act is exploited varies at least in part as a function of the degree of visual impairment. The strongest effects are for requests and assertions, where visual impairment correlates with an increase in the use of request strategies and where visual function correlates with a greater and more enduring use of assertions. Visual dysfunction is also associated with attention getting and routines. Figure 6.1 indicates the relative proportion of requests for each child calculated as a mean for all sessions beginning with the session during which the strategy was first observed at the criterion level. Figure 6.2 presents similar data for assertions.

Request strategies are consistently highly exploited by the three most impaired children, frequently accounting for more than 20 per cent of the illocutionary acts used in any given session.

The difference in the number of requests produced by Teddy compared to Lisa and Julie, is probably due more to Teddy's early mobility and independence than to his blindness. Teddy has always been quite willing to move about the house and climb on and off furniture, whereas Julie and Lisa typically sought help during this period of development. It is this factor which makes Teddy's overall rate of requests lower than Lisa's and Julie's. While requests are well exploited by Lydia, the data as a whole are less skewed towards requests. A similar pattern emerges for Brett. The import-

[6] Offering strategies appeared later in Julie's development and were paralleled by Julie's increasing ability to exploit the minimal vision that she has. Both developments were fostered by special pre-school education programs.

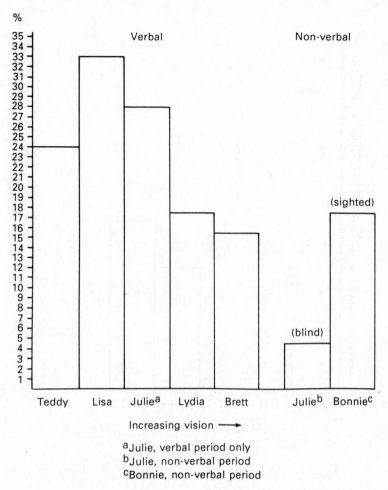

Figure 6.1 Mean proportion of requests relative to other acts.

ance of requests to the blind children presumably represents a highly adaptive strategy since blind children are inherently more dependent on others to help them obtain objects and to become more involved in the environment. This is even more evident if we compare the nature of requests performed by blind and sighted children.

The frequency of requests for objects is highly correlated with increasing visual dysfunction, and requests for actions/activities is correlated with visual function. Requests for routines are somewhat more frequent for the blind children. Table 6.10 indicates the number of object, action and routine requests for each child as a percentage of their total requests.

Although I have not quantified the data, the kinds of activities Lydia and

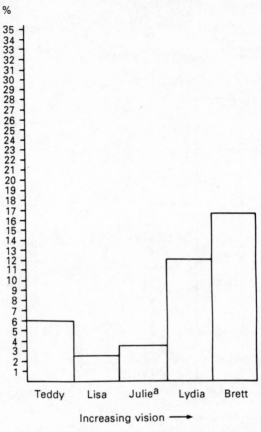

ᵃJulie, verbal sessions only

Figure 6.2   Mean proportion of assertions relative to other acts.

Table 6.10. *Proportion of total requests occurring as RqObj, RqRout and RqAct*

Child	% RqObj	% RqRout	% RqAct
Teddy	65.3	15	19.7
Lisa	47.4	12.9	39.8
Julie ᵃ	40.9	13.4	45.7
Lydia	22.5	2.8	74.6
Brett	20.9	8.9	70.1
Julie ᵇ (blind)		90	10
Bonnie (sighted)	38	24	38

ᵃ Julie verbal
ᵇ Julie non-verbal

Brett request are somewhat different from those of the severely blind children. Many of their requests are to join ongoing games and play; or they involve directions for others to become involved in their own ongoing play. For example, at 1;7;18 Lydia spent several minutes directing her grandmother to "hold the baby [doll]" "rock the baby," "hug the baby," "put the baby – put in rocking chair" and so on. In contrast, the action/activity requests produced by Teddy, Lisa and Julie are designed to satisfy a single personal need: requests to walk, to get on or off a chair, to be held and so on.

The non-verbal data from Julie are in line with the hypothesized importance of routines as a basis of early interaction between blind children and their parents. The data from Bonnie indicate that she is much more able than Julie to exploit gestures to gain access to both activities and objects. Thus, requests for routines are frequent in Julie's pre-verbal communicative strategies, and are more highly attested in verbal data from Teddy, Lisa and Julie than in the children with useful vision. It is possible that object requests are most attested in pre-verbal data for sighted children and verbal data for blind children. Such a tendency could be explained by two factors: (1) both groups have minimal accessibility to non-proximal objects because they are not yet fully mobile and (2) prior to language, the blind children have no satisfactory means for making requests.

The data on the use of assertion strategies suggest that access to visual information provides an incentive to represent events. While the overall use of assertions is lower for the three most impaired children, it is increasingly exploited during the final sessions. (The tables in appendix 4 present the frequencies with which different illocutionary acts occur for each session with each child.) The higher rate of assertions produced by Teddy compared to Lisa and Julie is probably the result of his more rapid language development.

Other differences in the relative use of various illocutionary acts by each of the children are presented in table 6.11.

As we would predict from the data presented in section 6.6, attention getting strategies are much more exploited by the visually impaired children, whereas they are virtually unattested in the data from the sighted children. Routines are also more important for the blind children. Lisa's mean proportion of routines is somewhat lower because they actually occur in only 12 of the 19 sessions for her (see appendix 4). While the proportion of routines generally declines with increasing vision, it is well attested in the non-verbal data from Bonnie, suggesting that routines are indeed important in early parent–child interaction.

There is no discernible pattern in the use of identification/description, though these continue to be important in the data from Brett throughout the study, whereas they are of decreasing importance to the other children. Note too that elicited identifications (Id +) are also quite high for Brett. However, we cannot assume a direct correspondence between I/D and Id + since I

Table 6.11. *Mean proportion for use of different illocutionary acts (averaged for all sessions from time of initial emergence on)*[a]

Child	Req	Q	AttnG	Soc	P/R/R/D	N-Resp	I/D	Id+	Asst	Rout	Rsp	Off/Shw	DrAttn
Teddy													
Mean	23.8	8.9	5.0	2.2	2.9	1.5	11.2	10.6	6.1	23.4	5.3	0	0
Range	2.7–75	.5–30.1	0–25	0–9.4	0–6.5	0–3.9	0–33.3	0–63.2	0–13.8	0–100	0–17.	0	0
Lisa													
Mean	33.2	4.7	4.0	.78	4.38	3.	17.3	5.4	2.5	8.6	2.7	0	0
Range	0–75.	0–18.2	0–22.2	0–3.8	0–25.2	0–12.5	8.8–44.4	0–23.1	0–3.1	0–57.1	0–5.8	0	0
Julie (verbal)													
Mean	27.7	.6	7.17	1.4	5.3	2.5	17.7	7.7	3.4	15.4	7.2	.45	0
Range	14.3–50.4	.4–2.	2.3–22.2	1.7–2.	2.6–13.5	.4–4.9	3.–44.	2.2–26.2	2.2–7.1	5.3–24.3	3.–24.	0–.9	
Lydia													
Mean	17.5	5.1	5.4	2.1	5.0	.06	8.2	1.3	12.0	7.5	5.4	4.9	0
Range	9.6–23.3	.8–12.6	2.3–8.7	1.5–3.2	3.–8.7	0–1.2	2.9–14.5	0–2.6	7.8–16.8	1.9–12.	.8–10.7	2.4–6.8	
Brett													
Mean	15.4	2.2	.5	3.7	.3	0	21.3	17.9	16.2	5.5	3.9	3.5	0
Range	1.7–37.3	0–5.1	0–1.	0–10.2	0–1.7	0	16.7–29.4	0–83.3	5.3–27.1	0–18.9	1.3–8	1.–10.4	
Julie (Non-verbal)													
Mean	4.5	0	16.6	0	0	0	7.4	0	0	15.1	0	0	0
Range	0–21.		0–50.				21.4–100			0–44.7			
Bonnie (Non-verbal)													
Mean	18.6	4.2	0	0	.85	1.05	.5	8.5	0	19.5	.73	25.2	25.6
Range	4.2–33.3	4.2			0–3.	0–2.1	0–3.	8.5		0–36.4	0–3.	12.1–44.7	9.–54.5

The tables in appendix 3 present actual frequency of each illocutionary act during each session for each child have not considered the parent's input in this study. It is possible that the other mothers tried to elicit as many or even more identifications but that their children failed to respond. Kekelis (1981) found that "requests for information," many of which were requests for identification, accounted for between 4 and 35 per cent of the mothers' surface speech acts in the language addressed to Teddy, Lisa and Julie during the period from 16 to 20 months.[7]

As was discussed in section 6.6, offer/show strategies are only attested in data from children with at least some useful vision, and attention drawing appears only in pre-verbal data from a visually intact child.

Thus, the most important differences in the exploitation of illocutionary acts are attributable largely to the degree of available visual information. In particular, the importance of requests for the blind children represents a highly adaptive strategy and the greater relative frequency of assertions for children with useful vision points to the importance of having access to ongoing events as a trigger for talking about them. Audio-kinesthetic information is clearly not a substitute for visual information in the earliest stages of language development. Yet, the blind children do come to depend on this information and in the final sessions for Teddy, Lisa and Julie, there is an increase in the use of assertions (see appendix 4). In chapter 5 the nature of the propositions encoded by assertive acts is analyzed.

6.8   Patterns in the use of utterance types

There are few discernible patterns of correlation between the type of utterance and the use of illocutionary force. Babbling and forms of expressive jargon are by definition non-interactive so they are never associated with illocutionary force. A similar pattern emerges for sound play (SP). Interactive vocalizations (IVs) are well attested for all children, but while they often perform a discourse-maintaining function they are almost never associated with illocutionary acts. Not surprisingly, IVs decrease as the children become more competent in their use of words.

Imitations are somewhat more communicative than simple vocalizations and convey illocutionary force 12 to 35 per cent of the time. Imitations are not unusually frequent for a particular illocutionary act just prior to or at the time that act first emerges for a child. This suggests that imitation may not facilitate the development of specific illocutionary acts in the way it has been seen to facilitate semantic development (see Bloom, Hood and Lightbown, 1974). However, the imitative code in their classification system captures instances when a child repeats a prior model utterance. A more detailed analysis of how and when children imitate specific illocutionary acts would be needed to further explore this relationship.

[7] Actual range is: 14%–27% for Teddy's mother; 11%–35% for Lisa's mother, and 4%–19% for Julie's mother (Kekelis, 1981, pp. 51–52). No information was available for Lydia's and Brett's mothers.

Table 6.12
Average frequency of utterance types: number and proportion with IF and
number of sessions in which type occurred.

	IV	TG	B	SP	IM	RIM	SpL	R	FI
Teddy: Number	527	27	124	48	510	19	1118	272	39
Number with IF	9	19	0	0	101	1	758	156	17
Percentage with IF	1.5%	70.3%			19.8%	0.5%	67.8%	57.3%	43.6%
Number of sessions	16	7	7	8	15	10	15	15	6
Lisa: Number	582	8	225	50	518	30	1474	162	13
Number with IF	10	7	0	0	155	3	1109	111	5
Percentage with IF	1.7%	87.5%			29.9%	10%	75.2%	68.5%	38.5%
Number of sessions	18	7	13	11	18	11	18	17	4
Julie (verbal): No.	806	49	199	16	274	18	720	142	2
Number with IF	22	39	0	0	92	3	560	109	0
Percentage with IF	2.7%	79.6%			33.6%	16.6%	77.8%	76.7%	
Number of sessions	8	6	7	4	8	7	8	6	1
Lydia: Number	685	8	68	18	123	3	764	78	5
Number with IF	1	7	0	0	28	0	491	56	1
Percentage with IF	0.1%	87%			22.8%		64.3%	71.8%	20%
Number of sessions	5	3	1	3	5	2	5	5	3
Brett: Number	481	46	56	14	315	3	728	32	0
Number with IF	9	38	0	0	38	1	406	21	
Percentage with IF	1.8%	82.6%			12.0%	33.3%	55.7%	65.6%	
Number of sessions	4	4	3	1	7	3	7	6	
Julie[a] (non-verbal):	379	42	119	3	17	5	16	5	0
Number with IF	17	30	0	0	3	2	6	0	
Percentage with IF	4.6%	71.4%			17.6%	40%	37.5%		
Number of sessions	7	4	3	2	4	5	5	1	
Bonnie: Number	822	224	6	0	25	0	58	2	0
Number with IF	5	221	0		4		33	1	
Percentage with IF	0.6%	98.7%			16%		56.9%	50%	
Number of sessions	6	6	1		6		5	2	

[a] During non-verbal period Julie also produced ritualized fussing that was credited as P|R|R|D

Repetitions (R) and spontaneous language (SpL) are the most strongly
associated with IF, as are turns consisting of conventionalized gestures
(TGs). TGs function as communicative acts an average of 70 per cent or
more of the time – nearly 99 per cent for Bonnie. The blind children use
gestures principally to participate in routines or to request routines.
However, all four blind children spontaneously use a rejection gesture in
which the child turns his or her face away from an entity and at the same
time, pushes the entity aside. Face turning occasionally occurred without the
pushing and seemed to signal displeasure. Since a similar gesture is regularly
observed in the sighted across many cultures, it may be an innate behavioral
response to an undesirable physical stimulus. Gestures are also used for
requesting and offering by Lydia, Brett and Bonnie and are used to draw
attention in Bonnie's pre-verbal data.

Spontaneous language is considerably more frequent than repetitions, but both are used to accomplish whatever illocutionary acts are in the child's repertoire at any given time. Frame-inserts are quite rare, though they are sometimes seen in data from Teddy and Lisa. However, there is too little evidence to suggest that this utterance type is more frequent in blind children.

Table 6.12 presents the frequency with which each utterance type occurred for each child and indicates the number and proportion of uses that conveyed illocutionary force across all sessions in which the type occurred. It also indicates the number of sessions in which instances of the utterance type are attested.

6.9   The effect of partial vision

Throughout the analysis a general tendency has been observed. Most phenomena, especially the relative use of object requests and of assertions, reveal a continuum of use between the totally blind and the fully sighted children. In these instances the two children with some residual vision fall between the ends of the continuum with Julie falling closer to the blind end and Lydia closer to the sighted end, as would be predicted by the degree of their visual dysfunction. Occasionally, phenomena are characterized by a division between the blind and sighted children, as is the case with offering strategies, and the use of the conventional gestural complex (pointing, reaching). In such instances Julie always behaves as a blind child, whereas Lydia patterns as a sighted child. This suggests that if vision is adequate enough to supply information about form and the relationships that obtain between forms (i.e., between objects and entities) and to provide the child with some information about the behavior of others, then the child will be motivated to maximally exploit this information.

6.10   Summary

The analysis reveals that there are indeed developmental trends in the use of illocutionary force. Moreover, the sequence for the emergence of illocutionary acts is remarkably similar for blind and sighted children, which suggests that certain fundamental (perhaps innate) needs actualize the use of various kinds of communicative functions. The observed sequence follows a logical progression where children first identify entities in the environment, then begin to make requests which transform the environment along familiar dimensions. The children then begin to comment on events and eventually to ask questions about events. The overall process of development is best captured through a set of implicational statements which articulate this logical progression.

What distinguishes the blind and sighted children is the relative frequency with which different communicative acts are used once these acts have been acquired. The usage patterns suggest that various adaptive strategies operate to provide the blind child with increased access to his or her invisible environment.

For example, the blind children make greater use of attention getting strategies since eye-gaze cannot be exploited for this purpose. Similarly, they produce a greater number of requests for objects since they have less access to the non-proximal environment. Routines are only slightly more frequent and enduring for the blind children. This suggests that they are most significant as a means of enabling blind children and their parents to engage in early interactive exchanges, but that they become less important as other kinds of interaction become possible through the emergence of language.

At the same time that the frequency of certain acts indicates that adaptive strategies are operating for the blind children, the relative infrequency of other acts, especially offers and assertions, points to the fact that much of the information that provides a catalyst for communication in sighted children is lost for the blind children and is in line with the findings reported in chapters 4 and 5.

The proportion of utterances which appear to have communicative force steadily increases for all the children once they have crossed a threshold point, roughly coincident with starting to combine a few words. Blind children consistently produce more utterances with illocutionary force than sighted children, possibly as a means of maintaining access to their environment. However, when the blind children do produce utterances which have no illocutionary force, the utterances often have no interactive purpose at all, that is, they do not even function to maintain discourse. It is suggested that sequences of non-interactive verbalizations are in fact early instances of role play. Verbal role play is reportedly the most frequent form of symbolic play in blind children (see chapter 2).

There appears to be little relationship between the type of utterance and the use of illocutionary force. Certain types are predictably more communicative than others (e.g., TG, SpL, R), but no particular utterance type seems specifically to foster the ontogenesis of illocutionary acts.

What is particularly clear from this analysis is that, while blind children are initially limited in their understanding of words and show less creativity in their early word combinations, they are able to convey messages through an increasingly sophisticated use of illocutionary force. These messages are often tailored to their very special needs. The only real difference between the blind and sighted children in the present context involves relative frequency of use, and not the order of acquisition for the illocutionary acts.

7   Conclusion

7.1   Summary

The preceding chapters have examined the role of visual information in three aspects of early linguistic development which form the core of "meaning" in semantic and pragmatic theory: the meanings of words; the construction of propositions; and the use of illocutionary force. These are also areas in ontogenesis where concept development and language development are especially interrelated. The major concern was to understand the extent to which visual information facilitates the process of language acquisition. A number of recurrent themes emerged from the analyses in which differences in the conceptual development of blind and sighted children are reflected in their early language, yet at the same time, certain adaptive strategies are clearly in operation. This chapter briefly summarizes the major findings of the investigation and in the final section, draws together the principal themes of the analysis in order to articulate the important role of visual information in the emergence of meaning and to identify some of the areas where non-linguistic conceptual development influences early language learning.

7.1.1   First words

The role of visual information in the acquisition of early lexemes appears to be significant. While superficially the blind and sighted children appear to have many similar forms, a closer examination of word use reveals differences that suggest the important role of vision as a stimulus in motivating children to construct hypotheses about the nature and meaning of words as symbolic vehicles.

The referents for which the children acquired their first 100 lexemes were fairly similarly distributed among ten mutually exclusive categories, regardless of the degree of visual impairment. Object words and words for actions predominated in the vocabularies of all four children who participated in the diary study, though terms extracted from routines or associated with sounds were more highly attested in the blind children's

155

lexicons, whereas deictic terms were better attested in the sighted child's vocabulary. Despite these similarities, there were three important qualitative differences that clearly distinguished the lexicons of the blind children from those of not only the sighted child in this study, but also the sighted population as widely described by others (e.g., Bowerman, 1978; Clark, 1973; Nelson, 1973a; Rescorla, 1980; Smith and Locke, 1986). First, there were no idiosyncratic forms in the blind children's lexicons and early words rarely fell into disuse. Secondly, words for action were restricted to self actions among the blind children, while sighted children use these terms to refer to a variety of activities involving other people and objects, as well as their own activities. Thirdly, the blind children used functional or relational terms (e.g., "no," "more," "again") to satisfy their own needs, but not to encode information about the dynamic state of entities, while sighted children clearly encoded a variety of transformations with these terms.

In addition to these basic differences, the analysis of the range of use for early lexemes revealed that the blind children's applications were in general more restricted than sighted children's are. The blind children overextended very few of their first words (8 to 13 per cent) and those that were overextended tended to be instances of categorical over-inclusion rather than associative complexes and were generally applied to only one or two referents in addition to the original referent. In contrast, the sighted child in this study overextended 41 per cent of his early words through both categorical overinclusion and associative complexes and frequently applied terms to a wide variety of referents, a profile which is typical of other sighted children as reported in the literature. The basis of overgeneralization was predominantly perceptual for all children, confirming other reports that perceptual attributes account for the majority of overextensions. The blind children's perceptual strategies reflected the relative importance of haptic-kinesthetic sensation for them.

Extensions within the normal domain of application were similarly restricted for the blind children and approximately one half of their first words were never generalized beyond their original context during the diary study. In contrast, the sighted child extended 95 of his first 100 lexemes, again consistent with other reports of extension in sighted children. Moreover, there was no evidence in spontaneous behavior or in sorting tasks that the blind children formed non-linguistic classifications, a strategy which is thought to underlie the process of lexical extension. Thus, behavioral and linguistic evidence are consistent and suggest that the process which enables young sighted children to abstract criterial features of a referent and extend the domain of application of early words is not functioning at the same level for blind children at the onset of language. Words tend to be associated with their original referent for a protracted period of time and when extensions do occur, they are contextually limited and center on the child's own activities rather than on activities of others.

The analysis suggests three general conclusions about how a lack of visual information affects early lexical development: (1) there is less objectification of the word–referent relationship (2) there is a failure to construct hypotheses about the meaning and nature of words, and in part as a result of this (3) there is a lack of extension paralleled by a lack of decentration.

7.1.2 The movement toward propositional structures

As with the acquisition of early words, the role of visual information in the emerging expression of semantic relations appears to be quite important. Although the children encode many of the same fundamental roles, there are significant qualitative differences which reflect how the relative inaccessibility of everyday events for the visually impaired children leads to their limited understanding of the relationships which obtain between entities and objects. Further, while the blind children produce increasingly complex structures, their language development begins to progress along a slightly different path during this period.

Sequences of semantically related single words were taken to be the first observable instances of proposition-like structures. Although these have received considerable attention in the developmental literature, they accounted for less than 5 per cent of the total corpus for each child. Lack of visual information distinguished the blind children in three significant ways: (1) vertical constructions emerged in request strategies for the blind children rather than in description of their own activities (2) some of the sequences referred to past events rather than centering on the "here and now," and (3) the blind subjects were more dependent on their mothers to help them build vertical sequences. The reliance on request strategies suggests that vertical sequences are a natural process in the development of meaning that has been adapted to the particular needs of the visually impaired children and emerges in the structures that they most highly exploit. Talking about shared past events allows the blind children to maximize the probability that they and their addressees have a common focus of attention, just as the use of visual cues aids sighted children in talking about the here and now. Moreover, it is possible that some of these events would have been previously encoded by someone else. Similarly, the mother's contributions may be necessary for helping the child establish reference since visual clues of attention cannot be used to affirm that a shared topic has been established (see Kekelis, 1981).

At the same time that the blind children begin to create horizontal constructions, they produce whole chunks of characteristic maternal speech in its appropriate context. The use of this stereotypic speech was unique to the three most visually impaired children. It was suggested that at least initially this language is interpreted by the children as part of the activity itself in much the same way that early words seem to be an intrinsic part of the referent. But stereotypic speech comes to be used in communicative situations, as when the children use their mother's prototypical offer structures to make requests (e.g., "You wanna go outside?" as a request to go outside). Despite its rather bizarre quality, this speech may actually help the blind children in several ways. In particular, it may enable them to recognize the component behaviors which constitute a single event (i.e., help them to understand part–whole relationships), and it may help them to conceptualize the environment and the events which occur in it. On the other hand, stereotypic speech seems to contribute to, or at least reinforce, the children's failure to understand the reciprocity encoded in pronominal deixis and it seems to reflect certain basic confusions about the roles of various people in the environment.

Perhaps the most important aspect of the investigation of early propositions involves the analysis of the semantic roles, and a few selected grammatical categories (e.g., negation, recurrence), that were expressed in the children's first multi-term utterances. The results indicate that the visually impaired children produced many of the same basic relations that have been identified in other studies of early combinatorial language for children acquiring a variety of different languages; however, only the sighted child produced all eight of the core relations proposed by Brown. The proportion of fundamental roles expressed by not only the verbal sighted child but also the two children with residual vision was within the normal range reported in previous studies (60 to 70 per cent of all their multi-term utterances) but the two children with no useful vision produced far fewer of these constructions and instead used a large amount of stereotypic speech and "want statements."

Examination of the information encoded in the semantic categories reveals several important differences that involve access to visual information. First, information about the location of events and objects and about the attributes (qualities) of entities is virtually unattested in the language of the four children with visual impairments. Their failure to discuss attributes corroborates the findings reported in chapter 4 that blind children seem to have difficulty in extracting the criterial features of referents leading to difficulty in lexical development that is paralleled by an absence of classification behavior. Secondly, although many of the core relations are expressed by the blind children, almost all of these constructions encode events in which the child is the principal agent or possessor. Again, this is compatible with the evidence in chapter 4 which revealed that the process of decentration is very restricted for young blind children. Thirdly, when the visually impaired children *did* encode the roles of other people, it involved requesting things of them or discussing shared past events. This points to an adaptive strategy in which the usual developmental progression occurs because the children exploit those aspects of language and the world which are most meaningful and most available to them. The analysis as a whole supports the theory that the expression of semantic categories does reflect an underlying conceptual framework of the fundamental relationships which obtain between entities and activities in the world.

7.1.3 Developments in the use of illocutionary force

In general, the role of visual information is much less dramatic with respect to the use of illocutionary force than with respect to the development of more purely semantic constructs, and many areas where differences were observed point to adaptive strategies on the part of the blind children.

In order to document the ontogenesis of illocutionary acts, an utterance analysis system was developed to take into account the interactional status of an utterance, the type of utterance (e.g., spontaneous use of language, imitation, sound play), and the accompaniments of the utterance as a basis for assigning it to one of 15 mutually exclusive illocutionary categories (including a category for "no illocutionary force"). These categories are based on standard adult illocutionary acts which have been subdivided to permit a fine-grained analysis that is sensitive to ontogenetic variation (e.g., it distinguishes between requests for objects, for actions, and for routines). Application of the system reveals a developmental progression which has been previously unrecognized, but which is compatible with changes in the use of language documented from a semantic perspective. The order of emergence of various illocutionary acts is best captured in terms of a set of empirically based implicational statements which hold for all children, both sighted and blind, and which can be explained by facts of language and of cognitive complexity. Very generally, the observed sequence follows a progression in which children first identify entities in the environment, then begin to make requests which transform the environment along familiar lines. Shortly, the children begin to comment on events and eventually ask questions about events. The number of utterances with illocutionary force increases as the children become more proficient with language and all of the children cross a threshold during the single-word period after which the proportion of utterances with no illocutionary force steadily declines. The two children with no useful vision produce the lowest proportion of utterances with no illocutionary force and I have suggested that this is because the blind children depend on language as a means of keeping in touch with their environment. However, when blind children do use utterances with no communicative force, they often engage in wholly non-interactive language sequences (e.g., babbling) and I have suggested that this represents the emergence of play strategies since verbal role play is thought to take the place of object play for blind children.

The principal distinction between blind and sighted children with respect to the development of illocutionary force is the relative frequency with which they use the various illocutionary acts once they have acquired them. The most important differences are attributable to the degree of available visual information. In particular, the relative proportion of requests is strongly correlated with visual impairment, while the relative proportion of assertions correlates with access to visual information. Offering and showing strategies are exploited only by the subjects who have useful vision, whereas attention getting strategies are more important for the blind children. The use of requests and attention getting devices by the blind children constitute a highly adaptive strategy since it enables them to increase their participation in and access to the environment. The infrequency of assertions points to the importance of having visual access to ongoing events as a stimulus for talking about them. Audio-kinesthetic information is clearly not a sufficient substitute for visual input in the early stages of language acquisition.

The overall picture is that blind children are able to convey a variety of messages through increasingly sophisticated use of illocutionary acts, and that the messages they produce reflect an adaptive strategy that is tailored to meet their need to gain access to, and information about, the world. The role of visual information with respect to the ontogenesis of communicative function is to provide an impetus for talking about the world, and this is lost to the blind children.

Taken together, the analyses presented in chapters 4, 5 and 6 reveal both adaptive strategies and cognitive deficits that emerge as the result of an absence of vision during the early stages of language development. In the following section these themes are drawn together in an effort to specify the role of visual information in the emergence of meaning.

7.2   Final comments

Adaptive strategies: There are at least four areas where the blind children's development points to their propensity to utilize those aspects of language and interaction which are most important to them and which increase their access to the invisible world. First, ritualized routines are exploited by the parents and children as a basis of early interaction (see Urwin, 1978a, b), and these are particularly well attested just prior to the emergence of words. Secondly, in ascribing meaning to words, the blind children depend largely on haptic-kinesthetic information in lieu of visual information. Although the process is highly restricted, it suggests that the children are struggling to utilize available information to make sense of their world. Thirdly, there is a predominance of requests among the blind children's illocutionary acts which indicate that they are actively seeking access to the environment. These request strategies have increasingly complex forms which demonstrate that development occurs in precisely those structures which are most useful to and in the control of blind children. Finally, the blind children produce the fewest number of utterances with no illocutionary force which suggests that they use language to maintain contact with others.

Cognitive deficits: There are three crucial ways in which the absence of visual information leads to significant cognitive deficits. First, vision seems to be a stimulus for abstracting criterial features necessary to construct categories and for constructing hypotheses about the meaning of words. There is an overwhelming tendency for the blind children to fail to generalize words or to objectify the vehicle–referent relationship, and it was suggested that many of the early forms which appear in their "lexicons" are more appropriately viewed as proto-words. Secondly, there is a later emergence of assertions among blind children which is a consequence of the children's lack of information about the world in general. Thirdly, and also as a result of paucity of their world knowledge, the blind children fail to encode information about semantic roles which do not directly involve them.

Ontogenetic universals: Examining the relationship between adaptive strategies and cognitive deficits provides evidence for the existence of certain universal propensities in the acquisition of language. For example, while extensions are rare in the blind children's early use of words, when they do occur they are based on such perceptual information as tactile and auditory sensation, which strongly supports the position that perceptual strategies are inherent in the organization of information. Further, many of the core semantic relations that have been proposed as universals are expressed by the blind children within the confines of the information available to them. This provides further evidence that these functions are intrinsic to human language. Similarly, the order of emergence of various illocutionary acts was strikingly similar across all subjects which suggests that these too may develop according to universal factors, perhaps relating to language and cognitive complexity, but this will depend on whether evidence from other investigations corroborates the hierarchy proposed in chapter 6.

Perhaps the most significant and intriguing finding pointing to an ontogenetic universal is the remarkable tendency for the blind children to progress from one "stage" of language to another, even though they apparently have not mastered the preceding stage or completed the developmental tasks typically associated with the earlier stage. This is discussed in detail in section 5.4. The key notion is that there may be a drive to express more and more elements of meaning (for example, combining words) even though the units being expressed are not well understood (for example, appreciating the expressive power of single words). This kind of developmental drive may aid communication in general and may be motivated by factors of language learning dexterity in children.

The role of visual information in the emergence of meaning: Taken together, the analyses provide considerable evidence that the earliest stages of language development depend on an underlying conceptual framework. However, the blind children appear to acquire certain (sometimes superficial) linguistic structures without having the conceptual framework to enable them to fully exploit these structures. For example, the blind subjects seem to acquire lexical forms for a long period of time before they fully recognize the nature of words. And, during the single word period, they never use words with the expressive power achieved by sighted children at this stage. From this shaky foundation, the blind children go on to combine words, but they cannot capitalize on the range of meanings that are discovered and encoded by sighted children. In short, the children without vision are severely limited to understanding and talking about those elements of an event which directly involve themselves. Because they progress to increasingly complex language structures without having fully worked through the antecedent stages, there is a cumulative deficit which must be reconciled. This reconciliation presumably comes about through language, specifically through what other people can explain to the children about the nature of a world they cannot see. But the role of language to amplify cognitive constructs comes about long after the emergence of meaning. Initially the absence of visual information inhibits the development of a realistic conception of the world and this in turn leads to deficits in the development of language.

The analyses suggest two general findings. First, from a cognitive perspective, the constrained pattern of conceptual development supports an epistemological theory that is both biogenetic and interactionist. The child's own actions on the world, and especially his observation of it, are essential to the construction of a meaningful concept of that world. From a linguistic perspective, the blind children's development indicates that what appears to be a universal ontogenetic progression in the acquisition of language cannot be fully actualized in the absence of a supporting conceptual framework. If anything, the importance of visual information in the emergence of meaning has been considerably underestimated, for it functions as a vital stimulus for activating the processes which underlie linguistic development, at least in the early stages.

The experiential deprivation resulting from a congenital absence of vision clearly affects aspects of lexical semantics, semantic (thematic) relations, and pragmatics. It is crucial to evaluate the next stages of language development for such children. If we find problems in formal or computational aspects of language as blind children begin to construct morphological and syntactic rules and higher level semantic rules, it will suggest an interrelationship between all aspects of language and other cognitive/conceptual processes. If on the other hand fewer problems are observed in formal areas of linguistics, findings may point to a possible separability of a formal computational component of language from other aspects of language competence.

Certainly, if we tried to picture the most precocious child orator we should never think of a blind child.

Appendix 1
Items in interview questionnaire

Child:
Parent:
Birthday:
Prenatal or birth difficulties:
Siblings:
Probable etiology of blindness:
    Estimated amount of vision: R_____ L_____
    Prognosis:
Child's general health:
Household composition:
Mother: Education____ ____ Occupation_____ 1st Language_____
Father: Education_____ Occupation_____ 1st Language_____

Motor development

Check if evidence of and give approximate age at onset if possible:
    sit without support
    rolls from back to stomach
    stand with support
    creep or crawl
    stand unsupported
    walk supported
    walk unsupported
    move from sitting to standing position without assistance
    stairs
    other

Language related

List familiar routines (e.g.: patty-cake, row your boat) and description of child's usual participation in them:

How does child get mother's or father's attention?

How does child express displeasure? Protest?

How does child express wants or needs (e.g.: for food, games, sleep)?

163

Language

Babbling sounds? Yes_____ No_____
Sounds mother reports:

Sounds observed:

Words? Yes _____ No _____
Description of first word (or first few words) and approximate age at onset?

Words child uses as reported by mother?

Words observed and probable reasons for speaking?

Objects

Does child play with toys? Describe kind of toys preferred and usual activities:

What does child usually do when given an object (i.e., exploration schema, etc.)?

Does child reach for nearby objects?

Does child ever give/offer/show objects to another?

Personal/social

Does child cooperate in dressing?

Does child help when eating? How?

Drink from cup? Holding cup or glass?

Things child especially enjoys doing:

Things child especially dislikes doing:

Describe a typical day:

1 Social awareness

1 Behavior towards persons is not different from behavior towards objects
2 Between 1 and 3
3 Responds briefly to social approach but when not approached directly by persons does not attend to them
4 Between 3 and 5
5 Responds to social approach and persons present, but less than half the time
6 Between 5 and 7
7 Responds to social approach and continues interest in persons present
8 Between 7 and 9
9 Behavior seems to be continuously affected by awareness of persons present

2 Responsiveness to strangers (circle one)

1 Avoiding or withdrawn
2 Hesitant
3 Accepting
4 Friendly
5 Inviting (initiating, demanding)

3 Social behavior with mother

1 Avoiding or withdrawn
2 Hesitant
3 Accepting
4 Friendly
5 Inviting (initiating, demanding)

4 Social behaviors observed

1 Initiating interaction
2 Expressing positive affect in social situation (laugh, smile, brighten)
3 Fussing, etc.

Appendix 2 Sample page of transcript

Teddy	Mother	Researchers	Non-verbal
Footage:			
	((E)) ¹³⁸No: way, Jose./		¹³⁸Sits up; M >TD: extends right leg outward
	¹³⁹Whoop?/ 'Scuse me./		¹³⁹TD bumps into slide and falls forward
[yu?dIdl:(t)]			¹⁴⁰Stands; walks away from slide towards M
'you did it'	What did you do?/		
[dIzufawdawml?wlædl]			
'did you fall down ( ) ladder'			¹⁴¹Turns away from M
	Yeah, you did fall down on the ladder./		
	((LF)) ((LFG)) Come here./	AD.//¹⁴²((HP)) Whoo;ps!/	¹⁴²TD bumps into videotape recorder
405	((HP)) Where are you going?/		
	There's//no coralling] him anymore. ¹⁴³	Yeah, I see that./	¹⁴³Reaches toward T
	((LF))¹⁴⁴Come he:re./		¹⁴⁴Stands
[kʌmhi:]	145		¹⁴⁵Walks backwards pulling TD
'come here'			
	((EI)) Please./		¹⁴⁶Stops pulling TD
	(146)		
[kʌm((SHT))hi:::r(bə)]	Ooh, you feisty¹⁴⁷ thing you./		¹⁴⁷Sits on chair
¹⁴⁸[we?di?kʰwiω]			¹⁴⁸Walks toward M, right arm extended

What?/[119] Where's-/[150]

[119]TD bumps in M's leg
[150]TD starts to walk to right of M
[151]M lifts and extends right leg, keeping TD from moving right
[152]M lowers leg; leans forward
[153]TD sticks right hand in mouth
[154]Bends forward

[151]
(1.) [wʌtyuː(b)]

((HP)) Where's your teeth?/[152]
(2.5)[153] A::h, there they a:re. ≠
((EI)) Good bo::y./

410

(1.3) [wɜsmaiʔtiːʃ]
'where's my teeth'

((HP)) Where's my teeth?/[154] Right here./

Appendix 3 Tally sheets for utterance analysis system

I

TOTAL: _____

T = _____
TG = _____
B = _____
B+ = _____
BW = _____
SP = _____
IM = _____
RIM = _____
SpL = _____
R = _____
FI = _____

II

CHILD _____
AGE _____
DATE _____

TOTAL ILLOC. ACTS: _____

TOTAL ? _____
****

REQUESTS = _____ ? = _____

_____ = RqObl = ?
_____ = RqRout = ?
_____ = RqAct = ?

Q _____ = _____ ?
AtnG _____ = _____ ?
Soc _____ = _____ ?
P/R/R _____ = _____ ?
N-Resp _____ = _____ ?
Id _____ = _____ ?
Asst _____ = _____ ?
Resp _____ = _____ ?
Id+ _____ = _____ ?
Rout _____ = _____ ?
Off _____ = _____ ?
DrAtt _____ = _____ ?

P/R/R + N-Resp = _____
N-Resp + Resp = _____
N-Resp + Resp + Asst = _____

Total I – II = _____

Average length of babble = _____
(B, B+, BW)
****

φ = _____ ? = _____

Tally sheet page 2

Utterance analysis system

Child.................Session number ....Date: ....Age: ....

	OFF	DR Attn	RQ OBJ	RQ ROUT	ACT	Q	ATTNG	SOC	P/R/R	N-RESP	ID	ID+	ASST	RESP ROUT	?	φ
T																
TC																
B																
SP																
IM																
RIM																
SpL																
R																
FI																

Appendix 4 Frequency of illocutionary acts for each session with each subject

Child: Teddy

Age	Total utts w/ Force	Req	Q	AttnG	Soc	P/R/R	N-Resp	I/D	Id+	Asst	Rout	Rsp	OfE/SH	?	DrAttn
0;9,29	3										2 66.6%			1 33.3%	
0;10,25	6	2 33.3%						2 33.3%	2 33.3%						
0;11,17	3										3 100%				
1;0,9	19	2 10.5%						3 15.7%	12 53.2%			1 5.3%		1 5.3%	
1;1,4	12	1 8.3%		1 8.3%					1 8.3%		6 66.7%	1 8.3%			
1;2,24	49	19 38.7%		2 4.1%	1 2.0%			13 26.5%	6 12.2%		3 7.5%			8 16.3%	
1;3,28	40	14 35%						10 25%	4 10%		3 7.5%			9 22.5%	
1;4,19	32	8 25%		8 25%	3 9.4%			1 3.1%			7 21.90%			5 15.6%	
1;5,8	133	38 28.6%		10 7.5%		1 1.0%		30 22.5%	4 3.0%	1 0.7%		1 0.7%		49 36.8%	
1;6,8	94	28 29.8%		2 2.1%	2 1.9%			18 19.1%	5 5.3%	13 13.8%	7 7.4%	7 7.4%		13 13.8%	
1;7,5	101	31 30.7%	4 3.9%	6 5.9%		5 4.9%	4 3.9%	9 8.9%	6 5.9%		15 14.8%	5 4.9%		14 13.9%	
1;8,24	207	36 17.4%	1 0.5%	2 1.0%	1 0.5%	5 2.4%	1 0.5%	19 9.1%	11 5.3%	18 8.7%	66 31.9%	8 3.9%		39 18.8%	
1;10,8	88	23 26.1%	1 1.13%		1 1.13%	5 5.7%	2 2.7%	1 1.13%	9 10.2%	5 5.7%	24 27.3%	7 7.9%		10 11.4%	
1;11,9	108	36 33.3%	1 0.92%			7 6.5%		2 1.9%		9 8.3%	9 8.3%	11 10.2%		27 25%	
2;0,8	93	22 23.6%	28 30.1%	2 2.1%					1 1.1%	2 2.1%	19 20.4%	3 3.2%		16 17.2%	
2;1;13	306	54 17.6%	51 16.7%	8 2.6%	16 5.2%		7 2.2%	4 1.3%	4 1.3%	29 9.5%	22 6.5%	52 17.0%		56 18.3%	

Frequency of illocutionary acts

Child: Lisa

Age	Total units w/ Force	Req	Q*	AttnG	Soc	P/R/R	N-Resp	I/D	Id+	Asst	Rout	Rsp	Off/SH	?	DrAttn
1;3,30	4	3 75%										1 25%			
1;4,13	22	6 27.3%	4 18.2%	1 4.5%			1 4.5%	7 31.8%						3 13.6%	
1;5,3	36	1 2.7%	3 8.3%	8 22.2%		4 11.1%		16 44.4%	1 2.7%					3 8.3%	
1;5,18	16	8 50%		1 6.2%		2 12.5%		2 12.5%			1 6.2%			2 12.5%	
1;6,7	22	9 40.9%						7 31.5%	4 18.2%		1 4.5%			1 4.5%	
1;6,27	26	5 19.2%	2 7.7%		1 3.8%			10 38.5%	6 23.1%			1 3.8%		1 3.8%	
1;7,17	49	23 46.9%	1 2.0%	1 2.0%		4 8.2%		10 20.4%	2 4.1%	1 2.0%				7 14.3%	
1;8,18	100	25 25%		10 10%	2 2%	1 1%	6 6%	10 10%	5 5%		7 7%	1 1%		33 33%	
1;9,11	81	15 18.5%		7 8.6%	2 2.5%	2 2.5%	2 2.5%	17 21.0%	5 6.1%	2 2.5%	17 21.0%			12 14.8%	
1;10,16	142	57 34.7%	1 0.7%	8 5.4%	1 0.7%	37 25.2%	14 9.5%	13 8.8%	2 1.4%	2 1.4%	2 1.4%	1 0.7%		15 10.2%	
1;11,14	132	80 60.6%		6 4.5%		10 7.6%		21 15.9%				2 1.5%		13 9.8%	
1;11,15	0														
2;0,0	7							2 28.6%	1 14.3%		4 57.1%				
2;0,15	NOT ANALYZED														
2;0,18	17	8 47%					1 5.8%	4 23.5%			2 11.8%	1 5.8%		1 5.8%	
2;2,2	196	112 57.1%			1 0.5%	8 4.1%	10 5.8%	28 14.3%	19 9.7%	6 3.1%	13 6.6%			9 4.6%	
2;3,13	173	91 52.6%	1 0.6%	6 3.5%	1 0.6%	8 4.6%	10 5.8%	9 5.2%	8 4.6%	3 1.7%	14 18.1%	4 2.3%		18 10.4%	
2;4,13	156	46 29.5%		8 5.1%	1 0.6%	6 3.8%	6 3.8%	4 2.5%	3 1.8%	14 9.0%	18 11.5%	20 12.8%	1(?) 0.25%	30 19.2%	
2;7,26	414	183 44.2%	2 0.48%	4 0.97%	1 0.24%	26 6.3%	15 3.6%	11 2.7%	5 1.2%	55 13.3%	12 2.9%	43 10.4%		56 13.5%	

* Early on, Lisa used the form "this" on a few occasions, and her mother always interpreted the utterance as a request for a label, hence a question. The behavior disappeared and Lisa only began asking real questions in the final session.

Child: Lydia

Frequency of illocutionary acts

Age	Total utts w/ Force	Req	Q	AttnG	Soc	P/R/R	N-Resp	I/D	Id+	Asst	Rout	Rsp	Off/SH	?	DrAttn
1:4.8	103	24 23.3%	13 12.6%	9 8.7%		9 8.7%		3 2.9%	1 0.97%	8 7.8%	2 1.9%	1 0.97%	7 6.8%	26 25.2%	
1:5.5	125	12 9.6%	1 0.8%	10 8%	4 3.2%	7 5.6%		15 12%	3 2.4%	21 16.8%	10 8%	1 0.8%	6 4.8%	35 28%	
1:6.7	131	23 17.5%	4 3.0%	3 2.3%	2 1.5%	4 3.0%		19 14.5%	3 2.6%	12 9.2%	10 7.6%	14 10.7%	6 4.6%	31 23.7%	
1:7.18	167	23 13.8%	5 3.0%	5 3.0%	4 2.4%	8 4.8%	2 1.2%	14 8.4%		28 16.8%	20 12%	8 4.8%	4 2.4%	46 27.5%	
1:8.18	260	60 23.1%	16 6.1%	13 5%	4 1.5%	8 3.1%		8 3.1%	1 0.38%	24 9.2%	21 8.1%	26 10%	16 6.1%	63 24.2%	

Child: Brett

Frequency of illocutionary acts

Age	Total utts w/Force	Req	Q	AttnG	Soc	P/R/R	N-Resp	I/D	Id+	Asst	Rout	Rsp	Off/SH	?	DrAttn
1:5;0	6							1 16.7%	5 83.3%						
1:7;11	59	22 37.3%	3 5.1%		6 10.2%	1 1.7%		8 13.6%	6 10.2%	12 20.3%		1 1.9%		1 1.7%	
1:8;10	53	9 17.0%	1 1.3%		2 3.8%			10 18.9%	5 9.4%	5 9.4%	10 18.9%			11 20.8%	
1:9;8	75	16 21.3%	2 2.0%		4 5.3%			14 18.6%	8 10.7%	4 5.3%		1 1.3%	3 4%	24 32%	
1:10;7	96	5 5.2%	2 2.0%	1 1%	3 3%			26 27.1%	9 9.4%	16 16.7%	4 4.2%	5 5.2%	10 10.4%	19 19.8%	
1:11;10	102	10 9.8%	2 2.0%		3 3%			31 29.4%		19 18.6%	4 3.9%	3 3%	1 1%	28 27.4%	
2;0;19	303	5 1.7%	8 2.6%					75 24.7%	7 2.3%	82 27.1%	2 0.7%	24 8.0%	6 2.0%	94 31.0%	

Child: Julie

Frequency of illocutionary acts

Age	Total utts w/ Force	Req	Q	AttnG	Soc	P/R/R	N-Resp	I/D	Id+	Asst	Rout	Rsp	Off/SH	?	Dr-Attn
1;10;17	27	1 3.7%		6 22.2%		8 29.6%					10 37.0%			2 7.4%	
1;1;14	8					8 100%									
1;2;26	5			1 20%		4 80%									
1;3;21	14	1 7.1%		1 7.1%		11 78.6%					1 7.1%				
1;4;26	14			2 14.3%		3 21.4%								9 64.3%	
1;4;28	38	8 21%		1 2.6%		12 31.6%					17 44.7%				
1;6;0	12			6 50%		4 33.3%					2 16.7%				
1;7;27	25	7 28%				1 4%		11 44%	1 4.0%		5 20%				
1;8;16	37	10 27%		2 5.4%		5 13.5%		8 21.6%	2 5.4%		9 24.3%	1 2.7%			
1;9;13	44	15 34.1%		1 2.3%				10 22.3%	5 11.4%		10 22.3%	2 4.5%		1 2.3%	
1;10;13	42	6 14.3%				2 4.8%		10 23.8%	11 26.2%		8 19.0%			5 11.9%	
2;0;19	228	115 50.4%	1 0.4%	12 5.3%	4 1.7%	6 2.6%	9 3.9%	7 3.0%	4 1.7%	5 2.2%	20 8.7%	7 3.0%		38 16.7%	
2;1;23	102	32 31.4%	2 2%	5 4.9%	2 2%	6 5.9%	5 4.9%	12 11.8%	9 8.8%		15 14.7%	9 8.8%		3 2.9%	
2;2;30	225	73 32.4%		50 22.2%		12 5.3%	1 0.4%	21 9.3%	5 2.2%	10 4.4%	12 5.3%	16 7.1%	2 0.9%	23 10.2%	
2;4;5	267	11 4.1%		27 10.1%	5 1.9%	18 6.7%	2 0.75%	15 5.6%	6 2.2%	19 7.1%	24 9.0%	64 24.0%		76 28.5%	

NON-VERBAL

Child: Bonnie

Frequency of illocutionary acts

Age	Total units w/ Force	Req	Q	AttnG	Soc	P/R/R	N-Resp	I/D	Id+	Asst	Rout	Rsp	Off/SH	?	Dr-Attn
1;0;25	33	11 33.3%				1 3%		1 3%			12 36.4%	1 3%	4 12.1%		3 9.0
1;1;25	72	12 16.7%									8 11.1%	1 1.4%	32 44.4%		19 26.4%
1;2;25	52	8 24.2%											5 15.1%	2 6.1%	18 54.5%
1;3;21	52	14 27%									13 25%		7 13.5%	7 13.5%	11 21.2%
1;4;26	47	3 6.4%				1 2.1%	1 2.1%				7 14.9%		21 44.7%	2 4.3%	12 25.5%
1;6;7	47	2 4.2%	2 4.2%						4 8.5%		14 29.8%		10 21.3%	7 14.9%	8 17.0%

References

Andersen, E. S., 1975, "Cups and glasses: Learning that boundaries are vague." *Journal of Child Language*, **2**, 79–103.

1978, "Lexical universals of body part terminology." In J. Greenberg (Ed.), *Universals of human language*, volume 3. Stanford, CA: Stanford University Press, pp. 335–368.

Andersen, E. S., Dunlea, A. and Kekelis, L., 1984, "Blind children's language: resolving some differences." *Journal of Child Language*, **11**, 645–664.

Andersen, E. S. and Kekelis, L., 1982, "Effects of visual impairment on early mother child communication." Boston University Conference on Language Development.

Anglin, J., 1977, *Word, object and concept development*. New York: Norton.

Antinucci, F. and Parisi, D., 1971, "Early language development: a second state." Paper presented at Conference on Present problems in Psycholinguistics, Paris.

1973, "Early language acquisition: a model and some data." C. Ferguson and D. Slobin (eds.), *Studies of child language development*. New York: Holt, Rinehart and Winston, pp. 607–619.

Arlman-Rupp, A. J. L., Van Niekerk de Haan, D., and van de Sandt-Koenderman, M., 1976, "Brown's early stages: some evidence from Dutch." *Journal of Child Language*, **3**, 267–274.

Atkinson, M., 1979, "Prerequisites for reference." In E. Ochs and B. Schieffelin (eds.), *Developmental pragmatics*. New York: Academic Press, pp. 229–250.

Austin, J., 1962, *How to do things with words*. New York; Oxford University Press.

1971, "Performative-constative." In J. R. Searle (ed.), *The philosophy of language*, London: Oxford University Press, pp. 13–22.

Barrett, M. D., 1978, "Lexical development and over-extension in child language." *Journal of Child Language*, **5**, 205–220.

1982, "Distinguishing prototypes: the early acquisition of the meaning of object names." In S. Kuczaj (ed.), *Language Development*, Volume I, *Syntax and Semantics*. Hillsdale NJ: Erlbaum.

1983, "The early acquisition and development of the meanings of action related words." In T. B. Seiler and W. Wannenmacher (eds.), *Conceptual development and the development of word meaning*. Springer–Verlag, pp. 191–209.

Bates, E., 1976, *Language and context*. New York: Academic Press.

1979, (in collaboration with L. Benigni, I. Bretherton, L. Camaioni, and V. Volterra), *The emergence of symbols*. New York: Academic Press.

Bates, E., Camaioni, L., and Volterra, V., 1975, "The acquisition of performatives prior to speech." *Merrill-Palmer Quarterly*, **21**, 205–226.

Bayley, N., 1969, *Bayley Scales of infant development*. New York: Psychological Corporation.

Benedict, H., 1979, "Early lexical development: comprehension and production." *Journal of Child Language*, **16**, 183–200.

Bernstein, D. K., 1978, "Semantic development in congenitally blind children." Unpublished doctoral dissertation, City University of New York.

Bigelow, A., 1982, "Early words of blind children." Paper presented at the International Conference on Infant Studies, Austin, Texas, March 1982.

1983, "Development of the use of sound in the search behavior of infants." *Developmental Psychology*, **19**, 317–321.

1986, "Early words of blind children." *Journal of Child Language*, **14**, 47–56.

Bloom, L., 1970, *Language development: form and function in emerging grammars*. Cambridge MA: MIT Press.

1973, *One word at a time: the use of single word utterances before syntax*. The Hague: Mouton Publishers.

1975, "Language development." In *Review of Child Development Research*, Volume 4, pp. 245–304.

1983, "Tensions in psycholinguistics", Review of *Language acquisition* (Wanner and Gleitman) in *Science*, **220**, 843–844.

Bloom, L., Capatides, J. B., and Tackeff, J., 1981, "Further remarks on interpretive analysis: in response to Christine Howe." *Journal of Child Language*, **8**, 403–412.

Bloom, L., Hood, L., and Lightbown, P., 1974, "Imitation in language development: if, when and why." *Cognitive Psychology*, **6**, 380–420.

Bloom, L. and Lahey, M., 1977, *Language development and language disorders*. New York: John Wiley and Sons.

Bloom, L., Lightbown, P., and Hood, I., 1975, "Structure and variation in child language." *Monographs of the Society for Research in Child Development*, **40**, (Serial No. 160).

Bloom, L., Rocissano, L. and Hood, L., 1976, "Adult–child discourse: developmental interaction between information processing and linguistic knowledge." *Cognitive Psychology*, **8**, 521–522.

Bohannon, J. N., 1986, Review of *Language and Experience*. *Language*, **62**, 446–450.

Bower, T. G. R., 1974, *Development in infancy*. San Francisco: Freeman.

1976, "Repetitive processes in child development." *Scientific American*, **235**, 38–47.

1977a, "Blind babies see with their ears." *New Scientist*, **73**, 255–257.

1977b, "Babies are more important than machines." *New Scientist*, **74**, 712–714.

1977c, *A primer of infant development*. San Francisco: Freeman.

Bowerman, M., 1973, *Early syntactic development: a cross-linguistic study with special reference to Finnish*. Cambridge: Cambridge University Press.

1976, "Semantic factors in the acquisition of rules for word use and sentence construction." In D. Morehead and A. Morehead (eds.), *Normal and deficient child language*, Baltimore: University Park Press, pp. 99–179.

1977, "The structure and origin of semantic categories in the language learning child." Paper prepared for Fundamentals of Symbolism, Symposium No. 74 of the Wenner-Gren Foundation for Anthropological Research, Burg Wartenstein, Austria.

1978, "The acquisition of word meaning: an investigation of some current conflicts." In N. Waterson and C. Snow (eds.), *Development of communication: social and pragmatic factors in language acquisition*, New York: John Wiley and Sons.

1979, "Semantic and syntactic development: a review of what, when and how in language acquisition." In Schiefelbusch (ed.), *Basis of language intervention*, 1, pp. 88–189.

de Boysson-Bardies, B., Sagart, L., and Bacri, N., 1981, "Phonetic analysis of late babbling: a case study of a French child." *Journal of Child Language*, **8**, 511–524.

Braine, M. D. S., 1970, "The acquisition of language in infant and child." In C. E. Reed (ed.), *The learning of language*, New York: Appleton-Century-Crofts, pp. 7–95.

1976, "Children's first word combinations." *Monographs of the Society for Research in Child Development*, **41**.

Braine, M. D. S. and Wells, R. S., 1978, "Case-like categories in children: the actor and some related categories." *Cognitive Psychology*, **10**, 100–122.

Braunwald, S., 1978, "Context, word and meaning: towards a communication analysis of lexical acquisition." In A. Lock (ed.), *Action, gesture and symbol: The emergence of language*, London: Academic Press, pp. 485–528.

Braunwald, S. and Brislin, R., 1979, "The diary method updated." In E. Ochs and B. Schieffelin (eds.), *Developmental pragmatics*, New York: Academic Press.

Brazelton, T. B., 1979, "Evidence of communication in neonatal behavioral assessment." In M. Bullowa (ed.), *Before speech*, London: Cambridge University Press, pp. 79–88.

Brazelton, T. B., Koslowsky, B., and Main, M., 1974, "The origins of reciprocity: the early mother–infant interaction." In M. Lewis and L. A. Rosenblum (eds.), *The effect of the infant on its caregiver*, New York: John Wiley and Sons, pp. 49–76.

Brieland, D. M., 1950, "A comparative study of the speech of blind and sighted children." *Speech Monographs*, **17**, 99–103.

Bronowski, J. and Bellugi, A., 1980, "Language, name and concept'.. In Seboek and Umiker-Seboek (eds.), *Speaking of apes: a critical anthology of two-way communication with man*, New York: Plenum, pp. 103–114.

Brown, R., 1973, *A first language: the early stages*. Cambridge MA: Harvard University Press.

Bruner, J. S., 1974/1975, "From communication to language – a psychological perspective." *Cognition*, **3**, 225–287.

1975, "The ontogenesis of speech acts." *Journal of Child Language*, **2**, 1–19.

1983, *Child's language: learning to use language*. New York: Norton.

Bullowa, M. (ed.), 1979, *Before speech.* London: Cambridge University Press.

Burlingham, D., 1964, "Hearing and its role in the development of the blind." *Psychoanalytic Study of the Child*, **19**, 95–112.

1965, "Some problems of ego development in blind children." *Psychoanalytic Study of the Child*, **20**, 194–208.

1967, "Developmental considerations in the occupations of the blind." *Psychoanalytic Study of the Child*, **22**, 187–198.

Carey, S., 1982, "Semantic development: the state of the art." In E. Wanner and L. Gleitman (eds.), *Language acquisition: the state of the art*. Cambridge: Cambridge University Press, pp. 347–389.

Carolan, R., 1973, "Sensory stimulation and the blind infant." *New Outlook for the Blind*, pp. 119–126.

Carter, A., 1978, "From sensorimotor vocalizations to words: a case study of the evolution of attention-directing communication in the second year." In A. Lock (ed.), *Action, gesture and symbol: the emergence of language*, London: Academic Press.

1979, "Prespeech meaning relations: an outline of one infant's sensorimotor morpheme development." In P. Fletcher and M. Garmen (eds.), *Language acquisition*, London: Cambridge University Press, pp. 93–104.

Chafe, W. L., 1970, *Meaning in the structure of language*. Chicago: University of Chicago Press.

Chamberlain, A. F. and Chamberlain, J., 1904, "Studies of a child." *Ped Sem II*, 264–291.

Chase, Joan B., 1972, *Retrolental fibroplasia and autistic symptomatology*. American Federation for the Blind.

Chiat, S., 1982, "If I were you and you were me: The analysis of pronouns in a pronoun-reversing child." *Journal of Child Language*, **9**, 359–380.

Clark, E. V., 1973, "What's in a word? On the child's acquisition of semantics in his first language." In T. E. Moore (ed.), *Cognitive development and the acquisition of language*, New York: Academic Press, pp. 65–110.

1975, "Knowledge, context and strategy in the acquisition of meaning." In D. P. Dato (ed.), *Georgetown University Round Table on Languages and Linguistics 1975*, Washington, DC: Georgetown University Press, pp. 77–98.

1977a, "Strategies and the mapping problem in first language acquisition." In J. Macnamara (ed.), *Language learning and thought*, New York: Academic Press, pp. 147–168.

1977b, "Universal categories: on the semantics of classifiers and children's early word meanings." In A. Juilland (ed.), *Linguistic studies offered to Joseph Greenberg: on the occasion of his sixtieth birthday*, Saratoga, CA: Anma Libri, pp. 449–462.

Clark, E. V. and Andersen, E. S., 1979, "Spontaneous repairs: awareness in the process of acquiring language." Paper presented at the Symposium on Meta-cognition, SRCD Biennial Meeting, San Francisco.

Clark, H. H. and Clark, E. V., 1977, *Psychology and language*. New York: Harcourt Brace Jovanovich, Inc.

Clark, R., 1974, "Performing without competence." *Journal of Child Language*, **1**, 1–10.

Cohen, L. B. and Strauss, M. S., 1979, "Concept acquisition in the human infant." *Child Development*, **50**, 419–424.

Cole, P. and Morgan, J. (eds.), 1975, *Syntax and semantics*, Volume 3: *Speech acts*. New York: Academic Press.

Coulmas, F., 1979, "On the sociolinguistic relevance of routine speech." *Journal of Pragmatics*, 239–266.

Cratty, B. J., 1971, *Movement and spatial awareness in blind children and youth*. Philadelphia: Lea and Febiger.

Cratty, B. J. and Sams, T. A., *The body image of blind children*. (Research Report) American Federation for the Blind, July, 1968.

Cromer, R. F., 1981, "Reconceptualizing language acquisition and cognitive development." In R. L. Schiefelbusch and D. D. Bricker (eds.), *Early language: acquisition and intervention*, Baltimore: University Park Press, pp. 51–137.

Cross, T., Johnson-Morris, J., and Nienhuys, T., 1980, "Lexical feedback and maternal speech: comparisons of mothers addressing hearing and hearing impaired children." *First Language*, **1**, 163–189.

Cruse, D. A., 1973, "Some thoughts on agentivity." *Journal of Linguistics*, **9**, 11–23.

Crystal, D., 1979, "Prosodic development." In P. Fletcher and M. Garmen (eds.), *Language acquisition*, Cambridge: Cambridge University Press, pp. 33–48.

Cutsforth, T., 1932, "The unreality of words to the blind." *Teachers Forum*, **4**, 86–89.

1951, *The blind in school and society: a psychological study*. New York: American Foundation for the Blind.

Demott, R. M., 1972, "Verbalism and affective meaning for blind, severally visually impaired and normally sighted children." *New Outlook for the Blind*, January.

Department of Health and Social Security (G.B.), 1972, "The incidence and causes of blindness in England and Wales 1963–1968." Reports on Public Health and Medical Subjects No. 128. Department of Health and Social Security. London: Her Majesty's Stationary Office.

Diebold, A. R., 1968, "The consequences of early bilingualism in cognitive development and personality formation." In E. Norbeck (ed.), *The study of personality*, New York: Holt, Rinehart and Winston.

Doll, F. A., 1947, *The Vineland social maturity scale: manual of directions*, New Jersey: Educational Testing Bureau.

1953, *Measurement of social competence: a manual for the Vineland social maturity scale*. New Jersey: Educational Testing Bureau.

Dore, J., 1974, "A pragmatic description of early language development." *Journal of Psycholinguistic Research*, **4**, 343–350.

1975, "Holophrases, speech acts, and language universals." *Journal of Child Language*, **2**, 21–40.

1978, "Conditions for the acquisition of speech acts." In I. Markova (ed.), *The social context of language*, New York: John Wiley and Sons, pp. 87–112.

1979, "Conversational acts and the acquisition of language." In E. Ochs and B. Schieffelin (eds.), *Developmental pragmatics*, New York: Academic Press, pp. 339–362.

Dore, J., Franklin, M. B., Miller, R. T., and Ramer, A. L. H., 1975, "Transitional phenomena in early language acquisition." *Journal of Child Language*, **3**, 13–28.

Dunlea, A., 1982, "The role of visual information in the emergence of meaning: a comparison of blind and sighted children." Unpublished doctoral dissertation, University of Southern California.

1984, "The relation between concept formation and semantic roles: some evidence from the blind." In L. Feagans, C. Garvey and R. Golinkoff (eds.), *The origins and growth of communication*, Norwood, NJ: Ablex, pp. 224–244.

Dunn, J. B. and Richards, M. P. M., 1977, "Observations of the developing relationship between mother and baby in the neonatal period." In H. R. Schaffer (ed.), *Studies in mother–infant interaction*, London: Academic Press, pp. 427–456.

Eaves, L. and Klonoff, H., 1970, "Comparison of blind and sighted children on an actual and performance test." *Exceptional Children*, **37**, 269–279.

Edwards, D., 1973, "Sensory-motor intelligence and semantic relations in early child grammar." *Cognition*, **2**, 395–434.

Eichel, V. J., "A taxonomy for mannerisms of blind children." *Journal of Visual Impairment and Blindness*, **73**.

Ewart, A. and Carp, F., 1962, "Recognition of tactual form by sighted and blind subjects." *American Journal of Psychology*, **76**, 488–491.

Fay, W. H., 1973, "On the echolalia of blind and of the autistic child." *Journal of Speech and Hearing Disorders*, **38**, 478–488.

Feldman, H., Goldin-Meadow, S., and Gleitman, L., 1978, "Beyond Herodotus: the creation of language by linguistically deprived deaf children." In A. Lock (ed.), *Action, gesture and symbol: The emergence of language*, London: Academic Press, pp. 351–414.

Ferguson, C. and Slobin, D. (eds.), 1973, *Studies of child language development*. New development in the child." *Papers and reports on Child Language Development*, **11**, Stanford University.

Ferguson, C. and Slobin, D. (eds.), 1973, *Studies of child language development*. New York: Holt, Rinehart and Winston.

Ferrier, C. J., 1978, "Some observations of error in context." In N. Waterson and C. Snow (eds.), *The development of communication*, New York: John Wiley and Sons, pp. 301–309.

Filmore, C. J., 1968, "The case for case." In E. Bach and R. T. Harms (eds.), *Universals in linguistic theory*, New York: Holt, Rinehart and Winston.

Fodor, J., Garrett, M., Walker, E., and Parkes, C., 1982, "Against definitions." *Cognition*, **8**, 263–367.

Fogel, A., 1977, "Temporal organization in mother–infant face-to-face interaction." In H. R. Schaffer (ed.), *Studies in mother–infant interaction*, London: Academic Press, pp. 119–151.

Fouts, R., 1974, "Language: origins, definitions and chimpanzees." *Journal of Human Evolution*, **3**, 475–482.

Fraiberg, S., 1968, "Parallel and divergent patterns in blind and sighted infants." *Psychoanalytic Study of the Child*, **23**, 264–300.

1971, "Intervention in infancy: a program for blind infants." *Journal of the American Academy of Child Psychiatry*, **10**, 381–405.

1974a, "Blind infants and their mothers: an examination of the sight system." In M. Lewis and L. Rosenbaum (eds.), *The effect of the infant on its caregiver*, New York: John Wiley and Sons, pp. 215–232.

1974b, "The clinical dimension of baby games." *Journal of the American Academy of Child Psychiatry*, **13**, 202–220.

1977, *Insights from the blind*. New York: Basic Books.

Fraiberg, S. and Adelson, E., 1973, "Self-representation in language and play: observations of blind children." *The Psychoanalytic Quarterly*, **42**, 539–562.

1975, "Self-representation in language and play: observation of blind children." In E. Lenneberg and E. Lenneberg (eds.), *Foundations of language: a multidisciplinary approach*, **2**, New York: Academic Press, pp. 177–192.

1977, "Self-representation in language and play." In S. Fraiberg (ed.), *Insights from the blind*, New York: Basic Books, pp. 248–270.

Fraiberg, S. and Freedman, D., 1964, "Studies in the ego development of the congenitally blind child." *Psychoanalytic Study of the Child*, **19**, 113–169.

Fraiberg, S., Siegel, B., and Gibson, R., 1966, "The role of sound in the search behavior of a blind infant." *Psychoanalytic Study of the Child*, **21**, 327–357.

Fraiberg, S., Smith, M., and Adelson, E., 1969, "An educational program for blind infants." *Journal of Special Education*, **3**, 121–142.

Freedman, D. G., 1964, "Smiling in blind infants and the issues of innate versus acquired." *Journal of Psychology and Psychiatry and Allied Disciplines*, **5**, 171–184.

1971, "Congenital and perinatal sensory deprivation: Some Studies in early development." *American Journal of Psychiatry*, **127**, 115–121.

Frege, G., 1962, "Sense and reference." *Philosophical writings.* (P. T. Geach and M. Black, trans.), Oxford: Blackwell.

Gentner, D., 1978, "What looks like a jiggy but acts like a bimbo? A study of early word meaning using artificial objects." *Papers and Reports on Child Language Development,* **15,** Stanford University, pp. 1–6.

Goldberg, S., 1977, "Social competence in infancy: a model of parent–infant interaction." *Merrill-Palmer Quarterly,* **23,** 163–177.

Goldin-Meadow, S. and Mylander, C., 1983, "Gestural communication in deaf children: noneffect of parental input on language development." *Science,* **221,** 372–373.

1984, "Gestural communication in deaf children: the effects and non-effects of parental input on early language development." *Monographs of the Society For Research In Child Development,* **49.**

Golinkoff, R. M., 1981, "The case for semantic relations: evidence from the verbal and nonverbal domains." *Journal of Child Language,* **8,** 413–438.

Golinkoff, R. M. and Harding, C. G., 1978, "Infants' perceptions of filmed events portraying case role concepts." Paper presented at the International Conference on Infant Studies, Rhode Island.

Gopnik, A., 1984, "The acquisition of 'gone' and the development of the object concept." *Journal of Child Language,* **11,** 273–292.

Gopnik, A. and Meltzoff, A., 1985a, "Words, plans, things and locations: interactions between semantic and cognitive development in the one word stage." In S. Kuczaj and M. Barrett (eds.), *The development of word meaning,* New York: Springer-Verlag, pp. 199–223.

1985b, "From people to plans to objects: changes in the meaning of early words and their relation to cognitive development." *Journal of Pragmatics,* **9,** 495–512.

1987. "The development of categorization in the second year and its relation to other cognitive and linguistic developments." *Child Development,* **58,** 1523–1531.

Gordon, D. and Lakoff, G., 1975, "Conversational postulates." In P. Cole and J. Morgan (eds.), *Syntax and semantics,* Vol. 3: *Speech acts,* New York: Seminar Press, pp. 83–105.

Gottesman, M., 1971, "A comparative study of Piaget's developmental schema of sighted children with that of a group of blind children." *Child Development,* **42,** 573–580.

1976, "Stage development of blind children: a Piagetian view." *New Outlook for the Blind,* **59,** 157–162.

Gratch, G., 1975, "Recent studies based on Piaget's view of object concept development." In L. B. Cohen and P. Salapatek (eds.), *Infant Perception,* **2,** New York: Academic Press.

Greenfield, P. M., 1978, "Informativeness, presupposition, and semantic choice in single word utterances." In N. Waterson and C. Snow (eds.), *Development of communication: social and pragmatic factors in language acquisition,* London: Wiley and Sons.

1979, "The role of perceptual uncertainty in the transition to language." Paper Presented in a symposium on the transition from sensorimotor to linguistic communication at the Biennial Meeting of the Society for Research in Child Development. San Francisco, March 1979.

1980a, "Going beyond information theory to explain early word choice: a reply to Roy Pea." *Journal of Child Language,* **7,** 217–221.

1980b, "Toward an operational and logical analysis of intentionality: the use of discourse in early child language." In D. R. Olson (ed.), *The social foundations of language and thought: essays in honor of Jerome S. Bruner*, New York: Norton, pp. 254–279.

Greenfield, P. M. and Dent, C. H., 1979, "A developmental study of the communication of meaning: the role of uncertainty and information." In P. French (ed.), *The development of meaning*, Pedolinguistic Series, Japan: Bunka Hoyron Press.

Greenfield, P. M. and Savage-Rumbaugh, S., 1984, "Perceived variability and symbol use: a common language–cognition interface in children and chimpanzees." *Journal of Comparative Psychology*, **96**, 201–218.

Greenfield, P. M. and Smith, J. H., 1976, *The structure of communication in early language development*. New York: Academic Press.

Greenfield, P. M. and Zukow, P., 1978, "Why do children say what they say when they say it?: an experimental approach to the psychogenesis of presupposition." In K. Nelson (ed.), *Children's language*, **1**, New York: Gardner Press.

Grice, H. P., 1957, "Meaning." *Philosophical Review*, **66**, 377–388.

1975, "Logic and conversation." In P. Cole and J. Morgan (eds.), *Syntax and semantics*, Vol. 3: *Speech acts*, New York: Seminar Press, pp. 41–58.

Griffiths, R. and Ritro, E., 1967, "Echolalia: concerning the dynamics of the syndrome." *Journal of American Academy of Child Psychiatry*, **6**, 184–193.

Gruaber, H. E. and Voneche, J. J., 1977, *The essential Piaget*, New York: Basic Books.

Gruber, J. S., 1967, "Topicalization in child language." *Foundations of Language*, **3**, 37–65.

1975, "The performative–constative transition in child language." *Foundations of Language*, **12**, 513–527.

Guillaume, P., 1927, *Imitation in children*. (E. P. Halperim, trans.), Chicago: University of Chicago Press.

1978, "First stages of sentence formation in children's speech." Reprinted in L. Bloom (ed.), *Readings in language development*, New York: John Wiley and Sons, pp. 131–148.

Halliday, M., 1975, *Learning how to mean*. London: Edward Arnold.

Hatfield, E. M., 1972, "Blindness in infants and young children." *Sight-Saving Review*, **42**, 69–89.

1975, "Why are they blind?" *Sight Saving Review*, **45**, 3–22.

Howe, C. J., 1976, "The meaning of two-word utterances in the speech of young children." *Journal of Child Language*, **3**, 29–48.

1981, "Interpretive analysis and role semantics: a ten-year mesalliance?" *Journal of Child Language*, **8**, 439–456.

Howlin, P., 1980, "The home treatment of autistic children." In L. A. Hersov, M. Berger and A. R. Nicol (eds.), *Language and language disorders in childhood*, Oxford: Pergamon Press, pp. 115–145.

Huttenlocher, J., 1974, "The origins of language comprehension." In R. G. Solso (ed.), *Theories of cognitive psychology*, Potomac, Maryland: Erlbaum, pp. 331–368.

Huttenlocher, J. and Higgins, E. T., 1978, "Issues in the study of symbolic development." In W. A. Collins, (ed.) *Minnesota Symposium on Child Psychology*, Volume II, Hillsdale, NJ: Erlbaum.

Huttenlocher, J., Smiley, P., and Charney, R., 1983, "The emergence of action categories in the child: evidence from verb meanings." *Psychology Review*, **90**, 72–93.

Huttenlocher, J., Smiley, P. and Ratner, H., 1983, "What do word meanings reveal about conceptual development?" In T. B. Seiler and W. Wannenmacher (eds.),

Conceptual development and the development of word meaning, Springer-Verlag, pp. 210–233.

Inhelder, B. and Karmiloff-Smith, A., 1978, "Thought and language." In B. Presseisen, D. Goldstein and M. Appel (eds.), *Topics in cognitive development*, Volume 2, (Language and Operational Thought), New York: Plenum Press, pp. 3–11.

Inhelder, B. and Piaget, J., 1964, *The early growth of logic in the child*. New York: Norton.

Jan, J., Freeman, R., and Scott, E. (eds.), 1977, *Visual impairment in children and adolescents*, New York: Grune and Stratton.

Kaye, K., 1979, "Thickening thin data: the maternal role in developing communication and language." In M. Bullowa (ed.), *Before speech*, Cambridge: Cambridge University Press, pp. 191–206.

Keeler, W. R., 1958, "Autistic patterns and defective communication in blind children with R.L.F." In P. H. Hoch and J. Zubin (eds.), *Psychopathology of communication*, New York: Grune and Stratton.

Keenan, E. and Ochs, E. 1974, "Conversational competence in children." *Journal of Child Language*, **1**, 163–185.

1977, "Making it last: uses of repetition in children's discourse." In S. Ervin-Tripp and C. Mitchell-Kernan (eds.), *Child discourse*, New York: Academic Press.

Kekelis, L. S., 1981, "Mothers' input to blind children." Unpublished master's thesis, University of Southern California.

Kekelis, L. and Andersen, E., 1984, "Family communication styles and language development." *Journal of Visual Impairment and Blindness*, **78**, 54–65.

Kernan, K., 1969, "The acquisition of language by Samoan children." Unpublished doctoral dissertation, University of California, Berkeley.

Kessen, W. and Nelson, K., 1978, "What the child brings to language." In B. Presseisen, D. Goldstein and M. Appel (eds.), *Topics in cognitive development*, **2** (Language and Operational Thought), New York: Plenum Press, pp. 17–30.

Kidwell, A. and Greer, P., 1973, *Sites, perception and the nonvisual experience: designing and manufacturing mobility maps*. New York: American Foundation for the Blind.

Klaus, H. M. and Kennel, J. H., 1970, "Human maternal behavior at first contact with her young." *Pediatrics*, **46**, 187–192.

Klima, E. and Bellugi, U., 1979, *The signs of language*. Cambridge MA: Harvard University Press.

Knight, J. J., 1972, "Mannerisms in the congenitally blind child." *New Outlook for the Blind*, Reprinted for the American Foundation for the Blind, pp. 297–302.

Kohler, I., 1964, "Orientation by aural clues." *Research Bulletin No. 4*, New York: American Foundation for the Blind, pp. 14–53.

Kuczaj, S., 1982, "Young children's overextensions of object words in comprehension and/or production: support for prototype theory of early meaning." *First Language*, **3**, 93–105.

Kuczaj, S. and Barrett, M. D. (eds.), 1986, *The development of word meaning: progress in cognitive development research*. New York: Springer–Verlag.

Labov, W. and Labov, T., 1974, "The grammar of *cat* and *mama*." Paper presented at the 49th Annual Meeting of the Linguistic Society of American, New York.

Lairy, G. C. and Harrison-Covello, A., 1973, 'The blind child and his parents: congenital visual defect and the repercussion of family attitudes on the early development of the child." Reprinted for the American Foundation for the Blind, *Research Bulletin*, no. 25.

Landau, B., 1981, "Language of the blind is not meaningless." Paper presented at the Symposium on Language and Communication of the Blind Child, University of Tübingen, West Germany.

1983, "Blind children's language is not 'Meaningless'." In A. Mills (ed.), *Language acquisition in the blind child*, London: Croom Helm.

Landau, B. and Gleitman, L., 1985, *Language and experience: evidence from the blind child.* Cambridge MA: Harvard University Press.

Landau, B., Gleitman, H., and Spelke, E. S., 1984, "Spatial knowledge in a young blind child." *Cognition*, **16**, 225–230.

Leonard, L. B., 1976, *Meaning in child language.* New York: Grune and Stratton.

Leopold, W. F., 1939–1949, *Speech development of a bilingual child* (4 vols.). Evanston IL: North-western University Press.

Lewis, D. K., 1900, *Convention: a philosophical study.* Cambridge MA: Harvard University Press.

Lewis, M. and Rosenblum, L. A. (eds.), 1974, *The effect of the infant on its caregiver.* New York: John Wiley & Sons.

Limber, J., 1980, "Language in child and chimp?" In T. Seboek and J. Umiker-Seboek (eds.), *Speaking of apes: a critical anthology of two-way communication with man*, New York: Plenum Press, pp. 197–220.

Lock, A., 1980, *The guided reinvention of language.* London: Academic Press.

(ed.), 1978, *Action, gesture and symbol: the emergence of language.* London: Academic Press.

Lord, C., 1974, "Variations in the pattern of acquisition of negation." *Papers and Reports on Child Language Developments*, **8**, 78–86.

Lowenfeld, B., 1956, *Our blind children: growing and learning from them.* Springfield, IL: C. C. Thomas.

1974, "History of the education of visually handicapped children." In B. Lowenfeld (ed.), *The visually handicapped child in school*, London: Constable.

Lyons, J., 1977, *Semantics* (2 vols.), Cambridge: Cambridge University Press.

McCune-Nicolich, L., 1981, "The cognitive bases of relational words in the single word period." *Journal of Child Language*, **8**, 15–34.

McGuire, L. and Meyers, C., 1971, "Early personality in the congenitally blind child." *New Outlook for the Blind*, **65**, 137–143.

McNeil, D., 1979, *The conceptual basis of language.* Hillsdale NJ: Erlbaum.

McShane, J., 1979, "The development of naming." *Linguistics*, **17**, 879–905.

Macnamara, J., 1972, "Cognitive basis of language learning in infants." *Psychological Review*, **79**, 485–491.

(ed.), 1977, *Language learning and thought.* New York: Academic Press.

MacWhinney, B., 1978, "The acquisition of morphophonology." *Monographs of the Society for Research in Child Development*, **43**.

Markova, I. (ed.), 1978, "The social context of language." New York: John Wiley and Sons.

Masur, E. F., 1982, "Mother's responses to infant's object-related gestures: influences on lexical development." *Journal of Child Language*, **9**, 23–30.

Maxfield, K. E., 1936, *The spoken language of the blind preschool child: a study of method.* Archives of Psychology No. 201.

Maxfield, K. E. and Buchholz, S., 1900, *A social maturity scale for blind preschool children: a guide to its use.* New York: American Foundation for the Blind.

Maxfield, K. E. and Fjeld, H. A., 1942, "The social maturity of the visually handicapped preschool child." *Child Development*, **13**, 1–27.

Meltzoff, A. and Moore, M. K., 1977, "Imitation of facial and manual gestures by human neonates." *Science*, **198**, 75–78.

Menn, L., 1976, "Pattern, control and contrast in beginning speech: a case study in the development of word form and word function." Unpublished doctoral dissertation, University of Illinois.

Menyuk, P., 1974, "Early development of receptive language: from babbling to words." In R. Schiefelbusch and L. Lloyd (eds.) *Language perspectives: acquisition, retardation, and intervention*, Baltimore: University Park Press.

Menyuk, P. and Menn, L., 1979, "Early strategies for the perception and production of words and sounds." In P. Fletcher and M. Garmen (eds.), *Language acquisition*, London: Cambridge University Press, pp. 49–70.

Mervis, C. B., Catlin, J., and Rosch, E., 1975, "Development of the structure of color categories." *Developmental Psychology*, **11**, 54–60.

Miller, G. A., 1963, *Language and communication* (Revised Edition). New York: McGraw-Hill Book Co.

Miller, M., 1979, *The logic of language development in early childhood*. New York: Springer–Verlag.

Miller, W. and Ervin, S., 1964, "The development of grammar in child language." In U. Bellugi and R. Brown (eds.), *The acquisition of language, Monographs of the Society for Research in Child Development*, **29**, 9–33.

Mills, A., 1983a, *Language Acquisition in the Blind Child*. London: Croom-Helm.

    1983b, "Acquisition of speech sounds in the visually handicapped child." In A. Mills (ed.), *Language acquisition in the blind child*, London: Croom-Helm.

    1987, Review of *Language and experience* (B. Landau and L. Gleitman). *Journal of Child Language*, **14**, 397–409.

Mills, A. and Thiem, R., 1980, "Auditory-visual fusions and illusions in speech perception." *Linguistische Berichte*, **68/80**, 85–108.

Miner, L. E., 1963, "A study of the incidence of speech deviations among visually handicapped children." *New Outlook for the Blind*, **57**, 10–14.

Mulford, R., 1980, "Talking without seeing: some problems of semantic development in blind children." Unpublished doctoral dissertation, Stanford University.

    1983, "Referential development in blind children." In A. Mills (ed.), *Language acquisition in the blind child*, London: Croom Helm, pp. 89–107.

    1986, "First words of the blind child." In M. D. Smith and J. L. Locke (eds.), *The emergent lexicon: the child's development of a linguistic vocabulary*, New York: Academic Press.

Nelson, K. 1973a, "Structure and strategy in learning to Talk." *Monographs of the Society for Research in Child Development*, **38** (Serial no. 149).

    1973b, "Some evidence for the cognitive primacy of categorization and its functional basis." *Merrill-Palmer Quarterly*, **19**, 21–39.

    1974, "Concept, word and sentence: Inter-relations in acquisition and development." *Psychology Review*, **81**, 267–285.

    1977, "The conceptual basis for naming." In J. Macnamara (ed.), *Language learning and thought*. New York: Academic Press, pp. 117–133.

Nelson, K., 1979, "Features, contrasts and the FCH: some comments on Barrett's lexical development hypothesis." *Journal of Child Language*, **6**, 139–146.

    1983, "The conceptual basis for language." In B. Seiler and W. Wannenmacher (eds.), *Conceptual development and the development of word meaning*, Springer–Verlag, pp. 173–188.

Nelson, K., Rescorla, L., Gruendal, J., and Benedict, H., 1979, "Early lexicons: what do they mean?" *Child Development*, **49**, 960–968.

Newport, E., 1979, "Constraints on structure: evidence from American sign language and language learning." In W. A. Collins (ed.), *Minnesota Symposium on Child Psychology*, **14**, Hillsdale NJ: Lawrence Erlbaum.

Nice, M. M., 1915, "The development of a child's vocabulary in relation to environment." *Pedagogical Seminary*, **22**, 35–64.

Nicolich, L. M., 1977, "Beyond sensorimotor intelligence: assessment of symbolic maturity through analysis of pretend play." *Merrill-Palmer Quarterly*, **23**, 89–99.

Ninio, A. and Bruner, J., 1978, "The achievement and antecedents of labelling." *Journal of Child Language*, **5**, 1–16.

Nolan, C., 1960, "On the unreality of words to the blind." *New Outlook for the Blind*, **54**, 100–102.

Norris, M., Spaulding, P. J., and Brodie, F., 1957, *Blindness in children*. Chicago: University of Chicago Press.

Ochs, E., 1979, "Transcription as theory." In E. Ochs and B. Schieffelin, (eds.), *Developmental pragmatics*, New York: Academic Press, pp. 43–72.

Ochs, E., Schieffelin, B., and Platt, M., 1979, "Propositions across utterances and speakers." In E. Ochs and B. Schieffelin (eds.), *Developmental pragmatics*, New York: Academic Press, pp. 251–268.

Patterson, F., 1977, "The gestures of a gorilla: sign language acquisition in another pongid species." In D. Hamburg, J. Goodall and R. McCown (eds.), *Perspectives on human evolution*, Menlo Park CA: Benjamin.

Pechman, T. and Deutsch, W., 1980, "From gesture to word and gesture." *Papers and Reports on Child Language Development*, **19**, Stanford University, pp. 113–120.

Pediatric Annals, 1977, "Pediatric ophthalmology I," January, vol. 6, no. 1, and "Pediatric ophthalmology II," February, vol. 6, no. 2.

Peters, A., 1974, "The beginnings of speech." *Stanford Papers and Reports in Child Language Development*, **8**, pp. 26–32.

1977, "Language learning strategies." *Language*, **53**, 560–573.

1980, "The units of language acquisition." *Working Papers on Lexicon*, **12**, University of Hawaii, pp. 1–72.

1983, *The units of language acquisition*. Cambridge: Cambridge University Press.

1985, "Routines as loci for language development." Paper presented at Boston University, October.

Piaget, J., 1926, *The language and thought of the child*. London: Routledge and Kegan Paul.

1927, "The first year of life of the child." Reprinted in H. Gruber and J. Voneche (eds.), *The essential Piaget*, New York: Basic Books, pp. 198–214.

1951, *The child's conception of the world*. London: Routledge and Kegan Paul.

1952a, *The language and thought of the child*. London: Routledge and Kegan Paul.

1952b, *The origins of intelligence in children*. New York: International Universities Press.

1955, *The construction of reality in the child*. London: Routledge and Kegan Paul.

1962, *Play, dreams and imitation in childhood*. New York: W. W. Norton and Company, Inc.

Piaget, J. and Inhelder, B., 1969, *The psychology of the child*. New York: Basic Books.

Pitman, D. J., 1965, "The musical ability of blind children." *Research Bulletin, No. 11*, New York: American Foundation for the Blind, pp. 63–79.

Premach, D., 1976, *Intelligence in ape and man.* Hillsdale NJ: Lawrence Erlbaum.

Press, M. L., 1974, "Semantic features in lexical acquisition." *Papers and Reports on Child Language Development*, **8**, Stanford University, pp. 129–141.

Pylyshyn, Z., 1977, "What does it take to bootstrap a language?" In J. Macnamara (ed.), *Language learning and thought*, New York: Academic Press, pp. 37–46.

Ramer, A., 1976, "Syntactic styles in emerging language." *Journal of Child Language*, **3**, 49–62.

Reibel, D. A., Mills, A. E., and Thiem, R., 1979, "Die Rolle der visuellen Information beim Spracherwerb." Unpublished research proposal, Department of English Philology, University of Tübingen.

Rescorla, L., 1980, "Overextension in early language development." *Journal of Child Language*, **7**, 321–335.

1981, "Category development in early language." *Journal of Child Language*, **8**, 225–238.

Retherford, K. A., Schwartz, B. C., and Chapman, R. S., 1981, "Semantic roles and residual grammatical categories in mother and child speech: who tunes in to whom?" *Journal of child Language*, **8**, 583–608.

Reynell, J., 1979, *Manual for the Reynell–Zinkin scales: developmental scales for young visually handicapped children, Part 1, Mental development.* Windsor, Berks.: NFER Publishing Company, Ltd.

Richards, M. P. M. (ed.), 1974, *The integration of a child into a social world.* London: Cambridge University Press.

Riciutti, H., 1965, "Object grouping and selective ordering behavior in infants 12–24 months old." *Merrill–Palmer Quarterly*, **11**, 129–148.

Robinson, G. C., 1977, "Causes, ocular disorders, associated handicaps, and incidence and prevalence of blindness in childhood." In J. Jan, R. Freeman and E. Scott (eds.), *Visual impairment in children and adolescents*, New York: Grune and Stratton.

Robson, K. S. and Moss, H. A., 1970, "Patterns and determinants of maternal attachment." *Journal of Pediatrics*, **77**, 976–985.

Rogdon, M. M., 1977, "Situation and meaning in one-and-two-word utterances: observations on Howe's 'The meanings of two-word utterances in the speech of young children'." *Journal of Child Language*, **4**, 111–114.

Rosch, E., 1973, "On the internal structure of perceptual and semantic categories." In T. E. Moore (ed.), *Cognitive development and the acquisition of language*, New York: Academic Press, pp. 111–144.

1975a, "Cognitive reference points." *Cognitive Psychology*, **7**, 532–605.

1975b, "Cognitive representations of semantic categories." *Journal of Experimental Psychology: General*, **104**, 192–233.

1977, "Human categorization." In N. Warren, (ed.), *Advances in cross-cultural psychology*, **1**, New York: Academic Press.

1978, "Principles of categorization." In E. Rosch and B. Lloyd (eds.), *Cognition and categorization.* Hillsdale NJ: Lawrence Erlbaum.

Rosch, E. and Mervis, C. B., 1975, "Family Resemblances: studies in the internal structure of categories." *Cognitive Psychology*, **7**, 573–605.

Rosch, E., Mervis, C. B., Gray, W., Johnson, D., and Boyes-Braem, P., 1976, "Basic objects in natural categories." *Cognitive Psychology*, **8**, 382–439.

Rosch, E., Simpson, C., and Miller, R. S., 1976, "Structural bases of typicality effects." *Journal of Experimental Psychology: Human Perception and Performance*, **2**, 491–502.

Rosenblatt, D., 1975, "Learning how to mean: the development of representation in play and language." Paper presented at the Conference on the Biology of Play, Farnham, England.

Rowe, E. M., 1958, *Speech problems of blind children*. New York: American Foundation for the Blind.

Rowland, C., 1980, "Communicative strategies of visually impaired infants and their mothers." Unpublished doctoral dissertation, University of Oklahoma.

1983, "Patterns of interaction between three blind infants and their mothers." In A. Mills, (ed.), *Language acquisition in the blind child*, London: Croom Helm, pp. 114–132.

Rumbaugh, D., 1980, "Language behavior of apes." In T. Seboek and J. Umiker-Seboek, (eds.), *Speaking of apes: a critical anthology of two-way communication with man*, New York: Plenum Press, pp. 231–260.

Ryan, J., 1974, "Early language development." In M. P. M. Richards, (ed.), pp. 185–214.

Sachet, G., 1979, *Observing behavior*, Part II. Baltimore: University Park Press.

Savage-Rumbaugh, S., 1986, *Ape language: from conditioned response to symbol*. Oxford University Press.

Schaffer, H. R. (ed.), 1977, *Studies in mother–infant interaction*. New York: Academic Press.

Schiffer, S., 1972, *Meaning*, London: Oxford University Press.

Schlesinger, I. M., 1971, "The production of utterances and language acquisition." In D. Slobin, (ed.), *The ontogenesis of grammar*, New York: Academic Press, pp. 63–101.

1974, "Relational concepts underlying language." In R. L. Schiefelbusch and L. L. Lloyd, (eds.), *Language perspectives–acquisition, retardation and intervention*, Baltimore: University Park Press, pp. 129–151.

Scollon, R., 1976, *Conversations with a one year old*. Honolulu: University of Hawaii Press.

1979, "A real early stage: an unzippered condensation of a dissertation on child language." In E. Ochs and R. Schieffelin (eds.), *Developmental pragmatics*, pp. 215–228.

Scott, E. P., Jan, J. E., and Freeman, R. D., 1978, *Can't your child see?* Baltimore: University Park Press.

Searle, J. R., 1969, *Speech acts: an essay in the philosophy of language*. Cambridge: Cambridge University Press.

1975, "A taxonomy of illocutionary acts." In K. Gundersen, (ed.), *Minnesota studies in the philosophy of language*, Minneapolis: University of Minnesota Press, pp. 344–369.

(ed.), 1971, *The philosophy of language*. London: Oxford University Press.

Seboek, T. and Umiker-Seboek, J., 1980, *Speaking of apes: a critical anthology of two-way communication with man*. New York: Plenum Press.

Shatz, M., 1974, "The comprehension of indirect directives: can two-year-olds shut the door?" Paper presented at the summer meeting, Linguistic Society of America, Amherst MA.

1978, "On the development of communicative understandings." *Cognitive Psychology*, **10**, 271–301.

Sinclair, H. J., 1978, "The relevance of Piaget's early work for a semantic approach to Language Acquisition." In B. Presseisen, D. Goldstein, and M. Appel (eds.),

Topics in cognitive development, Vol. 2, (Language and Operational Thought), New York: Plenum Press, pp. 11–16.

Sinclair-de-Zwart, H., 1973, "Language acquisition and cognitive development." In T. E. Moore, (ed.), *Cognitive development and the acquisition of language*, New York: Academic Press, pp. 9–25.

Slobin, D. I., 1971, *The ontogenesis of grammar*, New York: Academic Press.

1973, "Cognitive prerequisites for the development of grammar." In C. A. Ferguson and D. I. Slobin (eds.), *Studies of child language development*, New York: Holt, Rinehart and Winston, pp. 175–276.

1981, "The origins of grammatical encoding of events." In W. Deutsch (ed.), *The child's construction of language*.

Smith, M. D. and Lock, J. L. (eds.), 1986, *The emergent lexicon: the child's development of a linguistic vocabulary*. New York: Academic Press.

Smith, N. V., 1973, *The acquisition of phonology: a case study*. Cambridge: Cambridge University Press.

Snow, C., 1977, "The development of conversation between mothers and babies." *Journal of Child Language*, **4**, 1–22.

1981, "The uses of imitation." *Journal of Child Language*, **8**, 205–217.

1984, "Rejoinder." In L. Feagans, C. Garvey, and R. Golinkoff (eds.), *The origins and growth of communication*, Norwood NJ: Ablex.

Stampe, D. W., 1975, "Meaning and truth in the theory of speech acts." In P. Cole and J. Morgan, (eds.), pp. 1–38.

Starkey, D., 1981, "The origins of concept formation: object sorting and object preference in early infancy." *Child Development*, **52**, 489–497.

Stern, C. and Stern, W., 1928, *Die Kindersprache: eine psychologische und sprachtheoretische Untersuchung*. Liepzig: Barth.

Stern, D., 1974, "Mother and infant at play: the dyadic interaction involving facial, vocal and gaze behaviors." In M. Lewis and L. A. Rosenblum, (eds.), *The effect of the infant on its caregiver*, New York: John Wiley and Sons, pp. 187–213.

1977, *The first relationship: infant and mother*. Cambridge MA: Harvard University Press.

Stern, D. and Wasserman, G., 1979, "Intonation contours as units of information in maternal speech to pre-linguistic infants." Paper presented at the Society for Research in Child Development, Biennial Meeting, San Francisco, March.

Stinchfield-Hawk, S., 1944, "Moto-kinaesthetic speech training applied to visually handicapped children." *Outlook for the Blind*, **38**, 4–8.

Strawson, P. F., 1971, "Intention and convention in speech acts." In J. R. Searle, (ed.), *The philosophy of language*, London: Oxford University Press, pp. 23–39.

Sugarman, S., 1973, "A description of communicative development in the pre-language child." Unpublished honors paper, Hampshire College.

1983, *Children's early thought: developments in classification*, Cambridge: Cambridge University Press.

Swallow, R., 1976, "Piaget's theory and the visually handicapped learner." *New outlook for the blind*, 273–280.

Tait, P., 1972, "Play and the intellectual development of blind children." *New Outlook for the Blind*, **66**, 361–369.

Thompson, J. R. and Chapman, R. A., 1975 and 1977, "Who is 'Daddy' revisited: the status of two-year-olds' over extended words in use and comprehension." *Journal of Child Language*, **4**, 359–376. (Earlier version, appeared in *Papers and Reports on Child Language Development*, **10**, Stanford University, pp. 59–68.)

Tobin, M., 1971, *A study of the vocabulary of the young blind school child*. Monograph, Birmingham, Research Centre for the Education of the Visually Handicapped.

Tomasello, M., and Farrar, M., 1984, "Cognitive bases of lexical development: object performance and relational words." *Journal of Child Language*, **11**, 477–495.

Tronick, E., Als, H., and Adamson, L., 1979, "Structure of early face to face communicative interactions." In M. Bullowa, (ed.), pp. 349–372.

Urwin, C., 1976, "Speech development in blind children: some ways into language." Paper presented at Internationales Symposium des Blinden-und-Sehschwachen-Verbandes der DDR.

1977, "'I'm coming to get you: ready, steady, go!' – The development of communication between a blind infant and his parents." In G. Butterworth (ed.), *The child's representation of the world*, New York: Plenum.

1978a, "The development of communication between blind infants and their parents: some ways into language." Unpublished doctoral dissertation, Cambridge University.

1978b, "The development of communication between blind infants and their parents." In A. Lock (ed.), *Action, gesture and symbol: the emergence of language*. London: Academic Press, pp. 79–110.

1979, "Preverbal communication and early language development in blind children." *Papers and Reports on Child Language Development*, **17**, pp. 119–127.

Užgiris, I. and Hunt, J., 1975, *Assessment in infancy*. Urbana IL: University of Chicago Press.

Valvo, A., 1971, *Sight restoration after long-term blindness: the problems and behavior patterns of visual rehabilitation*. New York: American Foundation for the Blind.

Van Lanker, D., "Heterogeneity in language and speech." UCLA Working Papers. Papers.

Vygotsky, L. S., 1962, *Thought and language*. Cambridge MA: MIT Press.

Wales, R., 1979, "Deixis." In P. Fletcher and M. Garmen, (eds.), *Language acquisition: studies in first language development*, pp. 119–127.

Warren, D. H., 1970, "Intermodality interactions in spatial localization." *Cognitive Psychology*, **1**, 114–133.

1977, *Blindness and early childhood development*. New York: American Foundation for the Blind, Revised, 1985.

1978, "Childhood visual impairment: perspectives on research design and methodology." *Visual Impairment and Blindness*, pp. 404–411.

Warren-Leubecker, A., 1987, review of *Language and experience* (B. Landau and L. Gleitman). *Child Development Abstracts and Bibliography*, **61**, 219–220.

Weir, R. H., 1962, *Language in the crib*. The Hague: Mouton Publishers.

1966, "Some questions on the child's learning of phonology." In F. Smith and G. Miller, (eds.), *The Genesis of language*, Cambridge MA: MIT Press, pp. 153–168.

Wells, G., 1974, "Learning to code experience through language." *Journal of Child Language*, **1**, 243–269.

Welsh, J. R., 1964, "Psychoacoustic study of factors affecting human echolocation." *Research Bulletin No. 4*, New York: American Foundation for the Blind, pp. 1–13.

Werner, H., and Kaplan, B., 1963, *Symbol formation*. New York: John Wiley and Sons.

Wills, D., 1965, "Some observations on blind nursery school children's understanding of their world." *Psychoanalytic Study of the Child*, **20**, 344–364.

1970, "Vulnerable periods in the early development of blind children." *Psychoanalytic Study of the Child*, **25**, 461–480.

Wills, D. M., 1968, "Problems of play and mastery in the blind child." *British Journal of Medical Psychology*, **41**, 213–222.

Wilson, B., 1985, "The emergence of semantics of tense and aspect in the language of a visually impaired child." Unpublished doctoral dissertation, University of Hawaii.

Wilson, J. and Halverson, H. M., 1947, "Development of a young blind child." *Journal of Genetic Psychology*, **71**, 155–175.

Witkin, H. A., Olfman, P. K., Chase, J. B., and Freedman, F., 1971, "Cognitive patterning in the blind." In J. Hellmuth, (ed.), *Cognitive studies*, **2**, New York: Branner/Mazel.

World Health Organization, 1966, "Blindness: information collected from various sources." *WHO Epidem vital statistics report*, **19**, pp. 437–511.

Zukow, P., 1980, "A microanalysis study of the role of the caregiver in the relationship between symbolic play and language acquisition during the one-word period." Unpublished doctoral dissertation: University of California, Los Angeles.

1984, "Criteria for the emergence of symbolic conduct: when words refer and play is symbolic." In L. Feagans, C. Garvey, and R. Gobakoff (eds.), *The origins and growth of communications*, Norwood NJ: Ablex, pp. 162–175.

Author index

The following authors' work is either discussed in the text or is frequently cited. Occasional citations are not included in this index.

Subject index

DATE DUE

261-2500			Printed in USA